D0918476

WITHDRAWN FROM
NOREEN REALE FALCONE LIBRARY
LeMOYNE COLLEGE
DATE ___9/03/12___

Writing for Print

HARVARD-YENCHING INSTITUTE MONOGRAPH SERIES 112

Writing for Print

*Publishing and the Making of Textual
Authority in Late Imperial China*

Suyoung Son

Published by the Harvard University Asia Center
Distributed by Harvard University Press
Cambridge (Massachusetts) and London 2018

© 2018 by the President and Fellows of Harvard College

Printed in the United States of America

The Harvard University Asia Center publishes a monograph series and, in coordina-tion with the Fairbank Center for Chinese Studies, the Korea Institute, the Reis-chauer Institute of Japanese Studies, and other faculties and institutes, administers research projects designed to further scholarly understanding of China, Japan, Viet-nam, Korea, and other Asian countries. The Center also sponsors projects addressing multidisciplinary and regional issues in Asia.

The Harvard-Yenching Institute, founded in 1928, is an independent foundation dedi-cated to the advancement of higher education in the humanities and social sciences in Asia. Headquartered on the campus of Harvard University, the Institute provides fellowships for advanced research, training, and graduate studies at Harvard by com-petitively selected faculty and graduate students from Asia. The Institute also sup-ports a range of academic activities at its fifty partner universities and research insti-tutes across Asia. At Harvard, the Institute promotes East Asian studies through annual contributions to the Harvard-Yenching Library and publication of the *Harvard Journal of Asiatic Studies* and the Harvard-Yenching Institute Monograph Series.

Library of Congress Cataloging-in-Publication Data

Names: Son, Suyoung, author.
Title: Writing for print : publishing and the making of textual authority in late
    imperial China / Suyoung Son.
Other titles: Harvard-Yenching Institute monograph series ; 112.
Description: Cambridge, Massachusetts : Published by the Harvard University Asia
    Center, 2018. | Series: Harvard-Yenching Institute monograph series ; 112
    | Includes bibliographical references and index.
Identifiers: LCCN 2017032866 | ISBN 9780674983830 (hardcover : alk. paper)
Subjects: LCSH: Self-publishing—China—History. | Printing—China—History.
    | Censorship. | Authorship. | China—History—Qing dynasty, 1644-1912.
Classification: LCC Z285.5 .S638 2018 | DDC 070.5/930951—dc23 LC record available
    at https://lccn.loc.gov/2017032866

Index by Anne Holmes

∞ Printed on acid-free paper

Last figure below indicates year of this printing
22 21 20 19 18

Z
2855
.S638
2018

To my father, Sung-bae Son

Contents

Illustrations

Table

Figures

Acknowledgments

When I opened the first of the six volumes of Zhang Chao's collected letters, I did not anticipate what it would take to complete this long, arduous yet exciting journey. The seemingly haphazard assembly of short informal letters led me in ever-unfolding directions, from identifying letter writers to uncovering their local and interregional networks and coteries; from teasing out the minutiae of paper, money, and bookshops to exploring the relationship between publishing practices and textual production and circulation; from searching for original editions to analyzing the textual history comprising a multiplicity of textual forms and a proliferation of textual meanings; and from visiting libraries in China to recovering traces of the transregional flow of books in the libraries in Japan and Korea.

Whenever my research took an unexpected turn, teachers, friends, and colleagues guided me in the right direction. My doctoral advisor, Judith T. Zeitlin, and my committee members, Adrian Johns and Yuming He, continued to be unfailing sources of support and inspiration even after I finished my dissertation. Conversations with Ellen Widmer, Cynthia Brokaw, Patricia Sieber, Tobie Meyer-Fong, Sören Edgren, and Chong Min were inspirational in pushing me to delve into issues more deeply. I cannot thank individually every scholar and student with whom I shared my manuscript in its various stages in conferences, workshops, classes, casual talks, and email correspondence for their valuable comments, incisive questions, and suggestion of relevant materials, but I would like to express my particular gratitude to Wai-yee Li, Young Oh, Ross King, Manling Luo, and Pamela Crossley. I am also fortunate to have supportive colleagues at the University of Colorado at Boulder and Cornell University: I would like to thank Paul W. Kroll, Matthias L. Richter, Antje Richter, Terry Kleeman,

Andrew Stuckey, Laura Brueck, Haytham Bahoora, David Atherton, Ding Xiang Warner, Anne M. Blackburn, Keith Taylor, Robin McNeal, Arnika Fuhrmann, Chiara Formichi, Victor Seow, and Nick Admussen. Nick also read and commented on my introduction and conclusion in the most timely manner. Without the affectionate prodding by my friends, Heekyoung Cho, Rivi Handler-Spitz, and Jeehee Hong, this book could not have been finished. They not only provided the most useful suggestions from their book-writing experiences but also patiently lent their ears to my frequent expression of frustrations. Minhyea Lee, Yi Wang, and Jeongmin Song have become such good companions, constantly reminding me of the importance of creating a balance between work and family.

This book was based on several years of archival research in a number of libraries. I am indebted to specialists at libraries in China, Taiwan, Hong Kong, Japan, Korea, and the United States for their generous assistance, which enabled me to compile a detailed list of Zhang Chao's extant editions: the National Library of China, Beijing University Library, Shanghai Library, Zhejiang Library, the University of Hong Kong Library, the National Library of Taiwan, Taiwan University Library, the Cabinet Library of Japan, the Institute for Advanced Studies on Asia Library at the University of Tokyo, the National Library of Korea, Kyujanggak Library, Yonsei University Library, Korea University Library, Ewha Womans University Library, Harvard-Yenching Library, Princeton University Library, the University of Chicago Library, Columbia University Library, and Cornell University Library. I would like to offer special thanks to Zhou Yuan at the University of Chicago Library, Martin Heijdra at the Princeton University Library, and Daniel McKee and You Lee Chun at the Cornell University Library for their professional and kind help. In addition, financial sponsors from various institutions provided me ample time and resources to conduct research and write the manuscript. I gratefully acknowledge the Center for Asian Studies at Stanford University, the Northeast Asia Council of the Association for Asian Studies, the Center for Humanities and the Arts at the University of Colorado at Boulder, and the Department of Asian Studies and the East Asia Program at the Mario Einaudi Center for International Studies at Cornell University for their financial support. I also acknowledge the journal *Late*

Imperial China for permission to reprint chapter 1, an earlier version of which appeared in the journal in 2010. Jeong Kwanghoon and Shiau-Yun Chen kindly offered their help in taking some of the book photos in this book.

My family has sustained me during the ups and downs in writing this book with their warm support and deep understanding. Without the unconditional sacrifice of my parents and my parents-in-law, particularly my mother and my mother-in-law, who raised my infant son together with me during the first two years of his life, the book could not have been attempted. My brother Min-seok Son, and my sister-in-law Min-jeong Hong, my cousin Julia Son, and my niece Monica Yoon, always backed me up with their confidence in me. I simply cannot repay the constant love and unfathomable patience that my husband, Hyun-ho Joo, and my son, Benjamin Shiwon Joo, have shown me during the years of writing this book. Finally, I dedicate this book to my father, Sung-bae Son. As a self-made man, he might have had every reason to keep his daughter from pursuing an unfeasible scholarly pursuit in a foreign country. Nevertheless, he has had unwavering belief in me and has provided support in whatever form possible. I am just glad to show this book to him as a small token of my gratitude and affection before his memory grows too dim.

S. Y. Son, July 2017

Abbreviations

For complete bibliographical information, see the Bibliography.

CDOC   Zhang Chao. *Chidu oucun* 尺牘偶存. 1780 reprint edition in the Beijing University Library.

CDYS   Zhang Chao, ed. *Chidu yousheng* 尺牘友聲. 1780 reprint edition in the Beijing University Library.

TJCS   Wang Zhuo and Zhang Chao, eds. *Tanji congshu* 檀几叢書. Facsimile reprint of 1695 edition in Shanghai Library. Shanghai: Guji chubanshe, 1991.

ZDCS   Zhang Chao, ed. *Zhaodai congshu* 昭代叢書. Reprint of Daoguang 道光 Shikai tang 石楷堂 edition. Shanghai: Guji chubanshe, 1990.

Introduction

The writers of seventeenth-century China showed an unprecedented passion for publishing their works. Before that time, it was rare for living writers to see their works in print. Since a printed edition was considered a token of prestige granted only to a text of quality that deserved widespread transmission, most published works appeared posthumously, usually as a form of commemoration by the writer's family and disciples or after enough time had elapsed for the writer's reputation to become firmly established. Beginning in the sixteenth century, however, more and more writers, whether famous or obscure, saw their works published and circulated during their lifetimes.[1] They were no longer satisfied with only creating works—they were eager to have them printed. The firm belief in the immortalizing power of writing itself, epitomized in the eminent writer Su Shi's 蘇軾 (1037–1101) assertion that "writing is the only thing that does not perish along with the grasses and trees,"[2] gave way to writers' anxiety that without being published their names would perish in obscurity. Even the renowned and prolific writer Yu Huai 余懷 (1616–96) grumbled, "I am afraid that the works of my entire life will perish along with the grasses and trees unless I do something about [print] them."[3]

What gave rise to this shift of emphasis from writing to publishing in the seventeenth century? The simplest answer is the advance of print and its wide accessibility. After the invention of woodblock printing as

---

1. Ōki, *Minmatsu kōnan no shuppan bunka*, 35.
2. "惟文字庶几不與草木同腐。" Su Shi, "Yu Sun Zhikang ershou" 與孫志康二首, in *Su Shi quanji*, 3:1837.
3. "若不料理, 生平著作, 恐與草木同腐。" *CDYS* 6.10b. Yu Huai made similar remarks several times. See also *CDYS* 6.3a, 6.18b–19a.

early as the eighth century, the steady development of print technology and the growth of print culture reached a second high point in the seventeenth century,[4] along with a rise in population, expansion of the book market, increased access to education, and greater social mobility.[5] The sheer quantity and variety of printed books and their widespread geographic and social distribution in this period testify to not only the highly differentiated demands of an expanding readership but also book production across a range of official, private, and commercial sectors. In particular, private publishing by individuals became increasingly common. Because woodblock printing, which continued to predominate even after the invention of movable type in the eleventh century,[6] was done by pasting a page of a handwritten manuscript onto a block of wood and carving away everything but the text itself, it did not require the high capital investment and advanced technical tools that movable-type printing did.[7] In theory, anyone could publish a book as long as he had the capital to pay for wood, paper, and ink, and to hire carvers to make a set of printing blocks. The portability and relatively simple technology of woodblock printing combined with a

4. Scholars agree that the Song dynasty and the late Ming and early Qing period were two eras of momentum in the development of Chinese print culture. The print culture of the former period has been investigated less extensively than that of the latter, mainly owing to the paucity of materials, but new studies have emerged recently. See, for example, Chia and de Weerdt, *Knowledge and Text Production*; and Yugen Wang, *Ten Thousand Scrolls*.

5. See, for example, Brook, *Confusions of Pleasure*; Johnson, Nathan, and Rawski, *Popular Culture*, 3–33; and Rowe, "Political, Social and Economic Factors," 32.

6. Many scholars have pondered why woodblock print maintained preeminence over movable-type print in China up until the late nineteenth century, when the newly imported lithography from the West took the market by storm. Joseph McDermott, for example, offers the following explanation: first, Chinese woodblocks did not require any printing facilities or equipment, such as a foundry for casting type or printing and binding machines; second, carving woodblocks was much cheaper than casting and cutting Chinese characters into metallic type; and, third, labor costs significantly declined after the sixteenth century. He concludes that, "when compared with the cost of printing by movable type, it [woodblock printing] does seem to have been cheaper, particularly when the publisher was not willing to make a long-term investment in his printing enterprise." McDermott, *Social History of the Chinese Book*, 24.

7. For a detailed description of woodblock printing technology, see Tsien, "Technical Aspects of Chinese Printing."

significant reduction in paper and labor costs from the sixteenth century on contributed to the widespread popularity of self-publishing. As the renowned Ming scholar-official Tang Shunzhi 唐順之 (1507–60) noted, with some exaggeration, publishing was no longer limited to elites, such as "the rich, the noble, and successful civil examination candidates," but was being undertaken by whoever had a modicum of wealth, even "butchers and wine sellers."[8]

The surge in publishing by writers in the seventeenth century cannot be fully explained, however, by the wide accessibility of the means of printing alone. Scholars of Chinese print culture have made a thorough study of the impact of new printing technology on the economic, social, and political realms, but relatively few have devoted attention to the motives of the literary creators themselves and why they particularly chose print over the handwritten manuscript, though the latter remained a viable medium of textual production and circulation among the literati community.[9] In fact, the advent of print elicited ambivalent responses from scholars and writers. The technical capacity of print was initially identified with an unprecedentedly large number of books and access to them. Since print "did not require the efforts of hand copying as in the time before the Tang dynasty," scholars were able to "double their learning and writing ability" and "achieve more than they invested."[10] Along with awe and excitement, however, a great deal of anxiety about the widespread dispersal of books of problematic quality began to be voiced.[11] The Song poet Ye Mengde 葉夢得 (1077–1148), for example, worried that the limited numbers of authentic manuscript copies were being superseded by myriad incorrect printed copies: "Although printed books are often incorrect and not without errors, people in the world regard them as the correct versions. While

8. Tang Shunzhi, "Da Wang Zunyan" 答王遵巖, in *Tang Jingchuan wenji* 6.32b–36a.
9. Studies to date about the intimate relationship between print and literary production mainly focus on the commercial imprints that were targeted at a wider readership. See, for example, Hegel, *Reading Illustrated Fiction*; Lowry, *Tapestry of Popular Songs*; He Yuming, *Home and the World*; Shang Wei, "*Jin Ping Mei* and Late Ming Print Culture"; and Ding Naifei, *Obscene Things*, 47–79.
10. Wu Cheng, "Zeng yushu ren Yang Liangfu xu" 贈鬻書人楊良輔序, in *Wu Wenzheng ji* 34.19a.
11. See, for example, Cherniack, "Book Culture and Textual Transmission."

the stored [manuscript] books are gradually meeting their demise, the flawed [printed] versions cannot be corrected. How deplorable this is!"[12] In his view, the development of print resulted in the profusion of durable yet faulty texts. Another Song poet, Lu You 陸游 (1125–1210), shared Ye Mengde's apprehension by rhetorically rejecting the progress that print had supposedly made: "The flawed books are spread all over and fill the world, and they lead scholars to err more. It would be better not to print those books at all!"[13]

The Song literati's concern about the unreliable quality of printed books accelerated as the commercial book market expanded significantly following the sixteenth century. Although the merits of print were widely acknowledged as books "became easier to make, more indestructible, cheaper in cost, and handier to collect,"[14] the literati frequently registered their contempt for shoddy commercial print editions. The Ming scholar and bibliophile Lang Ying 郎瑛 (1487–ca. 1566), for example, charged commercial publishers with sullying the original meaning and eloquence of texts. Detesting the plethora of undeserving books (lanshu 濫書), he even compared print's devastating effect to that of the book burning (fenshu 焚書) by the first emperor of the Qin dynasty (259–210 BCE).[15]

In short, literati did not necessarily perceive the advance of print as an inevitable consequence of its technological breakthrough.[16] Writers were invariably aware of print's high production capability and wide reach, yet they did not consider print a superior medium to manuscript copies, instead noting the widespread dispersal of books of unchecked quality as a serious problem that print had caused. In

12. "板本初不是正不無訛誤, 世既一以板本為正而藏本日亡, 其譌謬者遂不可正, 甚可惜也。" Cited in Hu Yinglin, *Shaoshi shanfang bicong*, 44. For more examples of similar sentiments, see Zhang Xiumin, *Zhongguo yinshua shi*, 1:135–36.

13. "錯本書散滿天下, 更誤學者, 不如不刻之愈也!" Cited in Qian Daxin, *Shijia zhai yangxin lu* 19.1a.

14. "易成難毀、節費便藏。" Hu Yinglin, *Shaoshi shanfang bicong*, 45.

15. Lang Ying, "Shuce" 書冊, in *Qixiu leigao*, 2:665. For the in-depth discussion of book burning and book making, see Ding Naifei, *Obscene Things*, 68–75.

16. For a definition of the "Printing Revolution" and the ensuing criticism and debate, see Eisenstein, *Printing Revolution in Early Modern Europe*; and Grafton, Eisenstein, and Johns, "AHR Forum."

this regard, the advantages and disadvantages of print created new possibilities and constraints that writers in the seventeenth century needed to consider as they engaged in textual production and circulation. As this study demonstrates, their publishing practice was often shaped by conflicting expectations with regard to the print medium: writers used it to target a small, exclusive readership consisting of one's chosen coterie and sought to obtain peer recognition of the value of one's text, yet they also strove to attain the broadest possible circulation in the commercial market network so as to secure fame, economic gain, and social influence. In other words, they attempted to use print to acquire two ostensibly opposed rewards—exclusive cultural prestige and broad popular appeal—in establishing the authority of their texts and positioning themselves favorably within the larger rearrangements of political, commercial, and cultural relations in late imperial China.

This book examines such seemingly contradictory publishing practices of seventeenth-century writers and their reverberations for eighteenth-century censorship. By laying emphasis on the use of print as mediated by elite writers' literary, economic, and social desires, it reassesses the widespread printing boom of the seventeenth century as a deliberate choice of appropriation rather than the inevitable outcome of technological ascendancy. In doing so, the book challenges the allegedly clear-cut division between manuscript and print culture. First, it breaks with the tendency to emphasize the rupture between manuscript and print culture, instead focusing on their overlapping interaction. In light of recent studies of print culture in both the West and China that have increasingly highlighted the viability of the manuscript tradition and its compatibility with print culture,[17] this study shows how much seventeenth-century writers' publishing practices maintained or mimicked those associated with manuscript production and circulation. Indeed, writers attempted to combine the cachet

---

17. See, for example, Love, *Culture and Commerce*; McKitterick, *Print, Manuscript and the Search for Order*; and Blair, *Too Much to Know*. For scholarship about China, see Nugent, *Manifest in Words*; Inoue, *Chūgoku shuppan bunkashi*; and McDermott, *Social History of the Chinese Book*.

of peer patronage, which was garnered through limited production and controlled circulation of manuscript copies, with the possibilities that print opened up, such as large-scale reproduction, greater profits, and access to a wider audience. By integrating select coterie circulation and broad market distribution, peer recognition and widespread fame, and gift exchange embedded in reciprocal sociability and impersonal economic transaction, the writers appropriated print to secure the textual authority that was increasingly eroded by the rapidly changing socioeconomic situation in the late imperial period.

Second, this book reconsiders the notion of printed text as a fixed entity, a notion that fails to appreciate the fluid and evolving nature of textual production and circulation. Seventeenth-century writers' publishing practices demonstrate that the perception of printed text— often defined, by default, in contrast to manuscript copy—as a product of mass consumption in immutable standardized form mainly derives from the system of industrial book production, which did not become standard until the modern era.[18] As Stephen Orgel points out in the context of early Renaissance print culture, the printed book was "less a product than a process."[19] Far from closing off the act of writing and authorizing the text, printing was, in fact, an integral part of making and reading the text in the sense that it constantly invited readerly interventions, editorial revisions, economic considerations, and political impact. In effect, the seventeenth-century writer's printed text was not the exclusive end product of a single author's intention but rather the embodiment of the intersection of more diverse forms of creative agency of readers, commentators, preface writers, financial donors, printers, and booksellers, thereby highlighting the open, collective, and social aspect of textual production and circulation.[20]

18. For a powerful critique of the myth of the standardization and fixity of printed text, see Johns, *Nature of the Book*, 1–40; and St. Clair, *Reading Nation*, 177–85.

19. Orgel, *Spectacular Performances*, 179.

20. McKenzie, *Making Meaning*, 6.

The Publishing Practices of
Zhang Chao and Wang Zhuo

This book focuses on the publishing practice of the two most popular and successful writers-cum-publishers in the early Qing, Zhang Chao 張潮 (1650–ca. 1707) in Yangzhou and Wang Zhuo 王晫 (1636–ca. 1707) in Hangzhou, along with their coteries active in the economically and culturally vibrant lower Yangzi river delta region called Jiangnan 江南. As typical examples of literati who self-published in the seventeenth century, Zhang Chao and Wang Zhuo shared similar life trajectories: both had enough education and talent to pass the initial level of the civil service examinations in their youth, but their repeated failures to advance further eventually caused them to give up the idea of having a career in officialdom and turned their energies toward collecting, writing, and publishing books.

It appears that publishing was a viable alternative career for literati such as Zhang Chao and Wang Zhuo, members of the educated elite who had been traditionally privileged by the centralized bureaucracy and social hierarchy but had become increasingly diversified and stratified owing to the political instability, rapid commercialization, and heightened social mobility from the mid-Ming period onward.[21] These intellectuals found publishing to be an effective way to assert their cultural taste, earn economic capital, and exercise social influence, thereby valorizing their versatile elite identity. Although the elite's involvement in publishing was not uncommon in the Song dynasty, what distinguished seventeenth-century literati publishing from earlier efforts was its large scale. Almost all literati self-published or participated in their coterie's publishing projects in one way or another. Aside from composing texts, they were deeply involved in the practical matters of publishing, including securing funding, editing, collating, and proofreading

---

21. The term "literati" encompassed a wide range of educated elites in the late imperial period, from officials of high and low rank, to reclusive scholars and writers who eschewed public service, to failed examination candidates and students from the families of nouveau riche merchants as well as from scholarly lineages. For the shifting status of the literati in late imperial China, see, for example, Brook, *Praying for Power*, and idem, *Confusions of Pleasure*; Clunas, *Superfluous Things*; and Chow, *Publishing, Culture, and Power*.

the manuscripts, hiring carvers and printers, and distributing the printed copies. Therefore, literati publishing in this period took a variety of forms, from just a sporadic activity to the basis of a livelihood, from individual undertaking to a quasi-corporate venture, and from scholarly activity to pecuniary business, blurring the distinctions between the conventional tripartite categories of Chinese printing, that is, official (*guanke* 官刻), commercial (*fangke* 坊刻), and family or private publishing (*jiake* 家刻 or *sike* 私刻).[22]

Zhang Chao and Wang Zhuo began modestly, printing their own works as well as those of their late fathers. In contrast to those affluent literati who could afford to run large-scale publishing houses, they employed carvers, printers, and illustrators on an ad hoc basis, as did most writers of the time, because of limited resources. The favorable reception of their early imprints, however, led each to consider expanding: this took the form of deciding to work together and making a large volume of compendia. Heavily indebted to the participation of the widening web of their coterie, they collected a huge number of contemporary pieces and printed them as a compilation in a series of installments under the titles *Tanji congshu* 檀几叢書 (Collectanea of a Sandalwood Desk, 1695–97) and *Zhaodai congshu* 昭代叢書 (Collectanea of a Glorious Age, 1697–1703).

Despite the significant political break in the tumultuous transition from the Ming to the Qing, the compilation project of Zhang Chao and Wang Zhuo retained the defining features of late Ming print culture in terms of the varying kinds and wide scope of the included materials.[23] Unlike earlier elite publishing, which had largely focused on the

22. Compared to the large number of in-depth studies of commercial publishing, there have only been a few studies of private publishing, mainly owing to the latter's ill-defined nature. For a recent study about the diverse activities of private publishing in imperial China, see Bussotti and Drège, *Imprimer sans profit?* For a comparative perspective, see Kornicki, *Book in Japan*, 149–53, on private publishing in Tokugawa Japan; and Sin Sang-mok, Chang Chae-sŏk, and Cho Ch'ŏl-lae, *Kanyŏksi ilgi*, on family publishing in Chosŏn Korea.

23. Contrary to the prevailing conception that the flourishing late Ming print culture lost momentum in the early Qing owing to the dynastic transition and the destruction of infrastructure, literati publishing in early Qing in fact had a close affinity with that of late Ming. See, for example, Barr, "Novelty, Character, and Community," 283–84. On the long-term impact of the Ming-Qing dynastic transition on

Confucian classics, mainstream scholarly and literary works, and re-prints of rare editions, the late Ming witnessed a significant diversification of what was printed, including miscellanies and traditionally less valued writings, such as short treatises, informal letters, anecdotes and classical tales, drinking games, manuals of taste and hobbies, and travel records. In addition, collections came to the fore, having broadened the scope of their contents. Those of a variety of genres of writings by a single author (*wenji* 文集) continued to be printed, but anthologies (*xuanji* 選集) and collectanea (*congshu* 叢書), the compendiums of independent works by several authors, also became popular. Because of the censorship by the Qianlong 乾隆 emperor (r. 1735–96) in the late eighteenth century, it is hard to know the exact number of anthologies and compilations published in the late Ming and early Qing periods, but extant anthologies of poetry alone exceed fifty, and each contains poems by fifty to five hundred poets—an unprecedentedly large number and size before this period.[24]

Building on the late Ming enthusiasm for anthologies of a wide variety of genres, the compilations of Zhang Chao and Wang Zhuo are notable for their inclusion of casual short prose, often called as *xiaopin* 小品, newly created by a number of contemporary writers. The diverse genres of short prose in these compilations, although tinged with hindsight unique to the aftermath of the fall of the Ming, reflected the vibrant jocular sociality of literati culture in general. Their compilations were widely circulated through their cross-regional literati network and via commercial market distribution, and, with *Tanji congshu* and *Zhaodai congshu* becoming two of the most popular and successful compendia, Zhang Chao and Wang Zhuo earned a reputation across the Jiangnan area, far beyond their locus of activity.[25]

Qing print culture, see Brokaw, "On the History of the Book," 23–33; and Chia, "Of Three Mountains Street," 140–42.

24. Xie Zhengguang and She Rufeng, *Qingchu ren xuan*, 3; Ōki, *Chūgoku Minmatsu no media kakumei*, 38–41.

25. The motives for assembling compilations in the early Qing were diverse, including political and literary purposes. For example, on the early Qing literati's efforts to memorialize the Ming and rebuild a sense of contemporary culture, see Meyer-Fong, "Packaging the Men of Our Times," and Pattinson, "Market for Letter Collections"; Li Xiaorong's discussion of anthologies of women's writing in "Gender

The impact of Zhang Chao and Wang Zhuo's publishing practices continued to reverberate in the eighteenth century, as their imprints traveled long distances, engendered new interpretations, and defined different ideological agendas. The popularity of their imprints outlived their deaths, expanding beyond the Jiangnan area to Beijing, which emerged as a new center of the book market in the eighteenth century, and from Beijing crossing the border to reach Chosŏn Korea via the tribute book trade. Unfortunately, their imprints became the targets of censorship campaigns in both Qing China and Chosŏn Korea in the late eighteenth century, although they contained scarcely any material that referred directly to political matters. Despite having different political backgrounds, both censorship campaigns testify to the conflict between the literati community and the state regarding who was to decide what kinds of text could be printed and circulated—a conflict that extensive literati publishing combined with the flourishing book market and active international book trade engendered.

Structure of the Book

This book is divided into two parts by its historical time frame: the three chapters in part 1 explore the production, circulation, and reception of the imprints published by Zhang Chao and Wang Zhuo and their enmeshment of manuscript and print culture in the seventeenth century. The two chapters in part 2 examine the response to the imprints of Zhang Chao and Wang Zhuo in the eighteenth century, focusing on the ways in which censorship in eighteenth-century Qing China and Chosŏn Korea, respectively, dealt with the ramifications of the literati publishing of the seventeenth century. Each chapter begins with a vignette to situate the central issue of the chapter within its concrete historical situation. These vignettes also underscore that the issues encountered by Zhang Chao and Wang Zhuo in their publishing

---

and Textual Politics" highlights the establishment of a gender-specific aesthetics. The compilations of Zhang Chao and Wang Zhuo, however, should not be seen as reflecting any single intention alone, given their social and collective nature of production and circulation.

practices were far from exceptional but were in fact shared by their contemporaries.

Chapter 1, "The Making of the Printed Text," provides a detailed description of the production of printed texts by Zhang Chao. Zhang Chao appropriated the manuscript convention of limited circulation to an exclusive readership so as to ensure the prestige of the elite community within which literati aspired to acquire their reputation. By reconstructing each stage of Zhang Chao's publishing process, such as the initiation of the project, the gathering of manuscripts, the editing and collating of texts, and the distribution of printed copies, this chapter demonstrates how much he relied on collaboration with his close circle of literati friends. Thus his publishing practice was an open and flexible process in which additions and changes were constantly incorporated into the text during the very process of printing. This collective effort, as the textual history of Zhang Chao's collection of aphorisms *Youmengying* 幽夢影 (Faint Dream Shadows, 1681–97) exemplifies, shaped the printed text as a communal artifact by and for a select elite coterie.

Chapter 2, "Publishing for Reputation," examines the ways in which Wang Zhuo made his printed texts to create a reputation for himself and establish their textual authority. The self-publishing boom posed a dilemma for seventeenth-century writers: it was seen as the most effective means to acquire a reputation, yet it simultaneously risked undermining that very reputation. This chapter considers Wang Zhuo's publishing of *Lanyan ji* 蘭言集 (Collection of Fragrant Words) and *Jin Shishuo* 今世說 (Contemporary *Tales of the World*, 1683) to be an attempt to work around this dilemma by incorporating the approval of his fellow literati community into his printed books internally and externally. Furthermore, a close examination of Huang Zhouxing's 黃周星 (1611–80) northern drama (*zaju* 雜劇) *Xihua bao* 惜花報 (Recompense for Cherishing Flowers), written at the request of Wang Zhuo, reveals that the authority of a writer's self-published text was vindicated not merely by coterie patronage but also through the acknowledgment of a widening readership for whom print provided open access.

Chapter 3, "The Economics of Print," explores economic considerations in the circulation of the two huge compilations of contemporary prose *Tanji congshu* and *Zhaodai congshu*, copublished by Zhang Chao and Wang Zhuo. It challenges the preconception of private publishing by elite writers as a purely literary undertaking, focusing on its close relationship with the commercial book market. Looking beyond the monetizing and popularizing aspects of the commercial book market, this chapter highlights the ways in which the socially grounded economy of gift exchange was compatible with impersonal monetary transactions and the cultural prestige of elite taste was translated into successful market appeal, thereby enabling Zhang Chao and Wang Zhuo to achieve the goals of reputation building and money making at once.

Chapter 4, "Censorship of Installment Publication in Qing China," discusses the censorship of Zhang Chao's anthology of classical tales *Yu Chu xinzhi* 虞初新志 (The Magician's New Records, 1683–1704). *Yu Chu xinzhi* was published in installments, a popular mode of book production in the seventeenth century. Despite its continuing popularity into the eighteenth century, however, it was not only excluded from the Qianlong compilation of *Siku quanshu* 四庫全書 (Complete Library of the Four Branches of Literature) but was also censored, resulting in the considerable alteration of its original shape. This chapter argues that the censorship was triggered not by the controversial political ideas of the book but rather by the potential danger that the format of installment publication might present—the wide circulation of a possibly uncontrollable collective voice of the literati.

Chapter 5, "Transnational Circulation of *Tanji congshu* and Censorship in Chosŏn Korea," examines the transmission of *Tanji congshu* from Beijing to Seoul through the tribute book trade and how this transnational book trade played a crucial role in shaping the private venue of book circulation among the literati community in the absence of a full-fledged commercial book market in eighteenth-century Chosŏn Korea. Responding to the widespread popularity of imported Chinese books among elite circles, King Chŏngjo 正祖 (r. 1776–1800) launched a censorship campaign in 1792. This chapter revises the monolithic understanding of the censorship as drastic political suppression and considers Chŏngjo's censorship as an attempt to reinstate the state monopoly on the circulation of books, ideas, and knowledge that was threatened by private channels of literati communication via the circulation of imported Chinese books.

This book intends to be not only a historical study that reconstructs the publishing practices of writers and their influence on textual production and circulation in late imperial China, but also a literary study that reexamines the textual meanings and interpretations that have been overshadowed to date by an emphasis on authorial intention and textual stability. Integrating the hitherto separate fields of history of the book, literary criticism, and bibliographical and textual studies, this study focuses on specific texts in each chapter—*Youmengying* (chapter 1); *Lanyan ji*, *Jin Shishuo*, "Kanhua shuyi ji" 看花述異記 (Record of the Watching of Flowers and the Telling of the Odd), and *Xihua bao* (chapter 2); *Tanji congshu* and *Zhaodai congshu* (chapters 3 and 5); and *Yu Chu xinzhi* (chapter 4). In doing so, it teases out the meanings of a given text not only in its finalized form, but also during the process through which the text was produced and circulated. In effect, this book hopes to provide an opportunity for the reconsideration of the modern notions of text, author, and reader and the proper relationship among them, thereby validating diverse and historically specific forms of textual practice.

PART I

*Publishing Practices of Writers
in the Seventeenth Century*

CHAPTER 1

The Making of the Printed Text

When one of the most scandalous novels in Chinese literary history, *Jin Ping Mei* 金瓶梅 (The Plum in the Golden Vase), first appeared in manuscript in the late sixteenth century, it inspired heated controversy over whether or not it should be printed. Feng Menglong 馮夢龍 (1574–1646), a renowned writer of short vernacular stories who was deeply involved in the book market, immediately recognized the commercial value of the manuscript. He foresaw that it would fetch a high price from a commercial publisher and strongly urged Shen Defu 沈德符 (1578–1642), who owned a copy, to print it. But Shen Defu flatly refused to have it printed and explained the reason as follows:

> My Suzhou friend Feng Youlong [Feng Menglong] was both surprised and delighted when he saw it [the manuscript of *Jin Ping Mei*]. He encouraged a bookstore to buy it at a high price and print it. At that time Ma Zhongliang [Ma Zhijun 馬之駿, 1588–1625] worked for Customs in Suzhou, and he, too, urged me to accede to the publisher's request and thereby fill my stomach. But I told him that, as for this kind of book, someone will surely print it, and yet once in print it will circulate from household to household, corrupting men's minds. And if one day Yama [the Lord of Hell] were to tax me with setting off this catastrophe, what excuse would I be able to offer? How could I possibly risk all the torments of Niraya [Hell] for the hope of a paltry profit? Zhongliang entirely agreed with me, so I finally locked the manuscript in a trunk.

吳友馮猶龍見之驚喜, 慫恿書坊以重價購刻。馬仲良時榷吳關, 亦勸予
應梓人之求, 可以療饑。予曰: 此等書必遂有人板行, 但一刻則家傳戶
到, 壞人心術, 他日閻羅究詰始禍, 何辭置對, 吾豈以刀錐博泥犁哉? 仲
良大以爲然, 遂固篋之。[1]

Shen Defu objected to printing the novel because he thought that his
fellow literati would attribute only a vulgar desire to his doing so—that
he was satisfying his avarice by selling the manuscript in "the hope of
a paltry profit." He did not want to be seen as being involved in such
a degrading financial transaction. Moreover, he was concerned that
printing would empower the text to "circulate from household to
household" and thus corrupt readers' minds. The novel's provocative
content made him particularly anxious about the social consequences
that might ensue if the text were circulated in print.

Despite Shen Defu's apprehension that wider circulation due to
print would "set off a catastrophe," however, the manuscript copy of
the text had already freely circulated, particularly within a close circle
of friends. It had been transmitted from the famous painter and
scholar Dong Qichang 董其昌 (1555–1636) to his friend Yuan Hongdao
袁宏道 (1568–1610), through their mutual friend Tao Wangling 陶望齡
(1562–1609); then from Yuan Hongdao to his brother, Yuan Zhongdao 袁中道 (1570–1623); and thereafter to their friends, such as Shen Defu
and Xie Zhaozhe 謝肇淛 (1567–1624).[2] This close-knit circle of friends
found the novel captivating, and some were impressed by its high
aesthetic quality.[3] They strongly encouraged one another to share it,
regardless of the putative power of the novel to debase their minds. On
hearing of the praise heaped on this text by the renowned Yuan Hongdao group, more and more literati eagerly sought out the manuscript,

1. Shen Defu, *Wanli yehuo bian*, 85. I have slightly modified Patrick Hanan's translation in his "Text of the *Chin P'ing Mei*," 47.

2. Hanan, "Text of the *Chin P'ing Mei*," 39–49.

3. See Xie Zhaozhe's "*Jin Ping Mei* ba" 金瓶梅跋 and Li Rihua's *Weishui xuan riji*
味水軒日記, in *Jin Ping Mei ziliao huibian*, ed. Hou Zhongyi and Wang Rumei, 216
and 223, respectively.

so that the novel had enjoyed quite a reputation long before it was eventually printed by a commercial publisher around 1618.[4]

The vigorous circulation of the manuscript within a limited literati group indicates that what concerned Shen Defu was not simply the wide transmission that print enabled; rather, it was the indiscriminate and uncontrollable nature of print distribution. In contrast to manuscript circulation, which was under the control of a chosen elite coterie, printing would allow the novel to travel far beyond the intended readers and enter the arena of an anonymous audience. Shen Defu and other literati who opposed the printing of the novel contended that, although *Jin Ping Mei* contained excessive sexual descriptions, its aesthetic value could be properly appreciated as long as the circulation of the manuscript remained among discerning elite readers. Once it was put into print, however, it could be easily passed down to the so-called commoners, who the literati believed lacked the intellectual capacity to distinguish the underlying theme of the novel from its superficial sexual descriptions.[5] By retaining the manuscript form as the sole means of circulation, therefore, the literati expected that they could control the transmission of the text and prevent indiscriminate access to it. In other words, disallowing its printing made it possible for the literati to hold tightly to their cultural monopoly on the text, which was undergirded by an exclusive exchange of the manuscript.[6]

The anecdote about the printing of *Jin Ping Mei* demonstrates the literati's anxiety about print and the effect that it was believed to bring about, that is, the shift of the book from the property of only a privileged

4. The literati who read the *Jin Ping Mei* in manuscript included, at a minimum, Wang Shizhen 王世貞 (1526–90), Wang Kentang 王肯堂 (1549–1613), Wang Zhideng 王穉登 (1535–1612), Qiu Zhichong 邱志充, Wen Zaizi 文在兹, Tu Benjun 屠本畯 (1542–1622), Liu Chengxi 劉承禧, Xue Gang 薛岡, and Wen Jishi 文吉士. See Roy, "Case for T'ang Hsien-tsu's Authorship," 51–53.

5. Shen Defu, *Wanli yehuo bian*, 85. Also see the excerpt of Yuan Zhongdao, "Youju shilu" 游居柿錄, in *Jin Ping Mei ziliao huibian*, ed. Hou Zhongyi and Wang Rumei, 220–21.

6. The commercial publisher of *Jin Ping Mei* appropriated the symbolic value that the exclusive circulation of the manuscript carried so as to enhance its commercial appeal. By directly referring to Yuan Hongdao and his praise for the manuscript, one of the printed *Jin Ping Mei* editions urged readers to share in the cultural prerogative that the reading of the novel assured. Suyoung Son, "Reading an Authorless Text," 448.

few to a commodity available to a wider reading public. With its technological capacity for the rapid reproduction of identical copies, print was believed to transform the production and circulation of texts from the private realm of a select community to the public realm of consumption. Awe and excitement about the unprecedented abundance and easy accessibility of books was accompanied by a feeling of vulnerability that the elite's exclusive prestige and privileges would be jeopardized by the open and uncontrollable production and circulation of books. For elite writers, the choice to have a given text printed was closely associated with issues of access and distinction, not necessarily those of speed and quantity.

This chapter focuses on the ways in which the technological attribute of print was appropriated by seventeenth-century writers to claim cultural prestige and social status. Rather than making full use of the technological merit to be found in rapidly multiplying texts, therefore, seventeenth-century writers employed print in the same way that manuscript was used, in the sense that the availability of a manuscript copy provided opportunities for controlling text circulation among a select coterie and for facilitating communication among members of a coterie that kept the writer in personal touch with his readers, thereby retaining the cultural exclusivity that the manuscript tradition evoked. In charting in detail the production process of Zhang Chao's printed texts, this chapter argues that writers appropriated print to ensure their privileged status as elites by virtue of their social connections and cultural distinctions, thus making printed texts as a communal effort by and for a coterie.

Zhang Chao and His Coterie

As a native of She 歙 county in Huizhou 徽州 prefecture, where the Zhang family had lived for seven centuries since the Northern Song dynasty,[7] Zhang Chao (*hao* Shanlai 山來, *zi* Xinzhai 心齋 and Sanzai

---

7. The Zhang family had been affluent, but they fell on hard times because Zhang Chao's grandfather Zhang Zhengmao 張正茂 (d. 1616, *zi* Songru 松如, *hao* Yuanchen 元晨), a *xiucai* 秀才 (budding talent) degree holder, died young. His eldest son,

daoren 三在道人) followed a typical literatus career path in his youth. His father, Zhang Xikong 張習孔 (b. 1606), attained the prestigious metropolitan graduate degree of *jinshi* 進士 (presented scholar) and held official posts in Beijing and in Shandong province. But he retired soon after his widowed mother died, and he moved to Yangzhou in 1671.[8] Xikong's second son,[9] Zhang Chao showed precocious talent by becoming a supplementary government student (*bu zhusheng* 補諸生) at age fifteen in 1663, but, despite more than twelve years of study, he failed to advance beyond the initial level and obtain any official post.[10] Instead of

Zhang Xikong, who was eleven years old at the time, had to support the family with his meager income from teaching at town schools. Not until Xikong passed the highest level of the civil examinations in 1649 could the family escape poverty. Since Zhang Xikong's success in the examinations was relatively late—at the age of forty-four (1649)—the family had been in poverty for over thirty years. Zhang Xikong, preface in *Xin'an Zhangshi xuxiu zongpu* 6b, and "Jiaxun," in *TJCS*, 82. A brief record about Zhang Zhengmao appeared in the *wenyuan* 文苑 category in "Renwu zhi" 人物志, in Liu Dakui, *Shexian zhi, juan 7*. He left behind a poetry collection, *Yuanchen shiji* 元晨詩集, and Zhang Chao put one of his grandfather's prose pieces, "Guitai wanyan" 龜臺琬琰, in the first collection of *TJCS*.

8. For Zhang Xikong's career, see Dai Tingjie (Pierre-Henri Durand), "Yasu gongrong," 545–48. Zhang Xikong successively held the posts of senior secretary of the Bureau of Judicial Administration (*Xingbu langzhong* 刑部郎中) and assistant education superintendent for Shandong province (*Shandong tixue qianshi* 山東提學僉事). After his retirement and relocation to Yangzhou, the family lived on the east side of the Mawang miao 馬王廟 in Yangzhou. See his "Jiaxun," in *TJCS*, 83; Chen Ding, "Xinzhai jushi zhuan," in *Liuxi waizhuan*, 561. Pierre-Henri Durand claims that, after Zhang Chao moved to Yangzhou, he was probably involved in the salt trade in some capacity such as managing or investing. Durand surmises that this would have been the source of ample assets for Zhang Chao to pursue his publishing. Dai Tingjie, "Yasu gongrong," 550–52.

9. Zhang Chao had three brothers. His elder brother, Shilin 士麟 (1636–58), who was fourteen years older than he, died young, and there is no record of him except a fleeting remark in *ZDCS*, 202. His two younger brothers, Jian 漸 (*hao* Jinye 進也 and Mushan 木山), who was a *xiucai* degree holder, and Chun 淳 (*hao* Dongyou 東圃 and Zhisheng 質生), were ardent collaborators with Zhang Chao in his publishing projects, and their records remain in several imprints of Zhang Chao.

10. Zhang Chao, "Bagu shi zixu" 八股詩自序, in *Xinzhai liaofu ji* 1.23a–25b. Many scholars insist that Zhang Chao held the minor post of *Hanlin yuan kongmu* 翰林院孔目, a librarian at the Hanlin Academy. But, in his biography of Zhang Chao, Chen Ding mentions that "Zhang Chao became an officer of the Hanlin Academy with money, but he did not take the job. He closed the gate [shut out guests] and wrote books" 以貲為翰林郎, 不仕, 杜門著書. This indicates that Zhang Chao never served

continuing the futile effort of studying for the exams, he engaged himself in collecting, editing, and publishing books. Publishing was familiar to him because his father had printed some of his own works, and Zhang Chao had assisted and supported his father's compilation and publishing projects.

Zhang Chao began his publishing on a small scale, printing works of his late father and his own works, as most writers did. In the early stage, from 1677 to 1682, he edited his late father's remaining works into collections and printed his own early works, such as two collections of drinking games, *Jiulü* 酒律 (Rules for Drinking) and *Xiajiu wu* 下酒物 (Games to Relish with Drinks); a collection of poetry games, *Tangshi jiudi* 唐詩酒底 (Tang Poems with Unrefined Drinks); and a collection of diverse genres of writing, *Xinzhai liaofu ji* 心齋聊復集 (Xinzhai's Collection of Casual Writings, 1682). After obtaining some experience, Zhang Chao seems to have gained confidence in his publishing enterprise and expanded its scope. He published a wide variety of genres of works, including riddles; game manuals; drama and popular songs; collections of letters, poetry, and prose; annotations of the classics; a treatise on phonology; elegies for his dead wife; and textbooks for women—in all more than one hundred volumes of more than forty titles.[11] He also planned to print more diverse genres such as daily encyclopedias, history, books on Buddhism and Daoism, and collections of examination essays.[12] In addition, he frequently supported his friends' publishing projects, both financially and technically. Books that he took charge of printing on behalf of his friends included Wu Sugong's 吳肅公 (1626–99) *Dushu lunshi* 讀書論世 (Reading Books and Discussing Current Matters),[13] Deng Hanyi's 鄧漢儀 (1617–89) *Caogong shi* 曹公詩 (Poetry of Master Cao),[14] Dai Mingshi's 戴名世 (1653–1713)

---

in any official post during his lifetime and that his only title, *Hanlin yuan kongmu*, was also a purchased degree. One of Zhang Chao's closest friends, Jiang Zhilan 江之蘭, strongly dissuaded him from taking up this purchased post in a very disparaging tone. See Chen Ding, "Xinzhai jushi zhuan," in *Liuxi waizhuan*, 561; Jiang Zhilan's letter in *CDYS* 4.36a. Also see Dai Tingjie, "Yasu gongrong," 554–55.

11. Zhang Yi, postscript in Zhang Chao, *Yu Chu xinzhi*, 1760 reprint. Not every book that Zhang Chao published is extant, however. See the appendix for the bibliographical details of the extant editions of Zhang Chao's imprint.

12. *CDOC* 8.18a–21a, 9.1b–3a.

13. *CDYS* 7.16b–17a, 7.26b, 7.38b, 8.6a, 8.40a, 9.8b, 9.31b.

14. *CDYS* 2.19a.

Youming lichao xiaotiwen xuan 有明歷朝小題文選 (Selection of Examination Essays from the Previous Ming Dynasty),[15] Zhuo Erkan's 卓爾堪 (b. 1653) *Sanjia shi* 三家詩 (Poems of Three Masters),[16] and Li Dacun's 李大邨 *Guyi shixuan* 古逸詩選 (Poetry Collection of Old Remnant Subjects).[17]

What earned Zhang Chao his reputation as a publisher, however, were his massive collections of contemporary miscellanies, a popular item among seventeenth-century writers. Amid a flurry of anthologies published in the early Qing, Zhang Chao's compilations were some of the most successful and popular. His *Tanji congshu*, composed of 157 miscellaneous pieces in three installments, was published in 1695 and again in 1697. Following the compilation of *Tanji congshu*, he published *Zhaodai congshu* in three installments in 1697, 1700, and 1703, each consisting of 50 miscellaneous pieces by contemporary writers. *Yu Chu xinzhi* brought together 150 short stories, anecdotes, and biographies by late Ming and early Qing writers in four installments from 1683 to 1704.[18] These collections gained such wide popularity that they circulated not only in Yangzhou, where Zhang Chao resided, but also in Suzhou, Hangzhou, Nanjing, and Beijing. They also found their way into Edo Japan and Chosŏn Korea almost immediately.[19]

The success of Zhang Chao's contemporary compilations was heavily indebted to his connection to a wide network of writers who submitted their works to him for publication. Although he had only passed the preliminary civil service examinations, he was a local celebrity in Yangzhou, renowned for holding poetry gatherings and playing host to sojourning literati.[20] Regarding Zhang Chao's sociability,

15. *CDOC* 7.11a, 7.16b.

16. *CDOC* 11.3a.

17. *CDOC* 9.30a.

18. Deng Changfeng, "*Yu Chu xinzhi* de banke yu Zhang Chao de shengping," in *Ming Qing xiqujia kaolüe xubian*, 157–60. See chapter 4 of the present book for details of the compilation process of *Yu Chu xinzhi*.

19. See chapters 3 and 5 for more details on the transmission of Zhang Chao's books to Japan and Korea.

20. *CDYS* 2.16a–b. Zhang Chao was also frequently invited to other poetry gatherings in Yangzhou. For the example of Zhang Chao's involvement in Kong Shangren's poetry gathering of sixteen Yangzhou writers in 1686, which was later edited as "Guangling tingyu shi" 廣陵聽雨詩, see Dai Tingjie, "Yasu gongrong," 556.

Chen Ding 陳鼎 (b. 1650), one of Zhang Chao's closest friends, offers the following description:

> Zhang Chao has a calm and tranquil personality with little desire for indulgence. He does not like delicious food or luxurious clothes but only likes guests, so guests always crowd his place. The wealthy merchants and business magnates from Huainan [Anhui] only revere luxuries and behave as arrogantly as they please. Even when men of letters visit, they are so insolent as to decline to see them. But Zhang Chao opens his door and invites them in. Literati from everywhere visit him and stay at his place, drinking and writing poetry. And over the years he has not shown any sign of weariness. He covers the expenses for his poor guests to travel or yieldingly helps them if their satchels run out of money. He has never been rich, but his fondness for guests prompts him to spend money on them.
>
> 居士性沉靜, 寡嗜慾, 不愛濃鮮輕肥, 惟愛客, 客嘗滿座。淮南富商大賈, 惟尚豪華, 驕縱自處, 賢士大夫至, 皆傲然拒不見, 惟居士開門延客。四方士至者, 必留飲酒賦詩, 經年累月無倦色。貧乏者, 多資之以往, 或囊匱, 則婉轉以濟。蓋居士未嘗富有也, 以好客故, 竭蹶為之耳。[21]

Aside from socializing in Yangzhou, Zhang Chao maintained a network of coteries by his active exchange of correspondence with members of diverse groups of literati. He collected these letters and printed them in several installments of two collections over a span of about thirty years, from 1677 until 1706:[22] *Chidu yousheng* 尺牘友聲 (Friends' Voices in Letters) gathered 1,009 letters sent to him, and *Chidu oucun* 尺牘偶存 (Random Preservation of Letters) printed 454 replies by Zhang Chao. He stated that he printed only the letters that happened to be left in his possession, but even so the total number of collected epistles reached 1,463 and came from more than three hundred literati, including princes, officials, writers, scholars, publishers, monks, painters, dramatists, and women poets from such diverse places as Yangzhou, Huizhou, Hangzhou, Suzhou, Shaanxi, Nanjing, and Beijing.

21. Chen Ding, "Xinzhai jushi zhuan," in *Liuxi waizhuan*, 561.
22. Gu Guorui and Liu Hui, "'Chidu oucun.'"

The sheer volume and wide network of writers who contributed to Zhang Chao's compilations indicate that he was able to mobilize and deploy at least three different types of communities: those consisting of his kin, his local coteries, and the cross-regional literati community scattered over the Jiangnan region. Above all, Zhang Chao's lineage members were faithful and stable collaborators throughout his publishing career. Huizhou, the Zhang family hometown in southern Anhui province, had been one of the important publishing centers since the Song dynasty, owing to its abundant production of high-quality paper, ink, and ink stones.[23] It was thus common for Huizhou literati with sufficient wealth and education to be engaged in printing, especially of genealogies.[24] The Zhang family had participated in the tradition of publishing family genealogies as well, the first of these genealogies being compiled by none other than Zhang Chao's father, Zhang Xikong, along with his eldest son Zhang Shilin 張士麟 (1636–58) in 1659.[25] It continued to be reprinted by their descendants Zhang Tu'nan 張圖南 and Zhang Kongcheng 張孔成 during the Kangxi and Qianlong periods.[26] The publishing endeavors of the Zhang family were not confined to putting the family genealogy into print but extended to publishing the writing collections of Zhang Xikong, who was the pride of the family and the hometown.[27] Under his studio name, Yiqing tang 詒清堂 (Studio of Bequeathing Purity), Zhang Xikong published scholarly books such as his commentary on the "Tangong" 檀弓 section of *Liji* 禮記 (Book of Rites), titled *Tangong wen* 檀弓問 (Questions of Tangong); a reprint of both Zhu Xi's 朱熹 (1130–1200) *Jinsi lu* 近思錄 (Reflections on Things at Hand) and his commentaries on Zhou Dunyi 周敦頤 (1017–73), Zhang Zai 張載 (1020–77), Cheng Hao 程顥 (1032–85), and

23. The publishing history of Huizhou can be traced back to the mid-Tang dynasty, but its fame as a locus of fine printing culminated in the late Ming. See Xie Zhaozhe, *Wuzazu*, 274; and Hu Yinglin, *Shaoshi shanfang bicong*, 44.

24. Xu Xuelin, *Huizhou keshu*, 46–54.

25. Zhang Xikong, preface in *Xin'an Zhangshi xuxiu zongpu*.

26. Liu Shangheng, *Huizhou keshu yu cangshu*, 125.

27. In the increasingly competitive civil service examination in the Ming and Qing dynasties, achieving the highest degree was an honor not only to the holder's family but also to his hometown. Zhang Xikong's name was listed as a *jinshi* holder in the Huizhou local gazetteers, and his poems and writings were recorded in several literary collections printed in Huizhou.

Cheng Yi 程頤 (1033–1107), titled *Jinsi lu zhuan* 近思錄傳 (Annotations to *Reflections on Things at Hand*, 1678); his discussion of *Yijing* 易經 (Book of Changes) titled *Da Yi bianzhi* 大易辨志 (Explications of the Meanings of the Great *Book of Changes*, 1663); and a collection of his writings, *Yiqing tang ji* 詒清堂集 (Collection of the Studio of Bequeathing Purity), which could not have been completed without the full support and collaboration of both his own family and his wife Chen's 陳 family, members of whom participated as collaborators and collators.[28]

After Zhang Chao inherited his father's studio, the family members involved in Zhang Xikong's projects continued to be steady supporters of Zhang Chao's publishing enterprise.[29] Members of his family who were close to him in age—particularly his younger brothers Jian 漸 and Chun 淳;[30] nephews Shaoji 紹基 (b. 1655), Zhaoxuan 兆鉉, and Yun 韻; a cousin on his mother's side, Chen Mengzheng 陳夢徵; and his distant relatives Zhang Yu'an 張迂庵 and Zhang Shikong 張師孔—played a considerable role in his publishing projects, especially in the early stages before his publishing career was firmly established.[31] For instance, an examination guide that Zhang Chao copublished with fellow Yangzhou publisher Zhang Yongde 張庸德

28. For example, the collation of every *juan* of Zhang Xikong's *Yiqing tang ji* was assigned not only to his sons but also to cousins on both his paternal and maternal sides, such as Zhang Yun 張沄, Chen Mengzheng 陳夢徵 (*hao* Suxin 素心), and Chen Qi 陳圻 (*hao* Kangshou 康疇).

29. Most of Zhang Chao's books retained the same physical characteristics as Zhang Xikong's imprints: white fore edge (*baikou* 白口), single borderline (*danbian* 單邊), a single fishtail (*yuwei* 魚尾), the words "Yiqing tang" below the centerfold (*banxin* 版心), a block size of approximately 18 × 13.5 cm, and leaves of nine lines and twenty characters.

30. Zhang Jian added comments to *Youmengying* and also helped compile the third collection of *Zhaodai congshu* when Zhang Chao experienced emotional distress and financial difficulty; Zhang Chun also added his comments to *Youmengying*.

31. Zhang Shaoji had a close relationship with Chen Ding and mediated the publishing projects between Zhang Chao and Chen Ding. Zhang Zhaoxuan was a close collaborator with Zhang Chao throughout his publishing career; see chapter 3 for details about his contribution. Zhang Yun collated and proofread Zhang Chao's manuscripts and imprints, and also collated the first collection of Zhu Guan's 朱觀 *Suihua jisheng* 歲華紀勝. Chen Mengzheng commentated and collated *Xinzhai zazu* 心齋雜俎. Zhang Yu'an commented on *Youmengying*. Zhang Shikong was a cousin

in 1697, *Sishu zunzhu huiyi jie* 四書尊注會意解 (Explication of the Annotations of the *Four Books*), was closer to a Zhang family project, since almost all of Zhang Chao's direct family members, such as his sons Shaozong 紹宗 and Shaoxian 紹先, grandsons Qingzeng 慶曾 and Fuzeng 復曾, younger brothers Jian and Chun, and nephews Shaoji, Yuzeng 愉曾, and Qizeng 啓曾, participated as proofreaders and collators.[32] The family continued to possess Zhang Chao's original woodblocks after his death, at least until the Qianlong period. Some of the reprints of *Yu Chu xinzhi*, *Chidu yousheng*, and *Chidu oucun* were advertised as being reprinted from Zhang Chao's original blocks by his descendants.[33]

In addition to the hands-on help, the family connection was always an important factor in recruiting contributors for Zhang Chao's imprint. Zhang Xikong's fame, as a highest degree holder, enabled Zhang Chao to build an extensive connection with high officials and nationally renowned scholars such as Zhou Lianggong 周亮工 (1612–72). Wu Weiye 吳偉業 (1609–72), one of the eminent poets of the early Qing, acceded to Zhang Chao's request to contribute a preface to his late father's writing collection because he was a distant relative of Zhang Chao's grandmother.[34] Moreover, the most influential commentator on *Jin Ping Mei*, Zhang Daoshen 張道深 (1670–98), better known by his pen name Zhupo 竹坡, played a decisive role in shaping Zhang Chao's collection of aphorisms, *Youmengying*, into its present form by attaching a number of comments. Although they had not met before, Zhang Zhupo quickly formed a close relationship with Zhang Chao when he stayed in Yangzhou in 1692, merely because they shared

of Zhang Chao's father. He collated *Heke Cao Tao Xie Sanjia shi* 合刻曹陶謝三家詩 with Zhang Chao and Zhuo Erkan 卓爾堪.

32. Zhang Chao and Zhang Yongde collaborated in completing *Sishu zunzhu huiyi jie* in 1697, but after nine years they argued over the property rights to the book. For the collaboration and dispute between Zhang Chao and Zhang Yongde, see Suyoung Son, "Between Writing and Publishing Letters," 878–99.

33. Zhang Yi, postscript in Zhang Chao, *Yu Chu xinzhi*, 1760 reprint; the cover pages of *Chidu yousheng* and *Chidu oucun* indicate that the printed copy was from the original block that Zhang Chao made by including such phrases as "definitive edition of Xinzhai [Zhang Chao]" (*Xinzhai dingben* 心齋定本) and "retention of the blocks" (*benya cangban* 本衙藏板).

34. Wu Weiye, preface in Zhang Xikong, *Yiqing tang ji*.

the same surname and the same family origin. Zhang Zhupo not only contributed eighty-three comments, or one-fourth of the total comments of the initial printed copy of *Youmengying*, but also helped Zhang Chao proofread and collate his imprints.[35]

Aside from his family network, Zhang Chao also maintained a close connection with the literati of his hometown, Huizhou. Although he left Huizhou at an early age, he retained a strong sense of local identity. He actively collaborated with his Huizhou friends Min Linsi 閔麟嗣 (1628–1704), Wang Shihong 汪士鋐 (1658–1723), and Chen Ding on several book projects about Huangshan 黄山, the sacred mountain in the region.[36] Most of his close friends were Huizhou natives, including not only Huizhou residents but also many who had migrated to Yangzhou. Because Huizhou merchants dominated the salt trade in Yangzhou, many Huizhou natives relocated to Yangzhou, contributing to its flourishing economy.[37] Zhang Chao made full use of his position as a native of Huizhou who had settled in Yangzhou when building his personal connections,[38] and he gathered a noticeably large number of writings from Huizhou writers for use in his printed compilations.[39]

35. *CDYS* 8.25a–b, 8.26b–27a. Wu Gan, *Jin Ping Mei pingdianjia*, 17 and 69. Because of their close connection, some scholars suspect that Zhang Chao might have written a preface to the *Jin Ping Mei*. See Andrew Lo, "Amusement Literature," 275.

36. Zhang Chao was involved in the publishing of Min Linsi's *Huangshan zhi dingben* 黄山志定本 (1679), Wang Shihong's *Huangshan zhi xuji* 黄山志續集, and Chen Ding's *Huangshan shilüe* 黄山史略 from their conception to the final stage. On the surge of seventeenth-century literati interest in Huangshan, see McDermott, "Making of a Chinese Mountain," 145–69.

37. Zhu Fuwei, *Yangzhou shishu*, 199–206; Finnane, *Speaking of Yangzhou*, 43–68.

38. Zhang Chao's Huizhou friends included Jiang Zhilan, Yao Man 姚曼, Li Ruogu 李若谷, Fang Qijin 方淇蓋, Jiang Zhu 江注, Zheng Jinde 鄭晉德, Wang Tang 王棠, Yin Shu 殷曙 (b. 1624), Hong Jiazhi 洪嘉植, Wu Wenjiong 吳雯炯, Cheng Jing'e 程京萼 (1645–1715), Xu Chengxuan 許承宣, and Xu Chengjia 許承家, to name but a few. Some of his Huizhou native friends, such as Cha Shibiao 查士標 (1615–98), Wu Ai 吳藹, Wang Ji 汪楫 (1628–89), Cui Ruyue 崔如岳, Cheng Sui 程邃 (1605–91), Jiang Shijie 姜實節 (1647–1709), Zong Yuanyu 宗元豫, Tan Zong 譚宗, Yang Lai 楊騋, and Wu Qi 吳綺 (1619–94), had migrated to and settled in Yangzhou.

39. Zhang Chao collected the works of a number of Huizhou literati not only in his *TJCS* and *ZDCS* but also in the third collection of *Shiguan*, which he edited on behalf of Deng Hanyi. Lu Lin, "Qingchu zongji *Shiguan*," 289–306; Lo, "Amusement Literature," 279.

Zhang Chao built a larger network of connections in Yangzhou as well. Because of its beautiful scenery, various entertainments, and renown as a cultural center, many literati from all parts of the country flocked to Yangzhou to sojourn and live.[40] As the eminent dramatist Kong Shangren 孔尚任 (1648–1718), also a friend of Zhang Chao, once remarked, "Guangling [Yangzhou] is a great inn for the literati of the world. Everyone who possesses talent and nourishes expertise stays in Guangling. It is like a market in which all kinds of artisans have set up shop."[41] Yangzhou provided Zhang Chao with ample opportunities to make friends on a wider interregional scale. The most renowned literati included Deng Hanyi, Gong Xian 龔賢 (1618–89), Yu Huai 余懷 (1616–96), Zhu Da 朱耷 (zi Bada shanren 八大山人, 1626–1705), Mao Xiang 冒襄 (1611–93), Ji Yingzhong 紀映鍾, Zhang Zong 張摠 (fl. 1682), Cai Xi 蔡璽, Hu Jingfu 胡靜夫, Sun Zhiwei 孫枝蔚 (1620–87), and the brothers Wang Gai 王概 (1654–1710), Wang Shi 王蓍 (1649–1734), and Wang Nie 王臬, all of whom became faithful contributors to and supporters of Zhang Chao's publication projects.

As demand for Zhang Chao's compilations rose, he also broadened his connections beyond his intimate coterie. Having heard by word of mouth about ongoing compilation projects, many writers who had not had any prior contact with him sent him their works. Book merchants and literati publishers also contacted him with offers of reciprocal cooperation. They included commercial publishers and literati publishers who were active in Yangzhou, such as Zhu Shen 朱慎, Wang Bin 王賓, and Zhang Yongde; the ones in Suzhou, Hu Qiyi 胡其毅 and Gu Sili 顧嗣立 (fl. 1712); and local bookstores such as Daibao lou 貸寶樓 and Baohan lou 寶翰樓 in Yangzhou and Jingde tang 經德堂 in Nanjing.[42] Their relationships cannot be fully defined as entrepreneurial, because they always worked on private and intimate terms. Nevertheless, his connections with those who were deeply involved in publishing and

---

40. On the flourishing literati culture in Yangzhou in the seventeenth century, see Meyer-Fong, *Building Culture*, and Finnane, *Speaking of Yangzhou*.

41. "廣陵為天下人士之大逆旅，凡懷才抱藝者，莫不萬舍廣陵，蓋如百工之居肆焉。" Kong Shangren, "Yu Li Wanpei" 與李畹佩, in *Kong Shangren quanji*, 2:1235.

42. *CDYS* 1.13a–b, 2.19a, 2.30a–b, 3.12a–b, 3.35a–b, 3.38a, 5.6b–7a, 7.27a–b, 9.7a–b, 9.15b–16b, 9.24b; *CDOC* 1.20b–21a, 4.15b–16b, 5.8a, 5.27b–28a, 10.22a, 11.19b.

the book market gave Zhang Chao a range of information and practical tips on publishing.

Zhang Chao's relationship with the Hangzhou literatus-publisher Wang Zhuo 王晫 (b. 1636) is a good example of how such connections were decisive in expanding the scope of his books. As I will discuss in detail in chapter 2, Wang Zhuo had already published a number of books and gained a reputation when Zhang Chao first contacted him to propose a collaboration making compilations. In addition to abundant experience and practical skills that Zhang Chao could rely on, Wang Zhuo's ties with the Hangzhou literati community contributed greatly to the expanded scale of Zhang Chao's compilations. His network of friends had spread so broadly that it included a number of Hangzhou writers of repute, such as Mao Jike 毛際可 (1633–1708), Mao Qiling 毛奇齡 (1623–1713), Fang Xiangying 方象瑛 (b. 1632), Lu Ciyun 陸次雲 (1636–1702), Wu Yiyi 吳儀一 (1647–1704), Xu Qiu 徐釚 (1636–1708), Chen Yuankun 沉元琨, and others.[43] Wang Zhuo introduced them to Zhang Chao, and they submitted their works for the compilations. Some exchanged letters with Zhang Chao via Wang Zhuo, who sent and received these letters using his own address.[44] A letter from the Hangzhou writer Chai Shitang 柴世堂 to Zhang Chao describes in amusing terms how he had been able to glimpse Zhang Chao's latest imprints at Wang Zhuo's studio and why he wanted to pursue a direct relationship with Zhang Chao:

> I got to read your newly engraved books piled up on the desk of Mr. Qiangdong [Wang Zhuo] yesterday. I felt deeply sorry that I had not sent my works earlier, since not one of my pieces is included in your books. I have enjoyed reading the books of famous people since I was young. Just as I cannot help drooling when I see a cart of malted wheat [for liquor] on the street, I never fail to purchase rare and extraordinary books. And yet your books are much more extraordinary! I have heard that your munificent [publishing] projects are quite numerous and that you do not stint on money [when it comes to printing]. How regretful I will be if I am not able to come by all the imprints that you have been printing.

43. *CDYS* 10.38a–b, 11.2a, 11.11a, 11.36b–37a, 13.14a, 13.27a, 15.14a–b; *CDOC* 6.17a–b, 7.23b, 8.8b–9a.

44. *CDYS* 11.11a, 11.30a, 11.36b, 12.34b, 15.30a, 15.34a; *CDOC* 7.22a, 10.15b, 10.17a.

Please send me all your books, as though giving a huge chunk of beef to a person who has not eaten for several days.

昨於牆東先生案頭得讀新刻裒然如許。深悔續寄逡巡，未得一附傳書也。弟少所嗜好唯見名人著述，不禁如道逢軥車流涎，希異以必購得而後已。然於先生述作爲尤甚! 向聞先生豪舉頗多，揮金不怯，兹何惜盡以先後所刻，種種悉取。寄惠俾旬飢者而得太牢耶。[45]

Once such connections were established, the relationships tended to grow on their own. For example, Hangzhou native Wu Chenyan 吳陳琰 (fl. 1698) became acquainted with Zhang Chao through Wang Zhuo's introduction. He showed great interest in Zhang Chao's publishing project and provided substantial help in gathering materials for compilation.[46] He not only submitted several unpublished works of his own,[47] but also encouraged the cooperation of his friends by introducing Zhang Chao to members of his cross-regional network of coteries, such as the Suzhou literatus-publisher Gu Sili; the Yangzhou salt merchant Guo Yuanyu 郭元釪 (d. 1722); the high official and writer Song Luo 宋犖 (1634–1713); and the fifth son of Zhou Lianggong and prefect of Yangzhou at the time, Zhou Zaidu 周在都 (b. 1655).[48] The chain of Hangzhou acquaintances, extending from Wang Zhuo to Wu Chenyan and thence to Wu Chenyan's circle, thus made Zhang Chao's compilations more copious and extensive, and also helped spread the reputation of the books in Yangzhou, Hangzhou, and beyond.

45. *CDYS* 15.15a.

46. *CDYS* 10.38a–b, 11.11a–12b, 11.30a–31a, 11.38b–39b, 12.34b–35a, 15.30a–b, 15.34a–b, 15.40b; *CDOC* 7.1a–b, 7.8b, 7.19b–7.20a, 10.5a, 10.10b, 10.15b, 10.16b–17a.

47. Wu Chenyan sent Zhang Chao his "Chunqiu sanzhuan tongyi kao" 春秋三傳同異攷, "Lansheng tu" 攬勝圖, "Dengke lu ji" 登科錄記, "Fangshenghui yue" 放生會約, and "Zashuo" 雜説 in the hope of being included in the ongoing projects, and, except for "Dengke lu ji," all of his submissions were included in either *TJCS* or *ZDCS*.

48. *CDYS* 15.30a–b, 15.34a–b.

The Collective Process of Publishing

Zhang Chao's network of literati continued to expand as his compilations gained popularity. A writer would introduce Zhang Chao to his coterie and then members of that group would often introduce him to other groups of friends successively. Some of these relationships extended from father to son, brother to brother, and husband to wife.[49] Zhang Chao's relationships were thus not confined to people with whom he had a close affiliation but stretched to include an increasingly wider pool of literati through intermediate ties woven through networks of friendship, kinship, and local and cross-regional communities of literati. With varying degrees of cohesion and participation, the succession of connections and relationships shaped Zhang Chao's publishing into a collective enterprise not just for the gathering of materials, but also for propelling a publishing project from the initial phase of production to actual distribution.

Although the details of the private publishing process are usually difficult to reconstruct owing to a lack of concrete records, the letters exchanged between Zhang Chao and his friends when he was publishing the compilations *Tanji congshu*, *Zhaodai congshu*, and *Yu Chu xinzhi* give us a glimpse of the general pattern that seventeenth-century writers' publishing followed in this period. These letters, which were later published as *Chidu yousheng* and *Chidu oucun*, show that Zhang Chao, far from being a solitary individual in charge of selecting, preparing, and marketing the books produced, solicited the communal endeavors of his coterie at almost every juncture.[50] In the following discussion, I

49. Father and son relationships included Huang Yun 黃雲 and Tailai 泰來, Mao Xiang 冒襄 and Danshu 丹書 (fl. 1675), You Tong 尤侗 (1618–1704) and Zhen 珍 (1647–1721), Yu Huai and Lanshuo 蘭碩, Zhou Lianggong and Zaidu, and Zhang Zong and his sons Yun 筠 and Chun 淳. Brother relationships included Wang Gai, Wang Shi, and Wang Nie, and Xu Chengxuan 許承宣 and Xu Chengjia 許承家. A female painter and poet, Wang Zheng 王正, who not only sent some letters to Zhang Chao but also wrote a couple of prefaces for his books, became acquainted with him because of Zhang's relationship with her husband, Li Ruogu. See the entry about her in Li Dou, *Yangzhou huafang lu*, 46.

50. For the communal nature of literati publishing in this period, also see Meyer-Fong, "Packaging the Men," 5–56; and Carlitz, "Printing as Performance," 283–90.

describe the steps in Zhang Chao's publishing process to demonstrate that every step was open to involvement and participation by groups of his fellow literati.

1. INITIATING THE PROJECTS

Zhang Chao first conceived the idea of compilations, but discussions with his coterie helped bring them to their final shape. When he first designed *Tanji congshu*, he consulted with his relatives Zhang Zhao-xuan and Zhang Yu'an, who had prior publishing experience. Based on information about publishing projects in progress, Zhang Zhao-xuan suggested niche markets in which Zhang Chao's books could gain success. Their advice and information about similar competing works eventually resulted in several changes to Zhang Chao's initial plan, first reducing its scope from a collection of famous prose of all historical periods to a collection of prose of the Ming and Qing eras, and eventually making it a collection of contemporary prose.[51]

Zhang Chao's imprints went through revisions not only during their conception but also in the printing stage. As soon as he printed out the first installment of *Tanji congshu*, Zhang Chao received criticism and advice on sequels from his readers. He accordingly adjusted the format and style of the subsequent imprints. For example, the punctuation used in the first and second installments of *Zhaodai congshu* was removed in the third because the elite readers questioned the necessity of punctuation. They considered that punctuated text was for a less educated audience and insisted that it was not suitable for such a compilation as *Zhaodai congshu*, designed principally for highly educated readers.[52]

51. *CDYS* 6.29a–30a; *CDOC* 3.27b–28a. See chapter 3 for details.
52. Zhang Chao, "Fanli" 凡例 (Editorial Principles), in the second collection of *ZDCS*, 183, and "Fanli," in the third collection of *ZDCS*, 343.

2. GATHERING THE MATERIALS

Zhang Chao collected materials for his compilations from several sources. He searched for them in a variety of printed books, including literary collections, anthologies of tales and anecdotes, and court gazetteers.[53] But he was more eager to find recently created pieces, often buying manuscripts from the book market or publicly soliciting the submission of works.[54] In one of the announcements calling for submissions, Zhang Chao wrote:

> In my life I have not encountered many rare books, but I did not quail at borrowing and transcribing them. When I happened to see extraordinary books, I desired them and purchased them on the spot. Yet I feel embarrassed that my collection is not wide; I feel even more ashamed that my selection is not numerous. If you have any new pieces, please send them to me promptly. If you live nearby, I beg you to give them to me directly. It would be enough if you would just let me know what you know [about newly composed pieces].
>
> 生平罕逢秘本，不憚假抄；偶爾得遇異書，輒為求購。第媿蒐羅未廣，尤慚採輯無多。凡有新篇，速祈惠教。並望乞鄰而與，無妨舉爾所知。[55]

Despite public announcements soliciting manuscripts from the anonymous reading audience, however, most works that Zhang Chao published were in fact collected from his existing network of friends and acquaintances, who voluntarily submitted their writings or those of members of their coterie. They usually sent transcribed copies, but some also sent a printed copy or engraved woodblocks.[56] Benefiting by the development of the postal service in late imperial China,[57] Zhang Chao was able to collect a significant portion of these manuscripts by mail rather than personal contact. Zhang Chao's brother Zhang Jian,

53. Zhang Chao's "Xuanli" 選例 (Selection Principles), in the first collection of *ZDCS*, 3; *CDYS* 4.16b; *CDOC* 7.1b, 7.18a, 7.23b, 8.7b; and also see the table of contents of Zhang Chao, *Yu Chu xinzhi*, 1760 reprint.
54. *CDYS* 14.1b; Zhang Chao, "Fanli," in *Yu Chu xinzhi* 3a.
55. Zhang Chao, "Fanli shize," in *Yu Chu xinzhi* 3a.
56. Zhang Chao, *Yu Chu xinzhi* 2.11b; *CDYS* 11.36b, 13.27a.
57. Brook, "Communications and Commerce."

who helped in collecting works for the third installment of *Zhaodai congshu*, described the flood of submissions from readers as follows: "Every day what the postal service brings is received at the courtyard; every day the beautiful and brilliant works are piled up on the desk."[58] Zhang Chao did not fail to give credit to the people who made contributions to the gathering of materials by mentioning their names one by one at the front of his imprint.[59]

3. TRANSCRIBING THE MANUSCRIPTS

After receipt, manuscripts were usually transcribed onto thin sheets of paper, known as "divided grids" (*huage* 劃格), which were ruled into columns and spaces for easy engraving.[60] Most literati-publishers hired professional transcribers (*shuyong* 書傭) on an ad hoc basis,[61] but Zhang Chao seems to have had a full-time secretary (*jishi* 記室) who was in charge of transcribing and sometimes printing in addition to basic duties such as assisting with correspondence and serving visitors.[62] Wang Zhuo, as a coeditor of the compilation, often sent Zhang Chao a carefully transcribed and collated transcription (*qingben* 清本) to save Zhang Chao some labor.[63]

4. CARVING WOODBLOCKS

Once transcribed, sheets of text would be placed on woodblocks, and a carver would cut around the written characters. Because carving was the most labor-intensive and expensive step of the publishing process, which dictated the quality of an imprint, hiring carvers was considered

58. "夫郵筒投贈之來，日接於庭；琳琅璀璨之篇，日盈於几。" Zhang Jian, "Xu," in *ZDCS*, 343.

59. See, for example, Zhang Chao, "Fanli," in *TJCS*, 205.

60. Tsien, "Technical Aspects," 18.

61. Jiang Long, "Fanli," in *Qingchu shiji*, in Xie Zhengguang and She Rufeng, *Qingchu ren xuan*, 182; Ōki, "Minshin ryōdai ni okeru shōhon," 249. Sometimes *shuyong* also did binding. See, for example, Tang Shunzhi's "Hu Mao guanji" 胡貿棺記, in *Tang Jingchuan wenji* 8.40b–42a.

62. *CDYS* 3.18a, 5.9b, 11.15b, 13.29b.

63. *CDYS* 13.29b.

very important.[64] Unlike a few affluent literati who maintained in-house carvers and printers,[65] budget-conscious literati-publishers usually hired carvers when the need arose.[66] Zhang Chao used craftsmen only when he needed to cut the blocks, which was an economical decision considering the relatively low wages and abundant supply of carvers in the region. The carvers from his hometown, She county in Huizhou, were particularly known for their superb skills and great mobility. Their reputation was such that, "when people have something to carve, they always ask for the carvers from She county."[67] Since they were famous for being mobile—farming during the season and carving during the off-farming season—they were hired ad hoc by literati-publishers.[68] The carvers also served as go-betweens, connecting Zhang Chao with commercial bookshops,[69] or as deliverymen carrying his imprints from Yangzhou to other cities.[70]

64. *CDYS* 10.21b. According to the Yangzhou Guangling guji keyinshe, the only traditional woodblock publishing company still operating in contemporary China, the ratio of collator to scriber to carver to printer to binder is usually 1:2:4:1:4. Miu Yonghe, "Mao Jin Jigu ge," 1:612.

65. For example, the eminent bibliophile Mao Jin 毛晉 (1599–1659) set up a publishing pavilion of eight rooms in his house. He engraved books in the lower rooms and the contiguous galleries of the pavilion and preserved the blocks in the upper rooms. He not only hired almost twenty full-time printers and carvers in his library called Jigu ge 汲古閣, but also asked his literati friends to collate the books in other pavilions such as Lüjun ting 綠君亭 and Erru ting 二如亭. Ōki, *Minmatsu kōnan*, 54; Miu Yonghe, "Mao Jin Jigu ge," 1:592–615.

66. For example, the Huizhou literatus-publisher Zhu Guan sojourned in Yangzhou, Hanshui 漢水, Zhangjiang 漳江, and Huizhou, and employed local carvers at each location for expediency. Zhu Guan, "Fanli," in *Guochao shizheng* 國朝詩正, in Xie Zhengguang and She Rufeng, *Qingchu ren xuan*, 287.

67. "時人有刻, 必求歙工。" Zhang Xiumin, *Zhongguo yinshua shi*, 356–57; Liu Shangheng, *Huizhou keshu yu cangshu*, 175–85.

68. Michela Bussotti argues that carvers' traveling to work outside Huizhou was a local cultural practice that went well beyond that of Huizhou's traveling merchants. See Bussotti, *Gravures de Hui*, 283.

69. *CDOC* 11.9a–14b.

70. *CDOC* 7.15a.

5. PROOFREADING THE SAMPLE COPY

After a proof-print was pulled from an engraved block, the sample copy (called *jianyangben* 見樣本 or *yangben* 樣本) was sent to members of the coterie for proofreading.[71] When Zhang Chao copublished *Tanji congshu* with Wang Zhuo, a sample copy was usually sent to Wang Zhuo to discuss any editorial decisions.[72] As the popularity of the compilations grew, some readers became impatient to read the final imprint and even tried to acquire a sample copy. Wang Zhuo once complained, "I beg you to send me more copies, since every friend wants to take away this book [i.e., *Zhaodai congshu*] when they see it. For example, the sample copy that you had sent me was already wrested away by a friend!"[73]

Some contributors to a collection would ask Zhang Chao to send them a sample copy of their work to collate and proofread, but not all works were collated by the authors themselves. Zhang Chao acknowledged each collator by carving his name next to that of the author at the front of each text that appears in *Tanji congshu* and *Zhaodai congshu*. This publicized the participation of a large number of literati in the project in addition to the authors themselves.[74]

6. SOLICITING PARATEXTUAL WRITINGS

While cutting blocks, Zhang Chao commissioned his coterie to send prefaces (*xu* 序), postscripts (*ba* 跋), and verse endorsements (*tici* 題詞) to or comments (*ping* 評) on his books. Particularly in the seventeenth century, it was a popular convention to attach paratextual materials by renowned friends or acquaintances of the author in order to enhance the value of the text.[75] What is noteworthy is that Zhang Chao usually

71. Zhang Chao, "Fanli," in *ZDCS*, 343.

72. *CDYS* 8.16b, 13.29b; *CDOC* 4.7a–b, 5.29b–30a.

73. "乞多惠數冊, 已友人見者, 無不欲搶欲奪也。即如所寄樣本, 已爲友人強要去矣!" *CDYS* 9.10b.

74. Zhang Chao's *TJCS* and *ZDCS*, for example, recorded more than a hundred literati as collators. Durand argues that the number of participating literati must have been exaggerated for marketing purposes. See Dai Tingjie, "Yasu gongrong," 607.

75. Following Gérard Genette's definition, I use the term "paratext" to mean anything in a book that lies outside the main text but constitutes part of the meaning of

carved the main text in advance and sent a printed copy of it along with his request for prefaces and comments instead of waiting for the paratextual materials to arrive and printing them together with the main text.[76] The literati involved also assumed that they would write the paratexts only after they received the printed copy. When Zhang Chao created *Youmengying*, he asked Wang Zhuo to write a preface to it. Wang Zhuo replied: "I will wait until you finish printing and add a few words to the sample copy that you will send."[77] The cutting of the blocks for paratextual materials was thus generally considered a separate task from the carving of the main text.

7. CORRECTING THE CARVED BLOCKS

Upon indications from writers or collators, the engraved woodblock was corrected by means of supplementary carving (*buke* 補刻). This was usually undertaken for two reasons: the first was to correct errors in the woodblock by scraping down wrong characters and adding plugs with the correct ones;[78] the second was to add new material, usually consisting of paratextual pieces. This was often achieved by inserting lines or characters in the empty spaces of the block. For example, Wang Zhuo often asked to add his comments in the middle. "Seeing that there are empty lines and empty [spaces on] the woodblock under each entry in the collection," he wrote, "I ventured to record a few short comments on a separate sheet for you to choose from."[79] Zhang Chao also intentionally left an empty space at the end of each section on the block while awaiting comments from his friends so as to be able to incorporate them later when he printed off more copies.[80]

---

the book. See Genette, *Paratexts*, 2–12. Paratextual materials such as prefaces, verse endorsements, postscripts, and commentaries became indispensable components of the book in the seventeenth century. See chapter 2 for details.

76. *CDOC* 2.3a.

77. "或俟先生刻成, 幸以刻樣見寄, 當跋數語。" *CDYS* 6.1b.

78. *CDYS* 11.13a, 11.32a, 13.22a.

79. "見集中各條下, 尚有空行留木者, 妄擬小批數則, 另錄別紙, 以備采擇。" *CDYS* 9.10a–b. For more examples, see *CDYS* 2.1b–2a, 9.30b–31a, 13.23a, 15.14a.

80. *CDYS* 2.1b–2a; *CDOC* 5.4a, 7.18a.

8. PRINTING AND BINDING

The collation of wooden blocks would normally be followed by print-ing and binding. For financial reasons, however, these steps were often left not to the publisher but to the people who wanted a copy of the book. Writers who lacked the money to defray printing and binding expenses forwarded their woodblocks directly to bookstores, where those who wished to own a copy would purchase paper and have the text printed and bound themselves.[81] Although Zhang Chao was able to manage printing a small number of copies for his coterie, he was unable to cover all the expenses of printing and binding once he was inundated with requests for his books. He mostly relied on financial donations from his friends[82] or entrusted the blocks to bookstores.[83]

As a final stage of book production, binding was a relatively simple task of cutting, pasting, and stitching a cover onto the pages. Since binding was considered a personalized activity that reflected individ-ual owners' taste, it was fairly common for printed copies to be distrib-uted rough-bound (*maozhuang* 毛裝) or unbound so that owners could do the final binding themselves.[84] Zhang Chao's books were often distributed unbound. A reader from Guanzhong 關中 once sent a letter to Zhang Chao stating that he would be willing to pay the bind-ing expense because the printed sheets of a book often arrived with the

81. Ye Dehui, *Shulin qinghua; Shulin yuhua*, 120; Zhang Xiumin, *Zhongguo yin-shua shi*, 71, 249.

82. *CDYS* 9.31b, 10.8a; *CDOC* 11.13b.

83. *CDYS* 10.27b–28a; *CDOC* 6.12b–13a. See chapter 3 for more details.

84. There are several examples in which the owner, not the publisher, of the books did the final binding. One of the closest friends of Zhang Chao, Gu Cai 顧彩 (fl. 1692), sent him a copy of Tang Chuanying's 湯傳楹 (1620–44) *Xiangzhong cao* 湘中草 and told him: "I heard that you were looking for a copy of *Xiangzhong cao*, so I especially searched for it in Wumen [Suzhou] and am sending it to you. But the copy is from the book market, so it is not in good shape. You should bind it yourself" 聞先生向欲覓湘中草一部, 特從吳門覓來奉敬。但其帙經市肆, 不甚美觀。先生自加裝潢可也. *CDYS* 3.10b–11a. For the convention of binding, see Edgren, "Fengmianye," 262; also see Sun Congtian (1692–1767), "Cangshu jiyao," 221. In the West, a book was also customarily sold as unbound sheets and then personalized for the pur-chaser with a custom-made binding. See Jardine, *Worldly Goods*, 140–41; and Knight, *Bound to Read*.

pages in the wrong order.[85] In short, the stages of printing and binding were not regarded as the obligation of publishers at the time but were only completed contingent upon the publisher's budget or at the request of readers.

9. DISTRIBUTING THE PRINTED BOOKS

Once printed, copies were shipped off via personal messengers, such as servants, itinerant monks,[86] visiting friends,[87] carvers,[88] or traveling booksellers.[89] Zhang Chao's books were first distributed among contributors, preface authors, collators, donors to publication expenses, and Zhang Chao's close circle, who in turn became voluntary distributors within their own groups of friends. The printed copies usually circulated in the form of gifts or reciprocal exchanges without monetary transactions, as was conventional in the socializing practices of literati. In Zhang Chao's case, social dissemination, consolidated by the reciprocity mandated in literati relationships, was a priority, but his publishing project was also enmeshed in the market-controlled distribution system, as I discuss in chapter 3.

In contrast to modern industrial book production, Zhang Chao's publishing process did not consider printing as the final stage of text production. Although each step appears to have been taken in linear order, it was more often the case that several steps would be executed simultaneously, particularly the stage of printing, which was constantly modified by interventions and additions from his coterie. As already noted, Zhang Chao often asked his friends to send in paratextual pieces not before but after he finished cutting the main text and printing the copy. He would then incorporate his friends' additions into the woodblock as he printed off more copies. Because of these

---

85. *CDYS* 13.3b. In another example, a friend Zhang Zong sent the copies that he acquired from Zhang Chao to his binder (*zhuanghuang zhe* 裝潢者). *CDYS* 5.32a–b.

86. *CDOC* 5.13a, 8.2a, 8.5a.

87. *CDOC* 9.8b.

88. *CDYS* 11.32a.

89. *CDOC* 8.11a, 8.29a, 8.29b.

continuous amendments, Zhang Chao's printed books often had different numbers of paratextual pieces depending on when the text was printed. For example, the number of prefaces and postscripts to Zhang Chao's collection of riddles *Xinzhai zazu* 心齋雜俎 (Miscellaneous Morsels from Xinzhai) increased from three to five from one impression to the next of the same edition.[90] The comments attached to *Xinzhai liaofu ji* also increased from two to five.[91] In addition, the number of prefaces and postscripts to *Youmengying* went up from three to five and eventually to six.[92] The multiple impressions of a single edition reveal that the augmentation of the prefaces and comments was done during the circulation of the printed copies. This created a circular process of printing a copy, getting comments, recarving the block, and then printing a new copy for further review and commentary by yet another friend or friend of a friend. Far from being produced and circulated as a fixed and complete artifact, Zhang Chao's printed book was formed into its final shape during the ongoing publishing process.

The flexible publishing process was due in part to woodblock printing, for text copying by woodblock allowed adjustments and revisions to be made relatively easily by direct carving on the wooden block.[93] Thus woodblock printing corresponded to a large extent to the

90. There are three extant copies of *Xinzhai zazu*, in the National Library of China, the Beijing University Library, and the Shanghai Library, which are all different impressions of a single edition. Whereas the Shanghai Library copy has only three prefaces, the Beijing University Library copy has four prefaces, and the National Library of China copy has four prefaces and one postscript.

91. Three extant copies of *Xinzhai liaofu ji* are available in the Beijing Normal University Library, the Fudan University Library, and the Naikaku Bunko in Japan. Given the number of attached comments, it is clear that the Beijing Normal University Library copy is a later impression than the other two. For example, one of the collected works, "Yanfu" 煙賦, is composed of Zhang Chao's own rhapsody on tobacco and comments from his friends. Whereas the other two copies have four comments, the Beijing Normal University Library copy contains five. The later appended comment is even long enough to require more space so that the Beijing Normal University Library copy actually has two "eleventh" pages ("eleven" 十一 and "another eleven" 又十一).

92. See the next section for details about the editions of *Youmengying*.

93. As scholars point out, woodblock printing was not fundamentally distinct from manuscript production because it is the reproduction of a manuscript, only on

malleability intrinsic to manuscript transmission, which often enabled editing, altering, and revising to become part of the textual composition. But, more important, Zhang Chao and his friends may well have brought this more fluid idea of the text to bear on the practice of publishing. Rather than delimiting and securing the final shape of a text once and for all, Zhang Chao and his coterie appear to have used print not much differently from manuscript production and circulation, in the sense that amendments and changes could be easily incorporated into the text if and as the need arose. Being immersed in the manuscript tradition, Zhang Chao's readers did not hesitate to ask him to correct works and add comments in the midst of the printing process, even after receiving a printed copy. By the same token, Zhang Chao was hardly interested in keeping his original text intact. Instead, he seems to have been prepared for his friends' participation, which was an indispensable part of the text-making process, even if it meant recarving and reprinting a text. Zhang Chao and his coterie took it for granted that, far from being a fixed copy, a notion that reflects the system of industrial book production that is standard in the modern period, a printed text was something fluid and thus could be supplemented and transformed, so that any copy of a printed book was not likely to be identical to any other copy.

Printing as Text Making of *Youmengying*

The flexible printing process made the participation of readers an integral part of text making and enabled a collaborative and cumulative effort in the production of a printed text. Since Zhang Chao's publishing process openly invited amendments and interventions by a later hand, writing and reading were often not discrete but mutually interactive tasks. Zhang Chao's printing of *Youmengying* is a good example of the way in which the versatility of the printing process was built into the sociality of making texts in the literati community in the seventeenth century.

---

a wooden block. See Kornicki, *Book in Japan*, 27–29; and Chia, *Printing for Profit*, 11–12, 25–33, and 42.

Youmengying is one of Zhang Chao's best known and most influential works, both among his contemporaries and in later periods up to the present day. Following on the popularity of casual short prose in the late Ming book market, *Youmengying* collects Zhang Chao's quick-witted and perceptive maxims and aphorisms in succinct sentences. Its entries cover subjects as varied as reading, books, friendship, poetry, calligraphy, landscape, the seasons, flowers and beauty, musical instruments, and meditation. These diverse themes of what could be called the aesthetic and trifling aspects of literati life, not necessarily related to a larger political and moral agenda, are considered a repository for highly refined sentiments toward material affluence, sophisticated taste, and a cultivated lifestyle represented by the late Ming and early Qing literati culture.[94]

Despite various approaches to this collection by later critics, critical interpretation of the text itself is often lacking, partly because of its loose structure and fragmentary theme.[95] The text is made up of entries written by Zhang Chao, not more than a couple of sentences in length, each followed by a series of comments appended by his fellow literati. Most modern reprints omit the attached commentaries and only include the entries by Zhang Chao, citing authorial intent as the most important criterion for interpreting the text, but the comments to *Youmengying* are too notable to be dismissed as a mere appendage. First, the number of comments nearly triples the length of the original entry: whereas Zhang Chao wrote 219 items, the number of attached comments ranges from 350 to 701, depending on the edition, with a single chain of comments often running twice the length of Zhang

94. For studies of casual short prose, see, for example, Wu Chengxue, *Wan Ming xiaopin yanjiu*; Clunas, *Superfluous Things*; and Wai-yee Li's two articles "The Collector, the Connoisseur," 269–302, and "Rhetoric of Spontaneity," 32–52.

95. The interpretation of *Youmengying* has varied over time along with changing perspectives toward *xiaopin*. Lin Yutang first pointed to *Youmengying*'s accomplishment of genre as a Chinese-style "essay" in conjunction with the New Culture Movement in the 1920s, defining it as an expression of the Chinese way of enjoying leisure and pleasure. Literary scholars such as Gōyama Kiwamu and Wu Chengxue have identified the emergence of personal and informal aesthetics in the text as being in opposition to ancient-style moral and formalistic literary arguments. See Lin Yutang, *Importance of Living*; Gōyama, *Yūmuei*; and Wu Chengxue, *Wan Ming xiaopin yanjiu*.

Chao's original entry. Second, most comments were less secondary derivatives from the original entries than independent extensions and variations.

The dual and asymmetrical structure of *Youmengying*, consisting of main entry and attached commentary, challenges the conception of the text as a unified, consistent whole in which an author takes a central position in controlling textual meaning. Rather, it is closer to an impromptu combination of disparate and heterogeneous voices of an author and readers. The comments usually touch on the theme that Zhang Chao presents, yet they often borrow his sentence structure or use the same words to skew the entry's original meaning or derail it altogether.[96] Indifferent to the original entry, many commentators also often wrote comments to other comments. The following example shows how the text of *Youmengying* is typically constructed (emphasis is mine):

> Planting flowers *serves to invite* butterflies; piling up rocks *serves to invite* the clouds; cultivating pine trees *serves to invite* the wind; keeping a reservoir of water *serves to* invite duckweed; building a terrace *serves to invite* the moon; planting banana trees *serves to invite* the rain; and planting willow trees *serves to invite* the cicada.
>
> Ni Yongqing [Ni Kuangshi 倪匡世] says, "Editing poetry *serves to invite* slander."[97]
>
> Pang Tianchi [Pang Bi 龐弼] says, "Lack of humaneness *serves to invite* wealth."[98]
>
> Cao Qiuyue [Cao Rong 曹溶, 1613–85] says, "Collecting books *serves to invite* friends."[99]
>
> Cui Lianfeng says, "Brewing wine *serves to invite* me."

---

96. The contemporary reader Jiang Zhilan pointed out the cacophonous nature of comments and urged Zhang Chao to remove them. *CDYS* 6.30b.

97. Ni Kuangshi printed *Zhenya tang huibian shizui* 振雅堂匯編詩最. Zhang Chao's thirty-four poems are included in *juan* 16.

98. See Pang Bi's letters in *CDYS* 15.1b–2b, 15.4a–b, 15.26b–27a.

99. Cao Rong was a high-ranking Qing official, writer, and book collector. He hailed from Jiaxing 嘉興 in Zhejiang province and became a *jinshi* in 1697. See his letter in *CDYS* 1.20a and Zhang Chao's reply, *CDOC* 1.5b–6a.

You Genzhai [You Tong] says, "Where can we find this wise host?"[100]
You Huizhu [You Zhen] says, "Who else can the wise host be but Zhang Chao?"[101]
Lu Yunshi [Lu Ciyun] says, "Accumulating virtue *serves to invite* heaven; laboring on a farm *serves to invite* earth. Then inviting without the intention of return is different from inviting fame and profit."[102]

藝花可以邀蝶，累石可以邀雲，栽松可以邀風，貯水可以邀萍，筑台可以邀月，種蕉可以邀雨，植柳可以邀蟬。

倪永清曰選詩可以邀謗。

龐天池曰不仁可以邀富。

曹秋岳曰藏書可以邀友。

崔蓮峰曰釀酒可以邀我。

尤艮齋曰安得此賢主人？

尤慧珠曰賢主人非心齋而誰？

陸雲士曰積德可以邀天，力耕可以邀地。乃無意相邀而若邀之者，與邀名邀利者迴異。[103]

On the surface, the attached comments are an apparent repetition of the original entry, using the same verb structure "serves to invite" (*keyi yao* 可以邀). Yet on closer examination they are not merely appendages to Zhang Chao's remarks that vividly capture the romantic mood and pleasure of proper harmony between different natural elements. Instead of repeating Zhang Chao's theme, the comments often

100. You Tong was a renowned writer and calligrapher in the seventeenth century. See the exchange of correspondence between him and Zhang Chao in *CDYS* 9.26a–b, 10.17b, 11.18a–b, 13.22a–b; *CDOC* 5.5b–7a, 5.22b–23a, 6.9b, 6.18a–19b, 7.14a–b.

101. You Tong's son, You Zhen, became a *jinshi* in 1681. See his letter in *CDYS* 11.28a–b and Zhang Chao's reply in *CDOC* 7.20b–21a.

102. Lu Ciyun hailed from Hangzhou. He took the special "broad learning and vast erudition" examination (*boxue hongci* 博學鴻詞) in 1679 but did not pass. See the exchange of correspondence between Zhang Chao and Lu Ciyun in *CDYS* 10.29a–30b, 10.31a–b, 11.19b–20b, 11.35a–b; *CDOC* 6.16b–18a, 7.8a, 7.13a–14a, 7.17b–18a, 8.7a–b.

103. Zhang Chao, *Youmengying* 1.8a, Beijing University Library edition. Zhang Chao's main entry is Lin Yutang's translation from his *Importance of Living*, 317. The translation of the commentaries is mine.

stray from the original point. The first few follow the same verb form, "serves to invite," but they gradually go beyond perfunctory repetition and move on to discuss friendship and sociability. For example, the comment by Cui Lianfeng, "Brewing wine serves to invite me," turns Zhang Chao's fanciful mood into a self-referential joke. And the comments by You Tong and his son You Zhen expand Cui Lianfeng's topic by complimenting Zhang Chao's sociability instead of responding to his original theme. The final comment by Lu Ciyun switches back to the original syntax but turns the word game of "serves to invite" toward a contemplation of the meaning of the phrase itself.

Undoubtedly, kinetic and performative composition of linked comments, tinged with a lively and casual tone, evokes a conversational atmosphere around the given topic and would have built a sense of community between author and readers, and among readers. Yang Fuji 楊復吉 (1770–1816), who made sequels to *Zhaodai congshu* after Zhang Chao's death and included *Youmengying* in them, describes the friendly milieu behind this particular method of composition of the text: "When ancient people wrote a book, they put commentary in the middle of the text. But interweaving commentary with the text proper is the new style that *Youmengying* creates. Elegant words and lofty intentions respond in concert back and forth, which makes readers feel as though they are sitting in a long row and having conversations with several guests."[104] As if Zhang Chao's readers had convened together at a social gathering, one comment often invites another, frequently using interrogative forms such as "How about it?" (*heru* 何如) or "Isn't it so?" (*yiweiranfou* 以爲然否).[105] By stimulating participation and dialogue among the readers of the text, the attachment of comments urges readers to add their own comments and further take part in the making of the text.

The conversational and collaborative structure of *Youmengying* was not, however, a product of a "new literary style," as Yang Fuji supposed.

---

104. "昔人著書, 間附評語, 若一評語參錯書中, 則幽夢影創格也。清言雋旨, 前於后喝, 令讀者如入真長座中, 與諸客周旋, 聆其謦欬。" Yang Fuji, postscript to *Youmengying*, in ZDCS, 3220.

105. See, for example, Zhang Chao, *Youmengying*, annot. Wang Feng, 47, 66, 77, 96, 101, 126, 128, and 161.

It was, in fact, the physical embodiment of the text-making process—that is, of the way in which the text was printed. It is unfortunate that the original imprint of *Youmengying* by Zhang Chao is not extant, but three different editions have survived, exposing the process whereby it came into being as a complete text: an early Qing edition, a Daoguang 道光 (1820–50) edition, and a Guangxu 光緒 (1875–1908) edition, which reveal a fair degree of variation. A close comparison of these three editions confirms that they are all later reprints based on different impressions.[106] For the most part, the ratio between the text proper and the comments remains the same, but the editions are distinct in terms of the number of paratextual pieces and particularly in terms of a cumulative increase in comments between editions.

In the early Qing edition in the Beijing University Library (fig. 1.1), the original entry by Zhang Chao (in columns 1 to 3 from the right) is carved in big, bold characters in a single vertical line within the column. It is followed by the comments of Ni Yongqing, Pang Tianchi,

---

106. Scholars such as Zhang Shenyu and Zhao Yi insist that there are only two extant editions of the *Youmengying*: the *ZDCS* edition from the Daoguang reign and the *Xiaoyuan congshu* edition from the Guangxu reign. See Zhang Shenyu and Zhao Yi, "Zhang Chao *Youmengying*," 143–58. But, according to my archival research, three editions survive as described above. The production dates and sequence of editions do not correspond to their printed dates. Even though the printing of the Daoguang edition was earlier than that of the Guangxu edition, it is surmised that the Guangxu edition is based on an earlier transmitted edition. First, it does not contain Zhang Jian's comments written in 1699. Second, there are eighteen fewer comments than in the Daoguang edition. However, it is also impossible for the Daoguang edition to be the direct successor of the Guangxu edition because the number of attached prefaces and postfaces and the order of comments between them are slightly different. According to the postface by Ge Yuanxu 葛元煦, who printed the *Xiaoyuan congshu* edition, he acquired an early transmitted manuscript copy at Liu Shiting's residence that must have been an earlier copy than the one that Yang Fuji acquired for the *ZDCS*. Even though library catalogs do not specify the exact dates, the early Qing edition is possibly the original copy of Zhang Chao or close to the original copy, judging not only from its format and typeface but from the attached comments. It contains the highest number of comments among the three editions, but it cannot be the last edition, following the Daoguang and Guangxu editions, because the number and order of comments are quite different. Thus it appears that these three editions do not belong to a single ancestral edition (*zuben* 祖本) but are the reprints of three different impressions of the original edition. See the appendix for bibliographical details about the three extant editions.

Cao Qiuyue, Cui Lianfeng, You Genzhai, and You Huizhu (in columns 3 to 5), which are cut and arranged in smaller and thinner characters in two lines within a column. An additional comment by Lu Yunshi appears in small characters in the upper margin (above columns 1 to 5). It would appear that these comments were carved in the order in which they were received (with Lu Yunshi's comment presumably last) because they are assigned to columns 3 to 5 in that order. However, when this edition is compared with others, it becomes clear that the comments of Ni Yongqing and Pang Tianchi were in fact submitted later—not first, as is the initial impression given by this edition. Since the space below Zhang Chao's original entry is usually empty, and the other two editions do not contain Pang Tianchi's comment, it is likely that the initial woodblock contained only the four comments by Cao Qiuyue, Cui Lianfeng, You Genzhai, and You Huizhu (in two lines within columns 4 and 5) and that Ni Yongqing's comment was added thereafter, followed by the comments of Lu Yunshi and Pang Tianchi.

The question then arises as to why the comments of Ni Yongqing and Pang Tianchi were engraved directly below the original entry by Zhang Chao, a placement that makes them appear to have been carved first. Given Zhang Chao's publishing process, as described earlier, a probable explanation is that Zhang Chao acquired Ni Yongqing's comment after the cutting of the woodblock was finished, that is, after the carving of the four comments in columns 4 and 5. It seems that he did not mind disrupting the neatness of the carving, perceiving that it was more important to incorporate Ni Yongqing's comment into the text, so he had it carved in the empty space in column 3 just below his own original entry. After carving Ni Yongqing's comment, Zhang Chao must have obtained the comment by Lu Yunshi and put it in the upper margin, called the "book eyebrow" (*shumei* 書眉) or "heavenly head" (*tiantou* 天頭). Eventually, he received the comment by Pang Tianchi and had to cut in the only remaining space—that is, next to Ni Yongqing's comment in column 3, below his own original entry.[107] More research is needed to ascertain whether this edition is from the original

107. The order of the comments is also confirmed by the images in figures 5 and 8 in Dai Tingjie, "*Youmengying* banke kaolun." But Durand did not specify from which edition those images came.

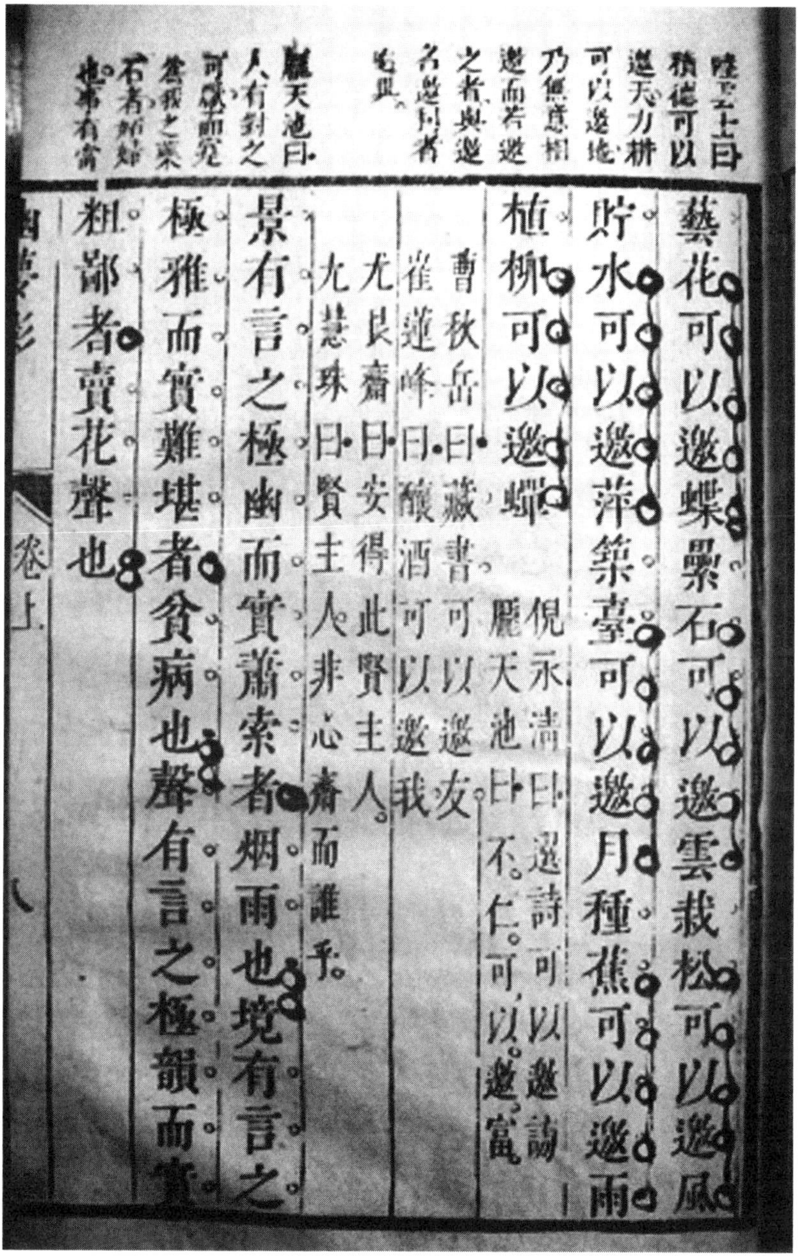

藝花可以邀蝶，纍石可以邀雲，栽松可以邀風，貯水可以邀萍，築臺可以邀月，種蕉可以邀雨，植柳可以邀蟬。

陸云士曰·積德可以邀天，力耕可以邀地，遷而若遷、乃無意相遷而遷者、與遷名遂別者竟此。

曹秋岳曰·藏書可以邀友。

倪永清曰·選詩可以邀謔。

麗天池比不仁，可以邀富。

崔蓮峰曰·釀酒可以邀我。

尤慧珠曰·賢主人非心齋而誰乎。

尤艮齋曰·安得此賢主人。

龐天池曰·人有對之可感而覚、者姉婦、地帛有窗、粗鄙者賣花聲也。

景有言之極幽而實蕭索者，煙雨也；境有言之極雅而實難堪者，貪病也；聲有言之極韻而實

幽夢影　卷上

Fig. 1.1. *Youmengying*, 1.8a. Beijing University Library edition.

block that Zhang Chao made. But, from simply examining the traces of this edition, it is evident that at least three more carvings were added to this single block and that more copies of the text were made from it after the initial carving and distribution of the printed copy were completed.

The textual evidence also supports the conclusion that there were several recarvings on the block of *Youmengying*. In one of the few textual studies of this work, Zhang Shenyu and Zhao Yi posit at least four stages in composition between 1681 and 1697: (1) Zhang Chao began writing it sometime before 1681; (2) the first draft was completed before 1694, and the preface of Yu Huai and the postscript of Zhang Zong were attached at that time; (3) Zhang Zhupo visited Yangzhou and added a great number of comments in 1696; and (4) the text was openly circulated from 1697 onward.[108] Following up, Pierre-Henri Durand argues that it is probable that Zhang Chao printed and reprinted *Youmengying* four times, adding more comments and prefaces in 1697, 1699, 1703, and 1705.[109] These stages of the printing and reprinting process indicate that comments were consistently added each time a printed copy was circulated. In effect, the text of *Youmengying* was completed through the accumulation of comments by more than one hundred literati in tandem with printing and reprinting processes that took place over more than twenty years. In other words, the printing of *Youmengying* was in fact an integral part of the very process of creating the text.

Publishing as a Coterie Enterprise

The textual production of *Youmengying*, in which text making and book making converged, attests to malleable print textuality in this period, raising the need to revise our assumptions about the relations among text, author, and reader. First, as Zhang Chao's publishing demonstrates, a printed copy, far from being a self-enclosed entity, often evolved and grew as it circulated. The continuous evolution of

108. Zhang Shenyu and Zhao Yi, "Zhang Chao *Youmengying*," 143–58.
109. Dai Tingjie, "*Youmengying* banke kaolun," 38–50.

printed copy not only militates against the modern distinction among manuscript drafts, authorized first-edition text, and revised reprint, but also challenges the emphasis on a definitive original edition that traditional bibliographical and textual studies (*banben xue* 版本學) have so treasured. In the case of *Youmengying*, how is one to decide which copy is the most authentic one? Is it the first printed copy, which contains Zhang Chao's original entry alone? Or is it the last one, which appends all the comments of his friends? The continuous printing and reprinting of *Youmengying* thus redirects our focus from the purity of text to the process of transmission and leads us to consider the multiple impressions of the book not necessarily as insignificant textual derivatives but as equally valid and important phases of the book's existence.[110]

Second, the malleable print textuality in this period refuses to identify the text as the final embodiment of authorial intention alone but instead opens the way for the creative agency of readers in shaping the book. The transmission of *Youmengying* was by no means a linear progression from composition to publication to reception. Rather, there was a simultaneous, organic convergence of writing, reading, and printing that proceeded in a spiral fashion. Far from being an individual and isolated process, *Youmengying* was formed over time as the product of collective and cumulative effort to which scores of readers contributed. This resituates the author from the central position of controlling all textual meanings to an interactive and interdependent relationship with readers, constantly re-creating textual meanings in tandem with them.

Admittedly, *Youmengying* as a collective enterprise does not necessarily mean that its composition was open to any reader. In fact, the text was first circulated exclusively within Zhang Chao's coterie for the purpose of eliciting participation. That is, his printed copy initially circulated only among a close-knit cohort—an identifiable literati readership rather than a random cross-section of readers. If someone who was not acquainted with Zhang Chao wanted to obtain a printed

---

110. For examples of the significance of a multiplicity of drama editions in the interpretation of drama, see West, "Text and Ideology," 237; and Li-Ling Hsiao, *Eternal Present*, 297.

copy, he could do so only through one of Zhang Chao's acquaintances. As the popularity of Zhang Chao's imprint increased, his friends frequently sent him letters asking for more copies to distribute to their own coteries. Chen Ding, a close friend of Zhang Chao, sent such letters several times:

> I am staying in Jiufeng temple [in Nanjing],[111] where not only the famous literati of Jiangnan gather but also the top literati who travel to the north or the south stay. Hence I could not help meeting them. They know that I am acquainted with you, so everybody asks about you. I cannot count the number of people who have asked me to give them your two compilations, *Zhaodai congshu* and *Tanji congshu*. People such as Wang Anjie, Gong Wensi, Wang Kunsheng, and Zhu Shaowen are all world-famous literati, and they have asked me to look for your books several times. In addition, the secretaries to the provincial treasurer and the provincial judge Wang Xianguan and Li Yunyi by turns asked me to look for your books. I do not know what to say to them. Apart from those literati, I declined the favor of the people who are not acquainted with me by saying that I did not make friends with you. They laughed at me for being a vulgar fellow, saying, "How could he not be a close friend of Mr. Xinzhai [Zhang Chao] given that he stayed in Yangzhou such a long time? He must be nothing but an ordinary fellow!"
>
> 茲弟現寓鷲峰寺中, 不特江南名士大集于寓, 即南來北往高流一駐足間, 未嘗不得見也。知弟與先生交好, 無不問詢起居而欲求先生之昭代、檀几兩叢書者, 難更僕數入。王安節、龔文思、王崐繩、朱少文, 此數公皆當世海內大名士也。囑之再三要索此書。而藩、泉兩臺幕中之王仙冠, 李雲衣輾轉相託索取此書。弟亦無此辭以對。其下不相知者, 概以不上交先生, 謝之。彼皆大笑以弟未鄙夫, 謂: "烏有在揚最久而不識心齋先生, 此一匹夫耳!"[112]

Such control over the distribution of printed copies was possible because Zhang Chao's printed books were not mass produced but cus-

111. Jiufeng si was a renowned temple built in the Tianshun 天順 reign (1457–64) of the Ming dynasty. It was one of the cultural centers of Nanjing literati in the seventeenth century, located in the vicinity of the famous Qinhuai 秦淮 area. Ōki, *Chūgoku yūri kūkan*, 58, 67, 73.

112. *CDYS* 10.18b–19a.

tom made. It appears that Zhang Chao would initially print about sixty or seventy copies, enough to distribute among his immediate circle of contributors, sponsors, and friends. He then stored the blocks in his home to be printed on demand. It was only after he received requests from friends such as Chen Ding that he would produce five or ten more copies.[113] Since he could not predict exactly how many copies would be needed, it saved time and money to initially print only a small number of copies. Although a single woodblock could produce between fifteen and thirty thousand copies in theory,[114] it was a common practice among publishers to make about ten copies at a time and keep the printing blocks for later use, as they were afraid to tie up capital by piling up printed books in stock.

At the same time, Zhang Chao's strategy of custom printing and highly controlled distribution bestowed cultural prestige on the members of his coterie. They shared a sense of privilege by being close to Zhang Chao and hence part of a select community that was distinct from the larger reading public. Not only did they participate in the making of the texts by composing paratextual pieces, but they also belonged to a select circle that made it possible for them to obtain printed copies. The literati who were able to submit their works to Zhang Chao's compilations or add comments to those submitted by others were mainly Zhang Chao's family members, friends, or friends of friends, and hailed in most cases from either Huizhou or Yangzhou. Although Zhang Chao emphasized that, for his two huge compilations *Tanji congshu* and *Zhaodai congshu*, he gathered the finest writings of the time, not necessarily following personal affinity, the selected writers turn out to have had direct or indirect personal or local connections with one or both the editors, Zhang Chao and Wang Zhuo, rather than simply being members of the anonymous reading public who had responded to the advertisement soliciting manuscripts. By exhibiting a strong affinity for locality and a specific group of literati, Zhang Chao's publishing instantiated exclusive sociability by reinforcing his social networks and cementing a sense of a chosen coterie centered on himself.

113. For example, *CDYS* 3.13a, 4.23b, 9.30a; *CDOC* 6.13a.
114. Tsien, "Technical Aspects," 23.

In this respect, Zhang Chao's publishing practices tried to reinstate the established prestige of manuscript transmission in the arena of the production and circulation of printed books. By limiting the distribution of his printed books to a close literati circle, Zhang Chao and his friends distinguished themselves from other groups and made their ties highly exclusive. As Chen Ding notes in his letter, they became not "ordinary fellows" but members of a chosen circle that communally created and shared items of cultural capital such as printed books. The cultural prerogative attached to Zhang Chao's printed books was promoted by the literati's endeavors to position themselves favorably within an economy of prestige by claiming a status distinction that was being increasingly eroded by the wide accessibility of print and the competitive book market in the seventeenth century.

CHAPTER 2

Publishing for Reputation

The late Ming collection of short vernacular stories *Xihu erji* 西湖 二集 (West Lake Stories, Second Collection) includes the story of a courtesan who helps her chosen mate achieve fame. Talented and clever Cao Miaoge 曹妙哥 recognizes the potential of Wu Erzhi 吳爾 知 as soon as she meets him despite his having no official position or mercantile wealth. Being familiar with the ways of the world, she teaches him how to make a fortune and, after he accumulates considerable wealth, advises him to enhance his reputation as follows:

> Since you do not possess any fame for your literary skills, people will talk about you and denounce you if you suddenly earn a *jinshi* degree. Why don't you discreetly ask a writer who is willing to write poetry and prose and attribute it to you? Then find a talented and renowned scholar to write a few fine prefaces and place them at the front of the book. They must praise and promote the book in whatever way possible. You should carve the manuscript on woodblocks, print copies, and then send or sell them to others. And when you build relationships with celebrities and officials who wear silk hats [i.e., who hold official posts], offer them a copy of this [printed book of] poetry and prose.
>
> 如今你素無文名, 若驟然中了一個進士, 畢竟有人議論包彈着你。你可 密請一個大有意思之人做成詩文, 將來妝在自己姓名之下, 求個有名目 的文人才子做他几篇好序在於前面, 不免稱之贊之、表之揚之, 刻成書 板印將出去, 或是送人, 或是發賣, 結交天下有名之人, 並一應戴紗帽 的官人, 將此詩文為進見之資。[1]

---

1. "Qiaoji zuofu chengming" 巧妓佐夫成名, in Zhou Qingyuan, *Xihu erji*, 2:389.

The course of action that Cao Miaoge recommends—namely, self-publishing—was nothing extraordinary at the time. It was a long-standing practice for the literati to resort to the publicizing of their talent in advance to gain success in the examinations and promote their official careers.[2] In particular, the publishing of their works became a widely used means of self-promotion in the seventeenth century.[3] In a rather comical exaggeration, thus, the story proceeds to show how Wu Erzhi's faithful adoption of the wily tactics Cao Miaoge suggests does indeed earn him a reputation as a skilled writer (*wenming* 文名), making him known among the literary community and successful in the exams, and resulting in his achieving a high official position in the end.

The happy ending of this story, however, also reveals how easily publishing for fame could be manipulated. As Cao Miaoge's strategy indicates, even a fellow of such meager talent as Wu Erzhi's could acquire a reputation as long as he followed the steps necessary for "buying a reputation by publishing" (*maiming keji* 買名刻集).[4] This was, in fact, one of the major criticisms of the self-publishing fad in the seventeenth century: it resulted in a proliferation of printed books, of which the quality varied widely, and even such cases as the ghostwritten book that Wu Erzhi published under his name. The esteemed scholar Tang Shunzhi was therefore worried that self-publishing opened the way to brash self-promotion by second-rate writers; publication was no longer the privilege accorded to works genuinely qualified for wide transmission in print. "Unless writings are done by a writer of literary merit, they tend to be useful only for covering jars," he said, attempting to dissuade a friend from publishing a collection of Tang's writings on his behalf. "Initially, no writer lacks the presumptuous intention of seeking immortality for his work. But his printed work only turns out to manifest his own vulgarity, which incites readers' ridicule. This is precisely what is meant by the calamity of wood[block printing]."[5]

2. Inoue, *Chūgoku shuppan bunkashi*, 131–34; Shields, *One Who Knows Me*, 95–101; and Linda Rui Feng, *City of Marvel*, 88–111.

3. See, for example, Chow, *Publishing, Culture, and Power*, 223–40.

4. "Qiaoji zuofu chengming," in Zhou Qingyuan, *Xihu erji*, 2:391.

5. "本非立言之人，而徒為覆瓿之用。彼其初作者莫不妄意於不朽之圖，而適足以自彰其陋，以取誚於觀者，徒所謂木災而已。" Tang Shunzhi, "Yu Bu Yiquan zhixian" 與卜益泉知縣, in *Tang Jingchuan wenji* 7.22a.

Despite the popularity of self-publishing by writers, therefore, the critical view of self-publishing as vanity publishing was prevalent among the contemporaries of Zhang Chao and Wang Zhuo. Early Qing poets such as Li Yi 李沂 and Shen Hanguang 申涵光 (1618–77), both of whom had works that were printed in *Zhaodai congshu*, warned fellow writers against reckless self-publishing:

> Nowadays people just print their poetry even before it has fully taken shape. Once they print it, it is transmitted throughout the country, and they cannot revise it. This is deeply deplorable. In fact, the desire for printing derives from the love of fame. If the poetry is indeed good, it will earn the author fame. But if the poetry has not taken shape and contains a lot of errors, people will reprimand and ridicule the author for its faults. Then what kind of reputation will he get?
>
> 今人詩尚未穩輒付梓, 付梓則播之通國, 不可復改, 深足惜也。原其付梓之意, 本因好名。若詩果佳, 斯得名矣。苟詩未穩兼多謬戾, 人將指摘非笑, 何名之可得?[6]

> You can make a collection of poetry and prose, but you should not print and circulate it. Even if for a time you disregard your teachers' and friends' advice [not to print it and you do indeed print it], you will eventually realize [that you should not have printed it] and your back will certainly drip with sweat [from shame]. Not until you have revised it from morning to evening for one or two years and received confirmation from a distinguished coterie should you print it. If you distribute the printed copies on an impulse and give them to all your relatives and friends, you will come to regret it. Why bother exhausting yourself to pursue publication? If possible, it is more decent not to print it at all.
>
> 凡詩文成集且勿梓行。一時所是師友言之不服, 久之自悟, 未必不汗流浹背也。俟一二年朝夕改訂, 復取證於高朋, 然後授梓。若乘興流布, 遍贈親知, 及予悔悟。安能盡人而追之耶! 若能, 不刻則更高。[7]

The widespread popularity and the concurrent criticism of self-publishing in the seventeenth century demonstrated the multivalent role that print played in textual production and circulation. On the one

---

6. Li Yi, "Jie qingzi" 戒輕梓, in *Qiuxing ge shihua* 秋星閣詩話, in ZDCS, 66.
7. Shen Hanguang, *Jingyuan xiaoyu* 荊園小語, in ZDCS, 414.

hand, writers' interest in self-publishing testified to the irrefutable centrality of publishing in literary production and circulation during this period. Neither Li Yi nor Shen Hanguang opposed the idea of publishing itself; they simply felt it ought to be restricted to deserving works. In other words, they construed publishing to be the sine qua non for the conferring of literary recognition. On the other hand, however, the rise of self-publishing posed a threat to the desired imprimatur that publication lent to a writer's work. When print was a rare and expensive medium of textual circulation, publishing was a token of honor granted only to a text of exceptional quality that deserved widespread transmission. But when writers were publishing and circulating whatever they wanted whether or not it was worthy of being widely transmitted, they were undermining the very authority of the printed text that they attempted to achieve through publishing and were diminishing the prestigious status for which they vied.

The debates over the self-publishing boom, in effect, forced writers of the seventeenth century to grapple with the dilemma of how to achieve a reputation by publishing without risking that very reputation. Cao Miaoge in the story above is aware that, unlike in the earlier period, publishing alone is not a surefire means for securing a reputation. She suggests that, after the manuscript has become a printed book, Wu Erzhi seek out various forms of public approval of its quality—peer support ("fine prefaces" by a "talented and renowned scholar"), wide dissemination in both the literati community and the book market ("send or sell them to others"), and coterie patronage ("build relationships with celebrities and officials" and "offering them a copy"). Otherwise, people might not trust the reputation that publishing had endowed and might "talk and denounce" the value of the book.

This chapter discusses publishing for reputation, with a focus on the way in which Wang Zhuo created a reputation for himself through self-publishing and sustained that reputation by attaining peer patronage. For Wang Zhuo, a local literatus who neither came from a prominent family nor held an official post, self-publishing was an effective means to establish his status in the literati community. But he was also conscious of the criticism that fame through self-publishing was often seen as disproportionate to a writer's literary prowess. Wang Zhuo's publishing of *Lanyan ji* and *Jin Shishuo* demonstrates how he attempted to resolve the dilemma that his self-publishing raised: he tried to validate the textual authority of his books by soliciting written endorsements by his coterie and also integrating them as an essential part of the narrative structure.

A close examination of the publication process of Huang Zhouxing's northern drama *Xihua bao* 惜花報 (Recompense for Cherishing Flowers), however, reveals that peer acknowledgment bestowed by a cohesive coterie was necessary but insufficient to establish public recognition. *Xihua bao* was created by the renowned contemporary writer Huang Zhouxing at Wang Zhuo's request to promote the latter's work of prose "Kanhua shuyi ji" 看花述異記 (Record of the Watching of Flowers and the Telling of the Odd). The carefully crafted theatricality was not merely designed to praise Wang Zhuo's literary talent. It also encouraged readers to confer upon Wang Zhuo a reputation that extended beyond his coterie. The need to make the leap from coterie patronage to public acknowledgment in establishing textual authority was aligned with the widening readership that the printing boom brought about, from a group of elites to the reading public at large, attesting to the newly emerging contestation of who decided what text was publishable.

Wang Zhuo and His Publishing Activities

Wang Zhuo (*zi* Danlu 丹麓, *hao* Mu'an 木庵 and Songxizi 松溪子) was a self-made Hangzhou writer who came from a relatively obscure background. Unlike Zhang Chao's father, who had earned the highest degree in the civil service exams and become an official, Wang Zhuo's family could claim no scholarly pedigree. Wang Zhuo's father, Wang Zhan 王湛 (1606–74), did not pass any examinations despite having received at least some education.[8] The eldest son Wang Zhuo became the hope for his family by becoming a supplementary student of the

8. Wang Zhuo's family was living in Zhangban alley 張版巷 in Hangzhou when he was born, but one month later Wang Zhan moved his family to the west of the Jiangzhang bridge 江漲橋 in Chengbei li 城北里 because almost all of their property was destroyed in a fire. Wang Zhuo's mother, née Yu 余, died when he was eleven years old. Wu Yiyi 吳儀一, "Benzhuan" 本傳, in Wang Zhuo, *Xiaju tang quanji dingben* 1b. This biography was reprinted in Li Huan, *Guochao shixian leizheng, juan* 473, *yinyi*

county school (*sibuxian xuesheng* 司補縣學生) at the age of thirteen in 1647. But in 1663, when he turned twenty-eight, his debilitating diabetes caused him to have to give up sitting for further examinations. Although he was recommended for the special *boxue hongci* 博學宏詞 (broad learning and vast erudition) examination in 1679, he declined to take it.

Despite officialdom being out of the picture for the rest of his life, Wang Zhuo was able to build his reputation by having a massive collection of books and an extensive coterie network. He kept tens of thousands of books in his studio Xiaju tang 霞舉堂 (Studio of Sunrise Glow) and later at Qiangdong caotang 墻東草堂 (Cottage on the East Wall), which was built in 1680.[9] His large book collection caught the attention of the literati in the local community. For example, Jiang Long 蔣鑨 (b. 1625) visited Wang Zhuo's library seeking materials for his compilation *Qingshi chuji* 清詩初集 (Qing Poetry, First Collection).[10] In addition, Wang Zhuo actively sought to become well connected to the men of letters in Hangzhou, which was facilitated by his family's deep roots in the area. Whenever he met talented scholars, he treated them "as extraordinary treasures" and enjoyed drinking, music, and poetry with them.[11] According to Wu Yiyi 吳儀一 (1647– ca. 1704), Wang Zhuo's close friend for thirty years and a famous song-lyric poet and drama critic in Hangzhou, Wang Zhuo's reputation spread far beyond his local coterie, and, whenever literati from other regions passed through Hangzhou, they were eager to establish a relationship with him. "Once having halted their carriages, they cannot bear to leave."[12]

隱逸 15.5a–8a. Wang Zhuo's other biographies were also included in *Hangzhou fuzhi*, 8:2762, and *Qingshi liezhuan*, 18:5689–90.

9. Wu Yiyi, "Benzhuan," in Wang Zhuo, *Xiaju tang quanji dingben* 1a–b. Qiangdong caotang was built in front of the residence of one of Wang Zhuo's sons in 1700. *CDYS* 11.22b. Wang Zhuo wrote about its scenic view in "Ji caotang shiliu yi" 紀草堂十六宜 in *TJCS*.

10. Jiang Long, "Fanli," in *Qingshi chuji*, in Xie Zhengguang and She Rufeng, *Qingchu ren xuan Qingchu shi huikao*, 182.

11. See, for example, Hong Yulin 洪虞鄰, "Yuanxu" 原序, in Wang Zhuo, *Xiaju tang quanji dingben*.

12. "停軺不忍去." Wu Yiyi, "Benzhuan," in Wang Zhuo, *Xiaju tang quanji dingben* 1b.

What contributed most to Wang Zhuo's prominence in the Hangzhou literati community, however, was his ardent publishing endeavors.
He produced more than eleven titles, most of which were prints or
reprints of his own works under his studio name. They included a
collection of stories about animals and insects that intended to incul-
cate Buddhist teachings, *Suisheng ji* 遂生集 (Collection of the Fulfillment of Life, 1660; rep. 1693);[13] a collection of his writings in diverse
genres, *Xiaju tang ji* 霞舉堂集 (Collection of the Studio of Sunrise Glow)
in thirty-five *juan*; a compilation of funeral orations for his late father,
Youguang ji 幽光集 (Collection of Dim Light) in two *juan*;[14] a collection
of his ten prose pieces, *Zazhu shizhong* 雜著十種 (Ten Miscellaneous
Works);[15] a collection of his 157 song-lyrics, *Xialiu ci* 峽流詞 (Song-
Lyrics of Gorge Stream);[16] a collection of his poetry and prose, *Qiangdong zachao* 墻東雜鈔 (Miscellaneous Writings of the Cottage on the
Eastern Wall);[17] a collection of 124 works of diverse genres by eighty

13. There is no extant edition of *Suisheng ji*, but Wang Zhuo's preface to the reprinted edition is included in *Xiaju tang quanji dingben* 3.2a–3a.

14. After the death of Wang Zhan in 1674, Wang Zhuo went to Yixing 宜興 to collect memorial writings, epitaphs, and celebratory remarks about his father and published them as *Youguang ji*. He also left a record of his journey to Yixing in "Xingyi
riji" 行役日記, in *Zazhu shizhong*. But there is no extant edition of *Youguang ji*.

15. *Zazhu shizhong* consists of ten pieces of miscellaneous prose: "Longjing" 龍經,
"Guzi jin" 孤子唫, "Songxizi" 松溪子, "Lianzhu" 連珠, "Yuyan" 寓言, "Kanhua shuyi
ji," "Xingyi riji," "Kuaishuo xuji" 快說續紀, "Qinyan" 禽言, and "Beishu zhuzhici" 北墅
竹枝詞.

16. *Xialiu ci* consists of three *juan*, each of which contains short, medium, and
long song-lyrics, totaling 157 song-lyrics under 123 tune titles. Prefaces by Cao Erkan
曹爾堪, Ding Peng 丁彭, and Mao Qiling and the table of contents are attached to
the first *juan*. The commentary by Mao Xianshu 毛先舒 and postscripts by Fang
Bing 方炳 and Wang Yongshuo 王用說 are attached to the last *juan*. *Xialiu ci* was also
included in the song-lyric anthology *Baiming jia cichao* 百名家詞鈔, edited by Nie
Xian 聶先 and Zeng Wangsun 曾王孫; it circulated widely during the Qing dynasty.

17. According to Wu Yiyi's preface, Wang Zhuo initially asked his son Yan to assemble and publish *Qiangdong zachao* because Wang Zhuo was ill, but he was not
satisfied with the resulting volume. Therefore, after he recovered from his illness, he
asked Wu Yiyi to recollate it. It contains a note that says "several colleagues commented and selected; Wang Zhuo from Hangzhou wrote; and his son Yan copied and
added commentary" 同學諸家評選 仁和王晫丹麓著 男言慎旃鈔附註. There are
copies in the National Library of China and Beijing University Library.

contemporary writers, *Wenjin* 文津 (The Crux of Writing);[18] and a collection of anecdotes on more than 370 contemporary personalities, *Jin
Shishuo* 今世說 (Contemporary *Tales of the World*, 1683). As was the
case with Zhang Chao, Wang Zhuo's family members played a crucial
role by supporting his publishing activities. His sons Nai 鼐 and Yan
言, brother-in-law Lu Jin 陸進, and son-in-law Xu Shiyong 徐士鏞 collated manuscripts, wrote prefaces, and added commentaries to Wang
Zhuo's imprints.[19]

Wang Zhuo's series of publication projects required a significant
outlay of capital. He frequently expressed concerns about publishing
expenses, but he contended that the money spent on publishing would
be compensated by the reputation that it earned him.[20] For example, he
stated that he had had to sell nine *mu* 畝 of land (54 acres) for 54 taels of
silver—which was still not enough to cover his publishing expenses. Not
until he borrowed additional funds from his friends could he get the
carving of one of his imprints finished.[21] He not only solicited financial
contributions from his friends,[22] but also collaborated with commercial bookshops to get books published. For example, his *Xiaju tang ji*

18. Wang Zhuo mentioned that one-third of the works in *Wenjin* were quotations
from books that he had bought at bookstores; one-fourth had been sent to him by his
friends; and the rest were pieces that his colleagues happened to show him at parties.
Wang Zhuo, "Liyan" 例言, in *Wenjin*.

19. For example, Wang Yan took charge of reprinting *Suisheng ji* and *Lanyan ji* on
behalf of his father, who was old and sick at the time; Wang Nai collated Wang
Zhuo's *Songxi manxing* 松溪慢興, *Chidu oucun* 尺牘偶存, and *Zazhu shizhong*, all of
which were included in *Xiaju tang ji*; Lu Jin collected Wang Zhuo's ten prose pieces
and asked Mao Jike to write a preface to *Zazhu shizhong*; and the collation of *Xiaju
tang ji* was done by both Wang Yan and Xu Shiyong.

20. Wang Zhuo, *Lanyan ji* 3a.

21. Ibid. Wang Zhuo also mentioned that he spent 300 taels of silver to have 1,400
sheets of paper printed for both the second installment of *Lanyan ji* and an anthology of examination essays, *Jingshi mingwen* 經世名文. See "Yu Shen Qujin" 與沈
去矜, in *Chidu oucun*, in *Xiaju tang ji*, in *Qingdai shiwen ji huibian*, 196.

22. Regarding Wang Zhuo's request for financial help from his friends, see, for
example, Wang Zhuo, "Jin Shishuo liyan" 今世說例言, in *Zhuye ting zaji*; *Jin Shishuo*,
141. Wang Zhuo's friend Wu Wenqing 吳雯清 (*jinshi* 1652) liked Wang Zhuo's *Suisheng ji*, and he transported one hundred copies to Beijing for circulation, paying the
printing cost out of his own pocket. See Wang Zhuo, "Yu Wu Fanglian Shiyu" 與吳
方漣侍御, in *Chidu oucun*, in *Xiaju tang ji*, in *Qingdai shiwen ji huibian*, 169.

was printed in at least three different editions, each of which reflected a different type of cooperation with bookstores. The first edition in thirty-five *juan* was financed, carved, and printed by Wang Zhuo on his own.[23] In 1680 he recarved the manuscript, and, although the woodblocks were in his possession, the copies were printed and sold by two bookshops—Huandu zhai 還讀齋 in Hangzhou and Wenzhi tang 文治堂 in Shulin 書林.[24] It is difficult to determine whether the association with these two bookshops was purely a business one, in part because their owners, particularly the owner of Huandu zhai, had close personal relationships with Wang Zhuo. As Ellen Widmer's study vividly demonstrates, Huandu zhai was one of the most successful bookshops in Hangzhou in the seventeenth century,[25] and its owner, Wang Qi 汪淇 (fl. 1600–68), was a close friend of Wang Zhuo. Wang Qi printed several letters to and from Wang Zhuo in his popular anthology of contemporary letters *Chidu xinyu* 尺牘新語 (New Letters), which he copublished with Xu Shijun 徐士俊 (1602–81) starting in 1663.[26] Xu Shijun was also a close friend of Wang Zhuo. Wang Zhuo printed several pieces by Xu Shijun in his anthology *Wenjin*,[27] and Xu

23. The National Library of China holds a copy of the first edition of Wang Zhuo's *Xiaju tang ji*. It does not have a cover page, but the table of contents is attached. Although the table of contents lists thirty-five *juan*, the extant edition contains only seven.

24. The second edition of Wang Zhuo's *Xiaju tang ji* is available in Beijing University Library. The cover page indicates that "Wang Zhuo of Hangzhou carved" 武林王丹麓梓 "Xiaju tang ji" 霞舉堂集, "Wenbu, Shibu, Ciyun, Chidu, Zazhu, Waibian" 文部 詩部 詞韻 尺牘 雜著 外編, and "Wenzhi tang and Huandu zhai printed and circulated" 文治堂 還讀齋 梓行; the preface by Wang Sihuai 王思槐 written in 1680, and the table of contents are attached. It includes six collections: "Nanchuang wenlüe" 南牕文略 (eight *juan*), "Songxi manxing" (ten *juan*), "Xialiu ci" (three *juan*), "Chidu" (two *juan*), "Zazhu shizhong" (ten *juan*), and "Mu'an waibian" 木庵外編 (two *juan*). That it was a newly carved edition is evident because the number of lines is different from the number in the first edition.

25. Widmer, "Huanduzhai," 77–90.

26. Wang Zhuo's letter was printed in Wang Qi and Xu Shijun, *Fenlei chidu xinyu*, vol. 2, *juan* 13, 2; his contemporaries' letters to Wang Zhuo were printed in ibid., *juan* 13, 6; *juan* 16, 4; *juan* 17, 1; *juan* 18, 2; and *juan* 19, 3.

27. Several writings of Xu Shijun were selected and printed in Wang Zhuo's *Wenjin*, and four letters from Wang Zhuo to Xu Shijun were printed in Wang Zhuo's *Chidu oucun, juanshang* 卷上, in *Xiaju tang ji*.

Shijun collated Wang Zhuo's *Xialiu ci*. The other bookshop, Wenzhi tang, also had close ties with Wang Zhuo. In addition to collaborating on the second edition of *Xiaju tang ji*, its owner worked on the collation and printing of *Qianqiu yadiao* 千秋雅調 (Fine Tunes of a Thousand Years), which had the alternate title of *Qianqiu sui changhe ci* 千秋歲唱和詞 (A Thousand Years of the Song-Lyric Singing in Harmony), the compilation of the poems and song-lyrics of 127 friends who celebrated Wang Zhuo's fiftieth birthday in 1685.[28] There are no extant records of exactly how these two bookshops—one in Zhejiang province and the other in Fujian—collaborated on the second edition of Wang Zhuo's *Xiaju tang ji*, but such interregional cooperation between bookstores was not uncommon in this period.[29]

Wang Zhuo's *Xiaju tang ji* was reprinted for the third time by Zhenxiu tang 振秀堂, another commercial bookshop in Shulin in Fujian province.[30] After the second edition had circulated for a time, the owner of Zhenxiu tang noted the growing demand for the book and approached Wang Zhuo, who had stored the woodblocks at his residence because he lacked funds to print more copies. The bookseller proposed that his bookshop take charge of printing, distribution, and sales. The third edition of *Xiaju tang ji* was eventually published bound together in a single volume with Wang Zhuo's poetry collection *Qiangdong zachao*, under the new title *Xiaju tang quanji dingben* 霞舉堂全

28. Zhu Rong, "Songxizi zhuan," in Wang Zhuo, *Qianqiu yadiao*. A decade later, Wang Zhuo was again feted on his birthday, his sixtieth, so an additional *juan* was attached to *Qianqiu yadiao*. Wang Zhuo, "Fanli," in *Lanyan ji* 2a. This additional *juan* is not included in the extant copy of *Qianqiu yadiao* in the National Library of China.

29. See, for example, Brokaw, *Commerce in Culture*, 189–267, and Chia, *Printing for Profit*, 184–85.

30. The third edition of Wang Zhuo's *Xiaju tang ji* is available in Naikaku Bunko, and there is a photo-reprint copy in the Hishi Collection of the Princeton University Library. It is nineteen *juan* in total. Attached at the beginning of the volume are the preface by Xu Zhuo 徐倬; four original prefaces to *Xiaju tang ji* by Mao Qiling, Fang Xiangying, Hong Ruogao 洪若皋, and Zhang Yanzhi 張彥之; a biography of Wang Zhuo by Wu Yiyi; a portrait of Wang Zhuo; editorial principles; foreword (*yinyan* 引言) and assorted commentaries of several friends (*pinglin* 評林); and the table of contents. On the cover page the following information is provided: "Written by Wang Zhuo of Hangzhou; selected and commented on by several colleagues; cocollated by Wang Zhuo's son Yan and his son-in-law Xu Shiyong" 武林王晫著; 同學諸家評選; 男言慎旂姪鈔 壻徐士鏞柯亭 仝校.

集定本 (Definitive Edition of the Complete Collection of the Studio of Sunrise Glow), and was sold in Fujian.[31]

Wang Zhuo's imprints became successful enough to firmly establish his reputation in literati circles. As Wu Yiyi noted, "People sought to buy or competed to copy every one of his writings. Thus his works were transmitted throughout the empire."[32] *Jin Shishuo*, published in 1683, was probably the most successful effort of Wang Zhuo's publishing career. Faithfully following the format of the fifth-century book of character appraisal *Shishuo xinyu* 世說新語 (A New Account of Tales of the World),[33] it gathered together the "beautiful remarks and exemplary conduct" (*jiayan yixing* 嘉言懿行) of more than 370 literati.[34] What set Wang Zhuo's *Jin Shishuo* apart from the numerous other sequels to *Shishuo xinyu* was its contemporaneity:[35] it only included the accounts of literati who were living and active in the late Ming and early Qing periods. The book was immediately circulated beyond Hangzhou, reaching Beijing, and helped establish not only Wang Zhuo's reputation but those of his contemporaries, anecdotes about whom he included in the book.[36] One reader even commented, "If you do not pay tribute to Wang Zhuo during your visit to Hangzhou, you are not a cultured scholar; if you are not paid tribute to by Wang Zhuo, you are not a cultured scholar either."[37]

31. Wang Zhuo, "Fanli," in *Xiaju tang quanji dingben* 1a.

32. "每一篇稿，就購求競寫，流傳海內。" Wu Yiyi, "Benzhuan," in Wang Zhuo, *Xiaju tang quanji dingben* 1b. For Wu Yiyi's biography, see Zeitlin, "Shared Dreams," 132, n. 17.

33. *Shishuo xinyu* collects 452 entries in thirty-six categories. Studies of *Shishuo xinyu* include Wang Nengxian, *Shishuo xinyu yanjiu*; Qian Nanxiu, *Spirit and Self*; Jack Chen, "Knowing Men"; and Wai-yee Li, "*Shishuo xinyu*."

34. Wang Zhuo, "Zixu" 自序, in *Zhuye ting zaji*; *Jin Shishuo*, 135. The 1683 edition was reprinted in *Xuxiu Siku quanshu*, vol. 1175.

35. On the popularity of sequels to *Shishuo xinyu* in the Ming and Qing periods, see Song Lihua, *Ming Qing shiqi de xiaoshuo chuanbo*, 263–70; and Qian Nanxiu, *Spirit and Self*, 256–82.

36. Mao Qiling, "Xiaju tang ji yuanxu" 霞舉堂集原序, in Wang Zhuo, *Xiaju tang quanji dingben* 2a.

37. "入杭若不賞識丹麓，必非佳士；或不為丹麓所賞識，亦非佳士也。" Lin Yunming's 林雲銘 (1628–97) comment, included in the beginning of Wang Zhuo, *Zhuye ting zaji*; *Jin Shishuo*, 137.

How to Establish a Reputation by Publishing

How did Wang Zhuo make a reputation for himself through publishing? Although it seems obvious that Wang Zhuo's publishing was mainly driven by his quest for fame, the self-image that he promoted in his imprints was that of a reserved hermit who had no interest in power, money, or fame, in other words, someone who was extremely unlikely to engage in shameless self-promotion. The anecdotes about Wang Zhuo in *Jin Shishuo* and other imprints present him in a variety of personas: a filial son who went through great difficulties to make a book commemorating his late father;[38] a popular publisher who printed books that scholars wanted to read "as hungrily as monkeys searching for fruit";[39] an eccentric who practiced necromancy for a friend;[40] a scholar who took pride in his poverty and valued it over power and money;[41] and a writer who was immersed in writing day and night.[42] Despite the apparent variation, all of these anecdotes eventually make the point that Wang Zhuo was a modest, unforthcoming, and covert talent. Typical are the examples in *Jin Shishuo*, one of his most popular imprints:

> Wang Zhuo's intention is profound, and he always humbles himself. When he talks with people, he never speaks first. Whenever famous scholars hold gatherings, he always attends them, but his modesty prevents everyone from noticing his presence until the party is over.
> 王丹麓意思深遠, 常有以自下。與人言, 未嘗先一語。名士宴集, 故未嘗不在, 竟日沖然, 若不知其在座者。[43]

> Wang Zhuo has been a cultured recluse since his youth, yet he enjoys the reputation of [being] a talented [scholar]. Zhao Qianwen [Zhao Yao 趙鑰, a 1658 *jinshi*] praised him highly and compared him to the hidden treasures of heaven and earth.
> 王丹麓蚤年高隱, 甚負才望。趙千文亟稱之, 比為天地私蓄。[44]

---

38. Wang Zhuo, *Zhuye ting zaji*; *Jin Shishuo*, 150.
39. Ibid., 155.
40. Ibid., 218.
41. Ibid., 212, 218.
42. Ibid., 180.
43. Ibid., 174.
44. Ibid., 184.

The image of Wang Zhuo as a cultured recluse (*gaoyin* 高隱) is even highlighted in a visual form. For example, his portrait *Songxi zhuren xiang* 松溪主人像 (Portrait of the Master of Pine Stream) appeared in his collection of various genres of writings *Xiaju tang quanji dingben*. It was painted in celebration of his seventieth birthday in 1705 (fig. 2.1),[45] portraying him as a sturdy elderly gentleman, sitting at ease and leaning against a rock. Wearing a Manchu-style fur hat, Wang Zhuo looks straight ahead. Contrary to the simple and bold lines of his clothing, his face is depicted in detail. One can notice his full moustache and flowing beard, the intricate lines of the wrinkles, and the calm and poised facial expression.[46] Holding a wide-open book, he seems to have just lifted up his head after being immersed in reading. The portrait's nod to the pictorial cliché of "leaning on a rock" (*pingshi* 憑石), which symbolized scholars' pastimes or their retirement in nature, reinforces Wang Zhuo's image as a serene and lofty figure.[47] In the colophon that he attached to the painting, Wang Zhuo declares: "How would it be appropriate for me to engage in worldly affairs? It simply suits me to distance myself from the human world and remain in solitude."[48] This visualization of Wang Zhuo as a detached hermit is in concert with what his autobiography, "Songxi zhuren zhuan" 松溪主人傳 (Biography of the Master of Pine Stream), relates. Wang Zhuo uses third-person narration to describe himself as a solitary scholar who has retreated to the countryside, enjoying himself in nature by sitting on a large rock and listening to the sound of a brook burbling beneath pine trees.[49]

It is, however, hard to accept the image that Wang Zhuo tried to advance via his books—that of a man of lofty detachment—as an authentic

45. Wang Zhuo had another portrait made, titled *Tingsong tu* 聽松圖. It was widely circulated, and in 1698 the collection of colophons attached to the painting was made into a book called *Tingsong tu tici* 聽松圖題詞 in six *juan*. Wang Zhuo, "Lanyan ji liyan" 蘭言集例言, in *Lanyan ji* 2a.

46. Wu Yiyi, "Benzhuan," in Wang Zhuo, *Xiaju tang quanji dingben* 3b–4a.

47. Park, *Art by the Book*, 130. The image of a literatus "leaning on a rock" is repeated in the portrait of Huang Zhouxing included in his literary collection *Xiawei tang bieji* (fig. 2.2).

48. "豈入世所宜乎? 只合離人而處於獨。" The back page of Wang Zhuo's portrait in *Xiaju tang quanji dingben*.

49. Wang Zhuo, "Songxi zhuren zhuan," in *Xiaju tang quanji dingben* 5.18a–19a.

Fig. 2.1. Portrait of Wang Zhuo titled *Songxi zhuren xiang*. Wang Zhuo, *Xiaju tang quanji dingben*, photo reprint of Naikaku Bunko edition in the Hishi Collection, Princeton University Library.

reflection of him because it so closely resembles the typical representation of the persona of a recluse (*shanren* 山人). This timeworn pose was frequently taken up by someone who wished to define his identity apart from the official sphere, instead seeking fulfillment in spiritual and cultural pursuit. Because of the noble connotation of the image, it was deployed shamelessly by educated men without official titles in the late Ming and early Qing periods in their self-fashioning, even including professional writers who ended up working for money in the late Ming book market.[50] In this sense, Wang Zhuo's constructed image was less that of a unique individual and more a hackneyed reproduction of the recluse that was fashionable in the era.

The authenticity of Wang Zhuo's self-image is further called into doubt by the fact that he himself published books that propounded this image. For example, *Jin Shishuo*, supposedly a historical record of leading contemporary literati, includes eighteen anecdotes about Wang Zhuo himself,[51] not to mention several entries about his father, brother-in-law, wife (née Zou 郫), and two sons (Ding 鼎 and Xiaoneng 小能, the latter having died prematurely)—obscure figures who would not have qualified for inclusion except for their personal ties to Wang Zhuo.[52] It also contains anecdotes about his close coterie, particularly the members of the Xiling shizi 西泠十子 (Ten Gentlemen of Hangzhou), the renowned poetry club active in Hangzhou at the time.[53] There are twenty-one entries about the leader of the poetry club, Lu Qi 陸圻 (1614–ca. 1688), which is the largest number about any one person in the collection.[54] What is more, anecdotes about other club members, including Mao Xianshu 毛先舒 (1620–88) and Ding Peng 丁澎 (b. 1622),

50. Chen Wanyi, *Wan Ming xiaopin*, 37–83; and Greenbaum, *Chen Jiru*, 172–76.

51. See *Zhuye ting zaji*; *Jin Shishuo*, 150, 167 (two entries), 174, 179, 180 (two entries), 183, 184, 192, 195, 197, 199, 208, 212, 213, 218 (two entries).

52. See the entries about Wang Zhan, in *Zhuye ting zaji*; *Jin Shishuo*, 147–48, 155; about Lu Jin, 157, 180, 185; about Xiaoneng, 189, 199; about Ding, 189; and about née Zou, 212.

53. Xiling shizi was a group of ten poets made famous by the publication of *Xiling shizi shixuan* 西泠十子詩選 in 1650. Chen Dakang, "Wang Zhuo he tade *Jin Shishuo*," 124.

54. See Lu Qi's biography in *Qingshi liezhuan*, 18:5684–85; and Deng Zhicheng, *Qingshi jishi chubian*, 2:257–60.

old friends of Wang Zhuo who wrote prefaces to or commentaries on his imprints, occupy a considerable proportion of the book.

To be fair, although *Jin Shishuo* looks like a brazen attempt by Wang Zhuo to promote himself and his coterie, the inclusion of entries about the writer and his acquaintances in self-published books was in fact a popular practice in the seventeenth century. For instance, the 1615 collection of words and quotes titled *Shehua lu* 舌華錄 (Record of Beautifully Spoken Words) contained a large number of quotes by its compilers, Wu Yuan 吳苑 and Cao Chen 曹臣 (b. 1583); the popular anthology series of contemporary letters *Chidu xinyu*, compiled and published by Wang Qi and Xu Shijun, included their own letters along with those by esteemed scholars and officials of the time; and Zhang Chao's friend Chen Ding inserted the biography of his mother in his collection of biographies of extraordinary figures, *Liuxi waizhuan* 留溪 外傳 (Unofficial Biographies by Liuxi [Chen Ding]).[55] Even the compilers of local gazetteers often put accounts of the lives of their relatives in the section of biographies of exemplary local figures.[56]

The wide popularity of the instrumental use of publishing did incur criticism. Particularly because *Jin Shishuo* focused more on praising than on criticizing figures,[57] it received little critical acclaim in the Qing period and afterward.[58] The Qing scholar Wu Chongyao 伍崇曜 (1810–63) commented that "Wang Zhuo flaunted his coterie in order to obtain a widespread reputation. So his writing was biased and honeyed, particularly lacking in fine selection."[59] In the same vein, the compilers of the eighteenth-century *Siku quanshu* denigrated the book, saying that, "in addition, most compliments [in *Jin Shishuo*] were overly exaggerated. This was a work that flaunted his coterie, which persisted as a convention of Ming poetry clubs. The inclusion

55. Chen Ding, "Chen jiefu zhuan" 陳節婦傳, in *Liuxi waizhuan*, 593.
56. Dennis, *Writing, Publishing, and Reading*, 9.
57. *Jin Shishuo* dropped the six categories of criticism that its model, *Shishuo xinyu*, had originally included. Wang Zhuo, "*Jin Shishuo* liyan," in *Zhuye ting zaji*; *Jin Shishuo*, 141.
58. Chen Wenxin, "*Jin Shishuo* yu Wang Zhuo xintai."
59. "蓋丹麓實游揚聲氣，以博取盛名，而文筆乃纖仄婉媚，殊乏雅裁。" Wu Chongyao, "*Jin Shishuo* ba" 今世說跋, in Wang Zhuo, *Jin Shishuo*, in *Aoya tang congshu*, 7:3388.

of anecdotes pertaining to his [Wang Zhuo's] own life in particular violated the standard [of proper selection]."[60]

Wang Zhuo for his part did not hide his sense of shame about including entries about himself in *Jin Shishuo*, saying that "nothing in my life is worthy of being recorded." But he foregrounded this with a principled stance against careerism, insisting that he had compiled the book with the attitude of a historian. He argued that, since *Jin Shishuo* was intended to be a supplementary record of those seventeenth-century men of letters whom the official history had left out,[61] he had collected verifiable facts in published sources alone, without culling anything from manuscript copies or from information orally passed on to him.[62] His reason for including the account about himself was the sheer abundance of published records about him submitted by his contemporaries: "Many literati from all around have presented me with their writings [about me], most of which conferred praise. My coterie excerpted one or two anecdotes and pressed me to include them in the collection. This indeed adds to my embarrassment."[63] He thus shifts the responsibility for the editorial decision away from himself to his peers.

Unlikely as it may sound, however, all the entries about Wang Zhuo in *Jin Shishuo* do appear to have been drawn from published materials. For example, six of Wang Zhuo's entries were quoted from

60. "所稱許亦多溢量，蓋標榜聲氣之書，猶明代詩社餘習也。至於載入己事，尤乖體例。" Yong Long et al., *Siku quanshu zongmu*, 2:1226. I have modified Qian Nanxiu's translation in *Spirit and Self*, 281. The official history of the Qing dynasty used almost the same wording in its criticism of *Jin Shishuo*. *Qingshi liezhuan*, 18:5690.

61. Wang Zhuo, "Zixu," in *Zhuye ting zaji*; *Jin Shishuo*, 135.

62. Wang Zhuo, "*Jin Shishuo* liyan," in *Zhuye ting zaji*; *Jin Shishuo*, 141. This was corroborated by his close friend Wu Yiyi's account: "When Wang Zhuo was editing *Jin Shishuo*, an assistant department magistrate, Luo Xianshou 羅賢手, made several bids to be included in it. But, by that time, Wang Zhuo had already finished making the selection and did not include any entry about Luo. Although Luo harbored a grudge, Wang did not mind." 丹麓撰今世說，羅參軍賢手數條頓首屬載，已盡真不錄。羅銜之，亦不顧。 Wu Yiyi, "Benzhuan," in Wang Zhuo, *Xiaju tang quanji dingben* 3a.

63. "至晔平生，本無足錄。向承四方諸先生贈言，頗多獎借，同人即為節取一二，強列集中，實增愧惡。" Wang Zhuo, "*Jin Shishuo* liyan," in *Zhuye ting zaji*; *Jin Shishuo*, 142.

Wu Yiyi's biography of him;[64] the Hangzhou literatus Mao Jike left a piece titled "Liang shuchi ji" 量書尺記 (Record of Book Measure), from which *Jin Shishuo* cites two anecdotes about Wang Zhuo;[65] and the comments of the eminent song-lyric writer Cao Erkan 曹爾堪 (1617–79) on Wang Zhuo's books were selected from Cao Erkan's preface.[66] It cannot be denied, therefore, that much of what he printed about himself came from the pens of others. Wang Zhuo must have been aware that it would be more effective if the records about him had already appeared in the published books of other writers. In other words, his self-promotion would not be authenticated unless it was shored up with the acknowledgment of his peers.

Seeking Endorsement by Peer Patronage

The validation of reputation by peer endorsement was a long-established convention, dating back to the Han dynasty (206 BCE–220 CE). Because the early bureaucratic system was built on selecting proper candidates for official posts via local recommendations, the ability to evaluate a person's character accurately and to be recognized by one's peers was valued initially for political purposes.[67] But fame soon became cultural and social power, allowing the recognizer and the recognized to form a social network centering on them.[68] In particular, when the excessively competitive civil service examinations, corrupt political system, and rapid commercialization of the late imperial period dismantled the traditional social hierarchy, a man's

64. For example, the anecdote on *Zhuye ting zaji; Jin Shishuo*, 150, was from Wu Yiyi, "Benzhuan," in Wang Zhuo, *Xiaju tang quanji dingben* 2a; the anecdote on 167 was from "Benzhuan" 1b; the anecdote on 174 was from "Benzhuan" 2a; the anecdote on 208 was from "Benzhuan" 2b; and the two anecdotes on 218 were from "Benzhuan" 2b.

65. The episodes on *Zhuye ting zaji; Jin Shishuo*, 167 and 218, respectively, were from Mao Jike, "Liang shuchi ji," in Wang Zhuo, *Lanyan ji* 11.4b.

66. The comment on *Zhuye ting zaji; Jin Shishuo*, 183, is from Cao Erkan, "Xialiu ci xu" 峽流辭序, in *Xialiu ci*, in Wang Zhuo, *Xiaju tang ji*, in *Qingdai shiwen ji huibian*, 125.

67. Henry, "Motif of Recognition."

68. Jack Chen, "Knowing Men," 60.

reputation among his peers became increasingly important as a barometer of his social and cultural status. As the renowned late Ming scholar and writer Yuan Hongdao remarked, reputation was considered even more crucial than official position for the literati in this period: "It is easy for people in this world to resign their official post but difficult to cast off their reputation. Since one can resign one's official post but not one's reputation, they hanker for reputation just as they hanker for official posts."[69]

One of the distinct characteristics of Wang Zhuo's self-publishing was his endeavors in integration of peer endorsement into his printed books. Peer acknowledgment of Wang Zhuo's literary prowess was thus an essential component of the book externally and internally. First, his imprints attached a large number of paratextual materials to the text proper, such as prefaces, postscripts, commentaries, and prefatory endorsements. It was common for writers to attach supporting materials by their coterie to their books, and the exchange of such materials was an important part of socializing, reciprocation, and status recognition in the literati community. The seventeenth century was notable for the inclusion of ever-increasing numbers of paratextual materials for various reasons, such as to guarantee a book's quality, market the book, or guide the textual interpretation. Even by the conventions of the day, however, the number of pieces Wang Zhuo attached to his imprints was excessive. His *Xialiu ci* had three prefaces, three postscripts, and 184 comments penned by more than one hundred men of letters.[70] And each of the ten short prose pieces in his *Zazhu shizhong* was preceded by a couple of prefaces, graced by several commentaries, and followed by a postscript, not to mention sprinkled with numerous interlinear commentaries, for a total of thirty extra-textual pieces added by his friends—three times the number of Wang Zhuo's texts themselves.[71]

69. "大約世人去官易，去名難。夫使官去而名不去，戀名猶戀官也。" Yuan Hong-dao, "[Letter to] Zhu Sili" 朱司里, in *Yuan Zhonglang chidu* 袁中郎尺牘, in *Yuan Zhonglang quanji*, 32.

70. *Xialiu ci* in *Xiaju tang ji*, in *Qingdai shiwen ji huibian*, 125–61.

71. Wang Zhuo, *Zazhu shizhong*, in *Xiaju tang ji*, in *Qingdai shiwen ji huibian*, 201–50.

Wang Zhuo's obsession with attaining a high degree of peer recognition by overloading his imprints with supporting materials culminated in his *Lanyan ji* in twenty-four *juan*. This work is a large collection of writings by members of his coterie—not written according to their own creative impulses but composed at Wang Zhuo's request—in response to his work. That is, *Lanyan ji* was made as a kind of dedicatory compendium extolling Wang Zhuo's talent. Each piece indicated to which specific work by Wang Zhuo it was responding, such as "Prefatory Piece Presented upon Reading *Xialiu ci*" (Du *Xialiu ci* tizeng 讀峽流詞題贈). It also identified when Wang Zhuo obtained each contribution: next to each title was an entry in small characters such as "received when we met for the fifth time" (*wujian* 五見). Despite collecting more than six hundred works in *Lanyan ji*, Wang Zhuo announced his plan to publish ten *juan* more because he still had unpublished manuscripts in his possession. He even urged his friends to submit manuscripts before he had completed the carving of the next installment of *Lanyan ji*.[72] Several of his contemporaries, among them Chu Renhuo 褚人獲 (1630–1705), Mao Jike, and Wu Yiyi, all recorded the huge accumulation of the manuscripts that Wang Zhuo diligently collected. On the last day of each year, Wang Zhuo measured the height of the gathered manuscripts: he was glad if the pile exceeded 6 *chi* 尺 (6.5 feet) in height and was disappointed with anything less.[73]

Wang Zhuo's mobilization of coterie patronage was also integrated into the textual composition. *Jin Shishuo*, for example, embedded coterie acknowledgment as an inlay in the narrative structure that represented the dynamics of recognizing and being recognized. Like its predecessor *Shishuo xinyu*, *Jin Shishuo* bolstered the reputation of the figures included in the collection, but the reputation in *Jin Shishuo* was made not only through the commendable conduct of the figure, but also through the acknowledgment of his peers. Here is a typical example of how reputation was shaped in *Jin Shishuo*:

72. Wang Zhuo, "*Lanyan ji* liyan" 蘭言集例言, in *Lanyan ji* 1b.

73. Chu Renhuo, "Liang shuchi" 量書尺, in *Jianhu ji*, 4:1285; Mao Jike, "Liang shuchi ji" 量書尺記, in Wang Zhuo, *Lanyan ji* 11.4a–b; and Wu Yiyi, "Liang shuchi ming" 量書尺銘, in *Lanyan ji* 11.8a–9a.

When Du Xiangcao [Du Shouchang 杜首昌, fl. 1699] from Huaihai visited Hangzhou, he toured the West Lake despite a snowstorm, which was deeply pleasant. The next day, a servant sent by Wang Zhuo came and invited him. They finally met each other and wrote calligraphy on the desk. At that time, the joint carriage of a provincial administration commissioner and a circuit intendant promptly arrived to pay a visit to him, but he declined their visit and did not meet them. The literati praised this highly.

淮海杜湘草過武林，冒雪游西湖，樂甚。次日適王丹麓使至，遂以相聞，據案作書。忽傳方伯、監司聯車到門，並謝不見。士論高之。[74]

On the surface, this anecdote compliments the famous calligrapher Du Shouchang by vividly depicting his integrity in accepting the invitation of Wang Zhuo, a scholar with no title, while resisting the flamboyant advances of the officials. But, on closer examination, it also insinuates that Wang Zhuo is such a remarkable figure that even Du Shouchang feels that it is worth declining the hospitality of the officials in order to spend time with him. Recognition in this episode is thus twofold: first Du Shouchang is recognized for his ability to value friendship with a scholar of no secular power yet of high cultural taste, and, second, Wang Zhuo is recognized for his extraordinary cultural refinement, meriting the recognition of Du Shouchang. The anecdote does not explicitly praise Wang Zhuo, but his reputation is legibly generated by the acknowledgment of Du Shouchang.

The importance of peer recognition in validating one's reputation is also shown in another example:

Yun Zhengshu [Yun Ge 惲格, 1633–99] and Zou Chengcun [Zou Zhimo 鄒祗謨, 1627–70] visited Hangzhou together. Zou did not stop talking about Wang Zhuo to Yun. Later, Yun paid Wang Zhuo several visits and saw him sitting upright in the room, always holding a brush and creating writings that he hoped would be remembered forever. After he returned, Yun told Zou what he had seen, and they alternately applauded Wang Zhuo as an extraordinary writer.

74. Wang Zhuo, *Zhuye ting zaji; Jin Shishuo*, 192.

惲正叔與鄒程邨同客湖上, 鄒向惲誦王丹麓不去口。後惲數過王, 見其
兀坐一室, 時時握管摻纂, 志在千古。歸與鄒言, 交歎為奇士。[75]

This anecdote involves three men of letters—the esteemed painter Yun
Ge, the renowned song-lyric writer Zou Zhimo, and Wang Zhuo.
Whose reputation does this episode solidify? As the last line indicates,
this account is designed to promote Wang Zhuo: "They alternately
applauded Wang Zhuo as an extraordinary writer." The recognition of
Wang Zhuo's quality as a writer is fortified not merely by his studious
mien, confirmed by his sitting "upright in the room, always holding a
brush and creating writings." But it is also made possible because this
behavior is seen by Yun Ge, whose established reputation in literati
circles authenticates his judgment of Wang Zhuo. Without the acknowledgment of his peer, the reputation of Wang Zhuo would remain
unconfirmed. Moreover, Yun Ge's recognition of Wang Zhuo was
bestowed only after he heard about Wang Zhuo from another writer of
renown, Zou Zhimo. Wang Zhuo's reputation was thus established by
the shared approval of the close coterie network, which connected Zou
Zhimo to Yun Ge to Wang Zhuo.

It is evident that the process of generating fame that *Jin Shishuo*
epitomizes is not unidirectional but mutual. In fact, the aforemen-
tioned anecdote of Wang Zhuo immediately follows two entries in *Jin
Shishuo* that highly praise Zou Zhimo's literary talent and extensive
reading.[76] While Zou Zhimo was the one who spurred Yun Ge to
recognize Wang Zhuo, Wang Zhuo also recognized Zou Zhimo by
selecting entries about him for *Jin Shishuo*. In this mutual recognition,
the boundary between the recognizer and the recognized becomes
blurry—that is, the recognizer becomes the recognized and vice versa.
By embodying a Möbius strip–like circuit of interdependent reputation, in which the fame of the recognized was generated by relying
on the fame of the recognizer, who in turn garnered more fame by
his act of recognition, the reputation that *Jin Shishuo* aimed to build
up became firmly grounded in the collective acknowledgment of the
coterie.

75. Ibid., 167.
76. Ibid., 166–67.

From Coterie Patronage to Public Recognition

Huang Zhouxing, a well-known Ming loyalist who managed to survive under early Qing Manchu rule, wrote in a variety of genres after the fall of the Ming in eking out a living via the commercial book market. He authored three dramas—one southern drama (*chuanqi* 傳奇) and two northern dramas.[77] Compared to the others, the four-act northern drama *Xihua bao* has received little attention, mainly because it is regarded as either a run-of-the-mill work without any compelling dramatic conflict[78] or a commonplace expression of Daoist transcendence in the face of tumultuous dynastic change.[79] Part of the reason for this neglect derives from the tendency to equate text with the artifact of a single authorial intention. But the condition of publishing of this drama raises the need to reconsider it not necessarily as the solitary religious or political expression of Huang Zhouxing but as the product of sociability between Huang Zhouxing and Wang Zhuo. More specifically, it was made and circulated as the response of Huang Zhouxing to Wang Zhuo's request to affirm Wang Zhuo's literary prowess. The drama was first printed in Wang Zhuo's compilation *Lanyan ji*, the tribute to Wang Zhuo's literary works, which recorded that *Xihua bao* was submitted "when they met for the second time" (*erjian* 二見).[80]

77. In 1676, Huang Zhouxing wrote the southern drama *Rentian le* 人天樂 (Earthly and Heavenly Happiness), the preface to which is a short treatise on drama theory called "Zhiqu zhiyu" 制曲枝語 (Techniques in Musical Writing). Besides *Xihua bao*, Huang Zhouxing also wrote the northern drama *Shiguan shuhuai* 試官述懷 (The Recount of an Examiner), a one-act play satirizing corruption in the examination system.

78. *Xihua bao* displays the typical characteristics of early Qing northern drama, including brevity and flexibility of format, decreased theatrical and dramatized elements, distribution of singing parts, and the use of southern music. On the development of northern drama in the early Qing, see Du Guiping, *Qingchu zaju yanjiu*, and Wang Ayling, "Ming Qing shuhuai xiefen zaju." The discovery of an extant copy was made relatively recently. See Pan Shuguang, "Ming yimin Huang Zhouxing"; and Wu Shuyin, "Dui 'Ming yimin Huang Zhouxing' de buzheng."

79. See, for example, Zhou Miaozhong, *Qingdai xiqu shi*, 86.

80. Wang Zhuo, *Lanyan ji* 10.1a–17b. It was later reprinted in Huang Zhouxing's own literary collection, *Xiawei tang bieji ciyu* 夏為堂別集詞餘. The version included in Wang Zhuo's *Lanyan ji* is the same as the one in *Xiawei tang bieji ciyu* in the National Library of China except that the latter omits the act titles. Huang Zhouxing

It is uncertain how Wang Zhuo became acquainted with Huang Zhouxing. They may have heard about each other through several mutual friends in Hangzhou and Yangzhou literati circles. Wang Zhuo was a friend of Wang Qi, who had worked with Huang Zhouxing on Wang Qi's several commercial imprints, including *Chidu xinyu* and *Xiyou zhengdao shu* 西遊證道書 (Journey to the West That Proves the Way), one of the most famous editions of the vernacular novel *Xiyou ji* 西遊記 (Journey to the West). Huang Zhouxing also formed a relationship with Zhang Chao around 1677. Their correspondence shows that Huang Zhouxing consulted with Zhang Chao while putting together his anthology of Tang poetry *Tang shikuai* 唐詩快 (Tang Poetry of Delight, 1679), which compiled 1,147 poems in sixteen *juan*,[81] and that Huang Zhouxing wrote some comments for Zhang Chao's *Youmengying*.

Aside from the tight-knit coterie connection, the reason Wang Zhuo asked Huang Zhouxing to create something for him must have been related to Huang Zhouxing's high reputation within the early Qing literati community. Huang Zhouxing was a *jinshi* degree holder (1640) and an official under the Ming dynasty, but, after the downfall of the Ming in 1644, he changed his pen name and withdrew from public service (fig. 2.2).[82] Despite being out of the public eye and earning a

---

gave Wang Zhuo one more prose piece, titled "Mu'an shuo" 木庵說 (Regarding Wood Cottage), which explicated the meaning of Wang Zhuo's pen name. See *Lan-yan ji* 11.5a–7b. It indicates that the work was received when the two men met for the third time (*sanjian* 三見).

81. With *Tang shikuai*, Huang Zhouxing followed the example of Zhang Chao's pastiche of Tang poetry lines titled *Ji Li Taibo shi* 集李太白詩 (Assorted Poetry from Li Bo). He invited Zhang Chao to publish with him, but Zhang Chao modestly declined to do so and participated only as a collator. After Zhang Chao pointed out the inappropriateness of one section title, Huang Zhouxing changed it accordingly. The initial divisions of the book were "Jingtian" 驚天 (Poetry That Frightens Heaven), "Qigui" 泣鬼 (Poetry That Makes Ghosts Wail), and "Yiren" 怡人 (Poetry That Delights Humans); following Zhang Chao's suggestion, the last section was changed to "Yiren" 移人 (Poetry That Moves Humans). *CDOC* 1.4b, 1.5a; *CDYS* 1.5a–b, 1.14a–b. *Tang shikuai* was sold at bookshops in Beijing. See Li Huan, *Guochao shixian leizheng* 13.31b.

82. Scholars argue that Huang Zhouxing's pen names after the fall of the Ming, such as Lüesi 略似 (Faint Resemblance), Banfei 半非 (Half False), Jiangjiu zhuren 將就主人 (Approximate Master), and Xiaocang zi 笑蒼子 (Master of Laughing at Heaven), all indicate his frustration and despair over the traumatic dynastic change as a typical

modest living by teaching, writing, seal carving, and commercial publishing, he was esteemed as a Ming loyalist in early Qing literati circles.[83] As his close friend Ye Mengzhu 葉夢珠 (b. 1624) mentioned, "Every time his [Huang Zhouxing's] works were finished, they were bought by bookshops, published, and circulated in the world."[84] His works were known across the Jiangnan region,[85] and in 1656 he published his own writing collection, *Xiawei tang ji* 夏為堂集 (Collection of Becoming Summer). This was expanded and reprinted by his son in 1688, eight years after Huang Zhouxing drowned himself to prove his loyalty to the fallen Ming dynasty. Wang Zhuo did not hesitate to flaunt his friendship with Huang Zhouxing in his several imprints, since the connection with Huang Zhouxing, an icon of integrity and loyalism, would endow his imprints with prestige.[86]

---

yimin 遺民 (remnant subject). For the interpretation of him as an *yimin* writer, see Widmer, "Between Worlds"; and Wai-yee Li, *Women and National Trauma*, 414–24.

83. The reputation that Huang Zhouxing enjoyed is evidenced by the number of biographies of him by his contemporaries. See Ye Mengzhu, *Yueshi bian, juan* 4 *mingjie* 名節 1, 105–8; Chen Shi, "Huang Jiuyan zhuan" 黃九煙傳, in *Daoshan tang houji* 4.5a–b, reprinted in *Qingdai shiwenji huibian*, 62:179; and Chen Ding, "Xiaocang laozi zhuan" 笑蒼老子傳, in *Liuxi waizhuan*, 552–53. Li Huan also collected together several biographies of Huang Zhouxing written by Wang Youdian 汪有典, Qu Yuanzhu 瞿源洙, Zhou Xiying 周系英 (1765–1824), Zhuo Erkan, and Du Jun 杜濬 (1611–87) in *Guochao shixian leizheng, juan* 473, *yinyi* 隱逸, 13.25a–33b.

84. "脫稿後，每為坊刻購去，梓以行世。" Ye Mengzhu, *Yueshi bian*, 107.

85. Huang Zhouxing produced poetry, prose, drama, and song-poems (*sanqu* 散曲). His record of an imaginary garden "Jiangjiu yuan ji" 將就園記, his treatise on drama theory "Zhiqu zhiyu," and a classical love story, "Bu Zhang Ling Cui Ying hezhuan" 補張靈崔瑩合傳, were widely transmitted because of their inclusion in *ZDCS, TJCS,* and *Yu Chu xinzhi.* See *ZDCS,* 45–49, 70–71; *TJCS,* 448–49; and Zhang Chao, *Yu Chu xinzhi* (Guji chubanshe), 155–60.

86. Wang Zhuo publicized his connection with Huang Zhouxing on multiple occasions: he printed his letter to Huang Zhouxing in his letter collections, quoted Huang Zhouxing's words in a literary collection, asked Huang Zhouxing to edit his writings, and included an anecdote about Huang Zhouxing in *Jin Shishuo.* See Wang Zhuo, "Yu Huang Jiuyan hubu" 與黃九煙戶部, in *Chidu oucun* 2.17b–18a, in *Xiaju tang ji,* in *Qingdai shiwen ji huibian,* 192; "Ji Huang Jiuyan xiansheng yu erze" 紀黃九煙先生語二則, in *Nanchuang wenlüe* 南牕文略, in *Xiaju tang ji,* in *Qingdai shiwen ji huibian,* 59; and *Zhuye ting zaji; Jin Shishuo,* 215. Huang Zhouxing edited Wang Zhuo's "Kuaishuo xuji" 快說續紀, a sequel to Jin Shengtan's 金聖嘆 (ca. 1610–61) "Kuaishuo" 快說 (On Pleasure). "Kuaishuo xuji," in *Zazhu shizhong,* in *Xiaju tang ji,* in *Qingdai shiwen ji huibian,* 239.

Fig. 2.2. Portrait of Huang Zhouxing titled *Jiuyan xiaoying* 久煙小影. Reprinted in Huang Zhouxing, *Xiawei tang bieji*, in *Qingdai shiwen ji huibian*, 37:10.

Granted that the exchange of supporting materials was part of literati sociability in this period, it is not surprising that Huang Zhouxing responded to such a request by Wang Zhuo. But some intriguing questions emerge. First, why did Huang Zhouxing choose the genre of drama? In fact, Huang Zhouxing's *Xihua bao* was the only drama among the hundreds of poems and song-lyrics in *Lanyan ji*. It was a much more elaborate endeavor than a poem or a song-lyric, the simple and swift form by which most chose to respond to a request from Wang Zhuo. In addition, *Xihua bao* adapted the plot of Wang Zhuo's prose piece "Kanhua shuyi ji," an account of his dream encounter with celestial female beauties written in 1688.[87] Wang Zhuo was eager to advertise this work not only by printing it himself but also by beseeching Zhang Chao to include it in *Yu Chu xinzhi*, despite the latter's initial objection.[88] But it did not garner any particular attention until Huang Zhouxing chose it as the basis for his *Xihua bao*. Why did Huang Zhouxing select "Kanhua shuyi ji" among many works of Wang Zhuo and decide to rewrite it in the theatrical form?

On the surface, Wang Zhuo's "Kanhua shuyi ji" presents a familiar topos of an encounter between a scholar and several celestial female immortals.[89] It opens with Wang Zhuo quietly savoring the beauty of the flowers in his friend's moonlit garden when he is approached by a maid of the fairy goddess Lady Wei (Wei furen 魏夫人). Lady Wei was a famous song-lyric poet of the Song dynasty, but in the drama she is transformed into a goddess of spring blossoms. She invites Wang Zhuo to her immortal paradise and introduces him to a number of historical and fictional beauties associated with flowers, music, and dance.[90] As

---

87. "Kanhua shuyi ji" was initially printed in *Zazhu shizhong*, which was later included in *Xiaju tang ji*. See *Qingdai shiwen ji huibian*, 224–27.

88. Zhang Chao opposed the inclusion of the fictional "Kanhua shuyi ji" in *Yu Chu xinzhi* because his collection proclaimed itself to gather only veritable records. But the constant requests from Wang Zhuo made him concede to including it in the end. *CDYS* 10.37a–b.

89. Hsieh, *Love and Women*, 59–110.

90. The beauties include Meifei 梅妃 and Yang Guifei 楊貴妃, the beloved consorts of the emperor Xuanzong of the Tang dynasty (Tang Xuanzong 唐玄宗); Yuan Baoer 袁寶兒, the palace lady who gave an extraordinary flower to Emperor Yang of the Sui dynasty (Sui Yangdi 隋煬帝); Xue Qiongqiong 薛瓊瓊, the palace lady of the

many contemporary readers mentioned,[91] the plot was very similar to that of the Tang scholar Wei Guan's 韋瓘 (789–ca. 862) ninth-century tale "Zhou Qin xingji" 周秦行記 (A Record of Travels through Zhou and Qin), in which a scholar enters a palacelike mansion (an imperial tomb in reality) and meets several legendary beauties.[92] Both stories focus on creating a literary fantasy that showcases prominent historical and imaginary female beauties who tell their stories through music and dance as a spectacle performed on the written page.

What made Wang Zhuo's "Kanhua shuyi ji" distinct from "Zhou Qin xingji" and other similar accounts is that the author, narrator, and protagonist are all the same person—namely, Wang Zhuo himself. Although the literary injection of real people into fictional narratives was common in the seventeenth century,[93] Wang Zhuo's first-person narrative makes it hard to distinguish the fictional Wang Zhuo from the real one. This mixture of fact and fantasy places Wang Zhuo at center stage, identifying him as an underappreciated talent. When in the story the character Wang Zhuo asks Lady Wei why he has been invited to the celestial realm of the flowers, she replies: "A beautiful woman is a flower's true form, and a flower is a portrait of a beautiful woman. Since you cherish flowers, you are invited here. Indeed, karma is not inconsequential. I have already asked Lady Wei 衛夫人 [the famous calligrapher from the Eastern Jin dynasty] to transcribe a copy of your piece 'Jie zhehua wen' 戒折花文 (Precaution Against the Plucking

---

Tang renowned for playing the zither (*zheng* 箏); Nongyu 弄玉, a daughter of Duke Mu of the Qin dynasty (Qin Mugong 秦穆公), who excelled at playing the fife (*xiao* 簫); and Jiangshu 絳樹, a legendary beauty who was talented at singing and dancing as well as other activities.

91. For example, see Lian Zhenji's 練貞吉 (fl. 1651) preface to "Kanhua shuyi ji," in Wang Zhuo, *Xiaju tang ji*, in *Qingdai shiwen ji huibian*, 223.

92. The protagonist of "Zhou Qin xingji" is the Tang scholar Niu Sengru 牛僧孺 (780–848), so the tale is often falsely attributed to Niu Sengru. See Wang Guoyuan, *Tangren xiaoshuo*, 213–17. For a discussion of "Zhou Qin xingji," see Hsieh, *Love and Women*, 71–72.

93. See, for example, the featuring of Dong Qichang and Chen Jiru 陳繼儒 (1588–1639) in Li Yu's 1653 drama *Yizhong yuan* 意中緣 and of Hou Fangyu 侯方域 (1618–54) and Li Xiangjun 李香君 in Kong Shangren's 1699 drama *Taohua shan* 桃花扇.

of Flowers) in standard script."[94] Wang Zhuo has been summoned because of this prose piece, which laments the fleeting nature of flower blossoms.[95] The piece has been neglected in the human world, but the heavenly goddess of flowers expresses her appreciation by orchestrating an exquisite performance by the flower beauties. In other words, Wang Zhuo's "Kanhua shuyi ji" is an imaginary fancy that celebrates his own literary accomplishment, "Jie zhehua wen."

Huang Zhouxing's *Xihua bao* supplements the gratuitous nature of the self-recognition in "Kanhua shuyi ji." At the end of the latter, the author Wang Zhuo cannot help but realize that it is nothing but an illusion. When the character Wang Zhuo within the story is startled by a rooster crowing at dawn, he finds out that it is time to awaken from the dream. After returning home and coming back to reality, he "sighs that affairs in the world have always turned out thus."[96] Since nothing has actually happened, the author Wang Zhuo feels bitter that self-recognition, no matter how glamorous it is in his fantasy, is futile. This frustrating ending of "Kanhua shuyi ji" is, however, transformed dramatically in *Xihua bao*. Overall, Huang Zhouxing's drama faithfully follows the first-person narrative of Wang Zhuo's "Kanhua shuyi ji," featuring Wang Zhuo as the male lead (*sheng* 生). In the first act, "Tuiju" 推舉 (Recommendation), Lady Wei of the Southern Mountain recognizes Wang Zhuo's piece "Jie zhehua wen" and asks her maid to invite Wang Zhuo to her immortal paradise. In act 2, "Jieyin" 接引 (Invitation), the maid delivers Lady Wei's invitation to Wang Zhuo and leads him into the celestial realm. There he encounters several legendary beauties associated with flowers and music. In act 3, "Guanle" 觀樂 (Watching Music), Lady Wei asks the beauties to perform the music, the lyrics of which are adapted from Wang Zhuo's "Jie zhehua wen." In the fourth and final act, "Zhengxian" 證仙 (Authenticated as an Immortal), Lady Wei appoints Wang Zhuo as an envoy for the protection

94. "美人是花真身，花是美人小影。以汝惜花，故得見此。緣殊不淺，向汝作戒折花文，已命衛夫人楷書一通。" Wang Zhuo, "Kanhua shuyi ji," in *Xiaju tang ji*, in *Qingdai shiwen ji huibian*, 226.

95. Wang Zhuo's "Jie zhehua wen" was printed in Wang Zhuo, *Xiaju tang quanji dingben* 7.1a–2b.

96. "因慨天下事，大率類是。" Wang Zhuo, "Kanhua shuyi ji," in *Xiaju tang ji*, in *Qingdai shiwen ji huibian*, 227.

of flowers (*huohua shizi* 獲花使子) and celebrates his heavenly official post with other male literary celebrities renowned for cherishing flowers.[97] Expanding on the literary allusions and references that Wang Zhuo had originally used in his piece, Huang Zhouxing's drama thus adds a completely new ending to magnify the celebration of Wang Zhuo's talent by elevating him as an immortal of flowers—someone to be remembered for eternity.

Aside from the glamorous ending in which Wang Zhuo becomes an immortal on the basis of his literary talent, the theatrical structure of *Xihua bao* serves to confer upon Wang Zhuo's work the recognition of Huang Zhouxing for which Wang Zhuo eagerly vies. According to the general convention of this type of drama, the climax occurs not in the final act but in the third act. It presents a scene in which the beauties all assemble before Lady Wei and Wang Zhuo to perform the musical rendering of Wang Zhuo's "Jie zhehua wen" in order to pay tribute to his accomplishment:

> *Huang Lingzheng*: All the beauties are here. Aside from Yongxin, Niannu's singing voice is the most superb. Have Niannu raise her voice, Jiangshu accompany her in the tune, Nongyu play the fife, Xue Qiongqiong pluck the guitar, Lüzhu blow the flute, Hongxian play the moon zither, and Xu Yuehua play the horizontal harp in harmony.
> (*Everyone responds*)
> *Niannu* (*holding a drum and a clapper*): I have made a song with lyrics from Wang Zhuo's "Jie zhehua wen." We will try to sing the song for him.
> *Lady Wei*: This will be even better!
> *Wang Zhuo* (*respectfully lowering his head*): The piece is worthless like the sound of crickets and frogs. How could it tarnish these beauties' lips?

97. These renowned literary celebrities include Cui Xuanwei 崔玄微, the protagonist of the well-known Tang story in which he encounters the flower fairies; Zhang Ji 張籍 (767–830), the eminent Tang poet renowned for his poems about flowers; Su Zhi 蘇直, a legendary doctor in the Tang dynasty; Song Zhongru 宋仲儒, famous for his exceptional skill at raising peonies; and Guo Tuotuo 郭槖駝, a fictional character who possessed a talent for planting trees in Liu Zongyuan's 柳宗元 (773–819) fabled prose. See "Cui Xuanwei," in Li Fang et al., *Taiping guangji*, 5:3392–93; and Liu Zongyuan, "Zhongshu Guo Tuotuo zhuan," 種樹郭槖駝傳, in *Liu Zongyuan ji*, 2:473–75.

Lady Wei: You are too modest. Beauties, play your instruments!
(*All play the music together*)
(*Niannu is singing to the tune of Dahefo*)

> In spring when every kind of charming flower blossoms,
> The fine scenery refreshes;
> Chilling wind and bitter rain, jealous of this beautiful season,
> Make fragrant souls cry;
> Human life is [fleeting] like a spring blossom,
> It is unbearable to watch such tender fragrance crumble into nothing
>   but dust;
> Please tell like-minded friends not to harm flowers
> Do not say it is because of my fondness for their allure
> You must know that the heavenly god fosters great virtue to live on.

旦：諸美人俱在此。除了永新，只有念奴歌聲獨絕。如今可令念奴發聲，絳樹接磬，弄玉吹簫，薛瓊瓊搊箏，綠珠等弄笛，紅線操月琴，徐月華彈臥箜篌以和之。

（眾應介）

淨執鼓板介：妾曾將王郎戒折花文，隱括成歌。今試為王郎歌之。

老旦：這箇更妙。

生躬介：蛩語蛙吟，何敢汙麗人香吻？

老旦：先生過謙了。諸姬每打動樂器者。

（眾奏樂介）

> 淨唱介[大和佛]
>
> 姹紫嫣紅爛熳春，淑景新。淒風苦雨妒良辰，泣芳魂。人生一世似春花放，忍看香艷化微塵。請把同心布告休侵損，莫道留情脂粉，須知道上帝生成大德存。[98]

Evidently, the lyric of the song is not a musical adaptation of Wang Zhuo's "Jie zhehua wen," as Niannu explains. In fact, it is newly composed by Huang Zhouxing—in other words, it is Huang Zhouxing's recasting of Wang Zhuo's "Jie zhehua wen." In this performance within a performance, therefore, Wang Zhuo watches not the performance of his own work but rather Huang Zhouxing's appreciation of Wang

98. Huang Zhouxing, *Xihua bao*, in *Xiawei tang bieji ciyu* 13b–14a.

Zhuo's work. As the title of act 3, "Watching Music," implies, Wang Zhuo becomes a spectator himself, watching his work being recognized by Huang Zhouxing in the drama.

Furthermore, the lyrics composed by Huang Zhouxing reveal that he does not read Wang Zhuo's "Jie zhehua wen" literally, as a lament over the fleeting nature of flower blossoms. Instead, he interprets Wang Zhuo's words in "Jie zhehua wen" as the lament of such an unrecognized talent as Wang Zhuo himself. In his reading, flower blossoms are the only companion of a scholar who "retreats into misery" (*bihu qiongju* 閉戶窮居), for flowers and scholars share the same destiny—unless they are recognized, they will soon be buried in oblivion.[99] Thus Huang Zhouxing has the beauties sing: "Human life is [fleeting] like a spring blossom / It is unbearable to watch such tender fragrance crumble into nothing but dust." By likening the fragility of the blossoms to the ephemerality of Wang Zhuo's life, Huang Zhouxing's drama recognizes Wang Zhuo's otherwise obscure presence as a talent, just as Wang Zhuo's "Jie zhehua wen" recognizes the transient blossoms of flowers. In this way, the script successfully shifts Wang Zhuo's self-recognition in "Kanhua shuyi ji" into recognition conferred by an eminent writer, Huang Zhouxing—which was probably what Wang Zhuo had hoped to obtain when he asked Huang Zhouxing to write something for him. As the title of Huang Zhouxing's drama insinuates, *Xihua bao* rewards (*bao*) Wang Zhuo's lament over being unrecognized (*xihua*), thus enabling self-conferred recognition to be upheld by peer recognition.

More important, however, Huang Zhouxing's *Xihua bao* does not stop at theatricalizing Huang Zhouxing's recognition of Wang Zhuo; it further amplifies the recognition of Wang Zhuo by garnering him the accolades of a much wider audience. Although *Xihua bao* was likely to be a "desktop drama" (*antou xi* 案頭戲)—that is, a script to be read rather than performed[100]—its theatrical setting intrinsically situates Wang Zhuo as an internal character who is supposed to be watched by

99. Wang Zhuo, "Jie zhehua wen," in *Xiaju tang quanji dingben* 7.14b.
100. There is no evidence that *Xihua bao* was ever performed, either during or after Huang Zhouxing's lifetime, probably because of its insufficient dramatic action and many actors, common characteristics of early Qing northern drama.

the audience. In other words, the audience watches Wang Zhuo watching the performance. Whether or not they intend to, therefore, the audience of the drama partakes in the recognition of Wang Zhuo by watching (*guan* 觀) the moment when recognition is conferred on him. The recognition of Wang Zhuo becomes a phenomenon designed to be shared by whoever views the drama, thereby transforming the illusory self-recognition into a real-life one that is being enacted at the moment of its watching. The progression from the recognition of "Jie zhehua wen" in Wang Zhuo's "Kanhua shuyi ji" to the recognition of "Kanhua shuyi ji" in Huang Zhouxing's *Xihua bao* thus results in the enlarging of the scope of the recognizer—from self-recognition of Wang Zhuo to the recognition of a peer such as Huang Zhouxing to that by a wider audience of the drama—thereby establishing a reputation via public acknowledgment.[101] In this way, Huang Zhouxing's drama refuses to remain as a static text but rather becomes a performative one with the goal of garnering public recognition of Wang Zhuo as a talent whose work deserved to be in print.

Conclusion

Wang Zhuo's publishing endeavors evidenced one of the most common anxieties of seventeenth-century writers with regard to self-publishing: the growing separation of merit and reputation. In an attempt to bridge the gap, Wang Zhuo's publishing used two strategies to bolster the worthiness of his imprints: with *Lanyan ji*, he externalized peer endorsement by gathering a great number of paratextual materials, and with *Jin Shishuo* he made peer recognition an integral part of a narrative structure that generated his fame. In short, Wang Zhuo relied on coterie patronage in establishing the authority of his imprints because he felt that reputation initiated through self-publishing had to be endorsed by a cohesive coterie whose members shared ideas, values, and standards of textual worth.

---

101. Indeed, *Xihua bao* must have deeply satisfied Wang Zhuo, because he not only printed it in *Lanyan ji* but also urged Zhang Chao to include it in *ZDCS* for wider dissemination. *CDYS* 10.37b.

But what if ideal readers, such as Huang Zhouxing, no longer existed and Wang Zhuo's cohesive coterie was dissolved? On one occasion Huang Zhouxing scoffed at the publishing boom, saying: "Whenever I see the recent printed anthologies, the names of the collators listed are so numerous that they run in the tens and hundreds. I laugh up my sleeve. Aren't they like a family register of sworn brothers or a record of pledges?"[102] His cynical attitude demonstrated that the traditional peer patronage on which Wang Zhuo's publishing endeavor sought to be grounded had become increasingly destabilized in seventeenth-century China, as economic, social, and political transformations accelerated the diversification and stratification of the literati community. In fact, Wang Zhuo's coterie was forced to defend "Kanhua shuyi ji" from attacks by other literati groups.[103] The competitive viability of reputation could no longer depend completely on coterie patronage but needed to be supplemented by other means, such as the acknowledgment of a widening readership that print made possible. Huang Zhouxing's theatricalization of the granting of recognition to Wang Zhuo attests to the necessity of achieving a more public form of approval as an alternative to the increasingly contested nature of coterie patronage in shaping textual authority in the seventeenth century.

102. "每見近日選刻, 臚列參閱姓字, 多至伯什。心竊哂之, 此非金蘭籍、香火簿?" Huang Zhouxing, "Xuanshi lilüe" 選詩例略 (Brief principles of selection of poetry), in *Chongding Tang shikuai.*

103. Mao Jike, "Zazhu shizhong xu" 雜著十種序, in Wang Zhuo, *Zazhu shizhong,* in *Xiaju tang ji,* in *Qingdai shiwen ji huibian,* 202. The eighteenth-century compilers of the *Siku quanshu* also downplayed it as a mere echo of "Zhou Qin xingji," saying that "'Kanhua shuyi ji' imitated Niu Sengru's 'Zhou Qin xingji' and gathered palace ladies from the previous dynasties and endowed them with sensual charm. It was especially inappropriate" 看花述異記, 摹仿牛僧孺周秦行記, 聚歷代妃主, 備諸冶蕩, 尤非所宜. Yong Long et al., *Siku quanshu zongmu,* 1:1140.

CHAPTER 3

The Economics of Print

For writers in seventeenth-century China, the boundary between literary fame and financial compensation was often porous. Wang Zhuo's *Jin Shishuo* records the following anecdote, which demonstrates the economic dynamics at work in this period, where financial capital is turned into symbolic capital and then back again.

> Mao Zhihuang [Mao Xianshu] was thinking of selling his farm in order to print his writing collection, but he was unable to make up his mind. Zhu Hu'nan [Zhu Kuangding 諸匡鼎, b. 1636] said to him, "If your asset is sold off, you are exempt from paying your land tax. And if your book gets recognition, you can earn profit. This serves two purposes and loses nothing at all." Mao smiled and nodded.
> 毛稚黄欲賣田刻集, 意猶未決。諸虎男曰: 產去則免役, 紙貴可以操贏, 是有兩得無兩失也。毛笑頷之。[1]

Mao Xianshu was considering selling his farm to raise the money that he needed to print his collected writings, but he was reluctant to do so because the farm was his only asset and the source of his livelihood. His fellow literatus Zhu Kuangding, however, pointed to the fact that printed books could earn Mao Xianshu fame, and that fame could be converted into a fortune large enough to recoup his investment. Mao Xianshu then agreed with him. Apparently Zhu Kuangding and Mao Xianshu recognized the necessity of having both a literary reputation

1. Wang Zhuo, *Zhuye ting zaji; Jin Shishuo*, 157.

and financial assets to ensure their elite status and further expressed the belief that the two were interchangeable.

More important, this anecdote points to the medium that enabled the interchange between financial capital and symbolic capital—print. In order to acquire "recognition" and consequently earn "profit," it was not enough to have simply *written* a manuscript; one had to have it *printed*. It was common for writers of the time to bemoan the fact that they could not afford to print their work once they had completed writing it. The eminent prose writer Zhang Dai 張岱 (1597–1684), for example, lamented his grandfather's futile efforts: "Now, if he were to spend another thirty years on this book, he would not finish it. And even if he were to finish it, he would not be able to have it printed. The brushes [that he has used] have piled up like a mountain, but his writing is only fit for covering jars!"[2] What made writers in seventeenth-century China consider writing to be worthless, "only fit for covering jars," unless it was put into print? What kind of profit did they expect to obtain by printing their work? It seems that print had emerged as a prerequisite to their work being recognized and becoming profitable—but how exactly did print enable this to happen?

This chapter examines the ways in which the economic dynamics of money and reputation intersected in the production and circulation of two large compilations of contemporary prose, *Tanji congshu* and *Zhaodai congshu*, that Zhang Chao and Wang Zhuo copublished. It begins with a critical reexamination of the prevailing perception of private publishing by elite writers as pure, free, and distinct from the soiling practices of the market and then goes on to reveal that the financial imperative was central to bringing about Zhang Chao's collaboration both with his fellow writer-cum-publisher Wang Zhuo and with commercial bookshops. But this chapter also confounds the simple reduction of the book market to thorough monetization and popularization. Instead, it sheds light on the complexity of the early modern book market in seventeenth-century China, where socially embedded gift giving was coopted by the impersonal business of

2. "今此書再加三十年, 亦不能成, 縱成亦力不能刻。筆冢如山, 只堪覆瓿!" Zhang Dai, "Yunshan" 韻山, in *Taoan mengyi*, 154. I have slightly modified Philip Kafalas's translation in his *Limpid Dream*, 32.

monetary transaction, which appropriated the cultural prestige of elite taste to serve broad marketing appeal. The economics of publishing thus enmeshed writers in the competitive book market yet also enabled them to differentiate themselves from it, thereby achieving the two ostensibly separate goals of reputation building and money making in the seventeenth century.

Financing Private Publishing

In studying Chinese print culture, the question of economics is a thorny one due to the scarcity of concrete evidence. Literati were usually reticent to discuss the economic factors that played into their publishing activities, mostly because the Confucian social order, based on the ideal of a self-sufficient agricultural economy, perceived commerce as a nonproductive surplus activity and therefore viewed a literatus's pursuit of money with moral contempt and as a socially inappropriate aspiration. Although the burgeoning book market from the fourteenth century onward had increased the number of writers involved in transactions between writing and money, and terms such as "farming with the brush" (bigeng 筆耕) and "inkstone rice field" (yantian 硯田) became common in the seventeenth century,[3] writing for money was still not completely free from the connotation that the author in question had become déclassé. For example, Chen Jiru 陳繼儒 (1558–1639), considered one of the most successful professional writers in the late Ming book market, concealed any trace of the financial transactions behind the commissioning of his works and also any records of payments he received.[4]

Writers also asserted that their reasons for publishing were unrelated to any financial motive, instead stressing their altruistic aims. One of the most common rationales for publishing was the wish to satisfy the increasing demand for their works. Writers often voiced their concern that they were not able to respond to readers' requests promptly enough through transcribed copies. For example, the publisher of a

3. Ho, "Late Ming Literati," 31.
4. Greenbaum, *Chen Jiru*, 108.

late Ming drama mentioned that "this book is only for spending spare time, not originally designed for profit. Since those who seek to read this book are numerous, I printed it to save them the trouble of making copies by hand."[5] By resorting to the technical capacity of print to produce copies in large quantities, the writers often insisted that their publishing was an act of philanthropy that allowed efficient dissemination of copies to the readers who aspired to obtain them.[6] Zhang Chao, too, refused to associate his publishing activities with any overt profit-seeking motive. When a friend congratulated him on the fact that his printed compilations were so popular as to produce profit over and above his original investment, Zhang Chao was so angered that he retorted:

> I printed the book because a number of friends sought to read it. I transcribed the copy on their behalf, and, because of this, I just put down myself as the collator. It was initially not aimed at making a profit. I am perplexed by what you meant by "earning too much profit to calculate" in your letter!
> 其所以付之棗梨者，亦因友人索看者多。聊代鈔錄，藉以就正云耳。初非侔利計也，台諭所云獲利不貲，僕竊惑焉![7]

5. "是編第以遣閒，原非規利。為索觀者多，借剞劂以代筆札耳。" "*Hudie meng* fanli" 蝴蝶夢凡例, in Cai Yi, ed., *Zhongguo gudian xiqu*, 2:1329.

6. For example, the Qing bibliophile Zhang Haipeng 張海鵬 (ca. 1840) described the merit of printing as follows: "Collecting books is not as good as reading books, but reading books is not as good as printing books. Reading benefits but one person, whereas printing is beneficial to other people. In terms of its relation to the past, it [printing books] preserves the spirit of the author for a long time; in terms of its relation to the future, it bestows benefits on posterity" 藏書不如讀書，讀書不如刻書。讀書只以為己，刻書可以澤人。上以壽作者之精神，下以惠後來之沾溉. Huang Tingjian, "Chaoyi dafu Zhangjun xingzhuang" 朝議大夫張君行狀, in *Di liu xianxi wenchao*, *juan* 4, in *Congshu jicheng chubian*, 2462:84.

7. *CDOC* 4.31a. The most popular and influential commentator of the novel *Jin Ping Mei*, Zhang Zhupo, similarly remarked, "How could I intend to profit by printing? I transmit [my book] in print so as to let the people of the world appreciate the beauty of the writing together" 吾豈謀利而為之耶？吾將梓以問世，使天下人共賞文字之美. Zhang Daoyuan 張道淵, "Zhongxiong Zhupo zhuan" 仲兄竹坡傳, in Hou Zhongyi and Wang Rumei, eds., *Jin Ping Mei ziliao*, 212.

Such public denials and denunciations of any financial incentive have contributed to the image of literati publishing as a purely academic or literary endeavor, incompatible with market demand. In keeping with the later modern romantic ideal of literature as genteel amateurism,[8] modern scholars have widened the supposed split between private publishing (*sike* 私刻) and commercial publishing (*fangke* 坊刻) by positing such binary oppositions as pure amateur undertaking versus professional commercial enterprise, lofty motives born out of love of learning versus blatant profit-seeking motive, and aesthetic or intellectual achievement versus mass-manufactured commodity.[9] But recently scholars have increasingly pointed out that the boundary between private and commercial publishing was hard to draw, and the rapidly expanding book market in seventeenth-century China made the interdependence between the two more and more inevitable and indispensable.[10] The focus of the inquiry should be shifted from how private publishing was distinct from the market practice to how writers negotiated the compelling market forces in their publishing practice—since money was a practical necessity in publishing books no matter what.

Turning a manuscript into a printed book required substantial financial investment to meet the expenses of compilation; the purchasing of blocks, paper, and ink; the costs of carving, printing, binding; and so forth. Scholars concur that the largest of these costs—purchasing the woodblocks and carving them—had decreased significantly since the sixteenth century, which made publishing a less expensive and more common task than before for anyone interested in pursuing it.[11]

8. Mary Poovey claims that the very triumph of the marketplace ironically gave rise to the Romantic notion of literature as pure amateurism that is incommensurate with market value. See her *Genres of the Credit Economy* for the historical formulation of the Romantic notion of literature.

9. The dichotomy between private and commercial publishing has been predominant in the scholarship of print culture. See, for example, Dai Tingjie, "Yasu gongrong," 545; Wang Guiping, *Qingdai jiangnan cangshujia*, 44–45; Katsuyama, "Mindai ni okeru bōkaku bon," 83–99; and Liu Hewen, *Zhang Chao yanjiu*, 163–64.

10. See, for example, Chow, *Publishing, Culture, and Power*, 62–63; and Carlitz, "Printing as Performance," 274, to name but a few.

11. Needham, *Science and Civilization*, 5.1:373. For the wages of a woodblock carver, see Zhang Xiumin, *Zhongguo yinshua shi*, 2:673–76; Yuan Yi, "Mingdai shuji jiage," 2:527; and Ye Dehui, *Shulin qinghua; Shulin yuhua*, 154–55.

But the financial burden was still not negligible. Except for a few affluent literati-publishers, most writers had to face financial pressures
while they published their books. In launching his own publishing
ventures, therefore, Zhang Chao emphasized that securing the wherewithal was the foremost task—in fact, it was more important than
anything else. In a letter to a friend who wished to publish, he listed a
number of members of his coterie who had either deferred an initial
publishing plan or abandoned a project unfinished owing to the financial difficulty:

> Chen Jiaofeng [Chen Yuji 陳玉璂, fl. 1681] from Changzhou made a selec-
> tion titled *Guochao wentong* (Succession of Writings of Our Dynasty)
> before,[12] and Yu Danxin [Yu Huai] made an anthology *Wenjiu* (Rescued
> Writings from Oblivion).[13] But they were not circulated. The only book
> disseminated was Qian Shifeng's [Qian Surun 錢肅潤, 1619–99] *Wenjie*
> (Pure Writings). Wang Danlu [Wang Zhuo] from Hangzhou also named
> his collection of classical short prose *Wenjin*. Aside from it, he also made
> an anthology of examination essays, in which the selected pieces were all
> elegant documents and brilliant writings.[14] But unfortunately he did not
> have the [financial] capacity to carve them, so he just recorded the list of
> titles. What is to be done about it?
> 毘陵陳椒峰先生曾有國朝文統之選, 余淡心先生有文救之選, 亦未見
> 行世。行世者, 惟錢十峰文潔而已。西泠王丹麓其所選古文小品名曰文
> 津。此外尚有大題文字之選, 所載者皆高文典冊、煌煌大篇。惜彼無力
> 付梓, 徒存書目而已。奈之何哉?[15]

12. Chen Yuji started to compile *Wentong* in 1667, but by 1694 he still could not
finish it. In a letter to a friend, he pleaded the lack of funding to complete his publishing. Chen Yuji, "Fengda Wei Xiangguo shu" 奉答魏相國書, in *Xuewen tang wenji*,
126:464–65. *Guochao wentong* is not extant, but some pieces of it are collected in
Zhang Chao's *Yu Chu xinzhi*.

13. Yu Huai came to Yangzhou from Suzhou to collect money to publish *Wenjiu*.
He asked friends and visited several bookshops for financial support, but his *Wenjiu*
was not published in the end. *CDYS* 6.10b, 6.18b. *Wenjiu* is not extant, but some
pieces of it are collected in *Yu Chu xinzhi*.

14. According to the only extant edition of *Wenjin* in the National Library of
China, Wang Zhuo seemed to have published it in 1664. It is not clear why Zhang
Chao mentioned that *Wenjin* was not printed, but perhaps he wrote this letter before
Wenjin was finally put into print.

15. *CDOC* 4.30b.

Zhang Chao then added this final advice for the novice publisher: "If you indeed have the intention [to engage] in this kind of work [publishing], you ought to secure the publishing expenses in advance before you close the doors and shut out visitors to make a book."[16]

Writers would come up with several ways to overcome the often meager funding. First of all, they tried to minimize publishing expenses as much as they could. The Ming playwright Zang Maoxun 臧懋循 (1550–1620), for example, moved from place to place looking for lower costs, such as hiring printing labor in the countryside and having the binding done in Changxing 長興, and then selling the finished books in Nanjing.[17] When compiling a poetry collection, some publishers limited the number of poems per poet,[18] the punctuation used, or the number of comments on each work so that more poems could be engraved on a block.[19] And when Nie Xian 聶先 (fl. 1679) published a large volume of contemporary poetry titled *Baiming jia shichao* 百名家詩鈔 (Poetry Collection of One Hundred Personages), which included poems by both Zhang Chao and Wang Zhuo alongside poems by renowned contemporary writers, he shortened the table of contents to keep the budget low.[20]

Writers were also eager to enlist sponsors to help mitigate the lack of funding from other sources. It was common to seek financial donations from officials with whom the writers had a connection[21] or to appeal to well-to-do friends.[22] It was also popular to solicit monetary contributions publicly. Wang Zhuo, for example, phrased

16. "今足下若果有意于此似，宜先籌剞劂所出，然後杜門却掃，勒成一書。" Ibid.

17. Idema, "Zang Maoxun," 21, 24–25.

18. Jiang Long, "Fanli," in *Qingshi chuji* 清詩初集, in *Qingchu ren xuan*, 181.

19. Wang Ergang 王爾鋼, "Fanli," in *Mingjia shiyong* 名家詩永, in *Qingchu ren xuan*, 236.

20. *CDYS* 5.4b. Nie Xian also included Zhang Chao's collection of song-lyrics, *Huaying ci* 花影詞, in his own large compilation of contemporary song-lyrics titled *Baiming jia cichao* 百名家詞鈔.

21. See, for example, Xu Qiu, "Ciyuan congtan xu" 詞苑叢談序, in *Ciyuan congtan jiaojian*, 6. For officials, donations were also a good way of getting recognition as members of the cultured elite without having to do anything themselves. See Greenbaum, *Chen Jiru*, 130–34.

22. See, for example, *CDYS* 5.8b, 7.4b, 8.15b, 14.20a; Xie Zhengguang and She Rufeng, *Qingchu ren xuan*, 167, 192, 200, 216, 238, 274, 288, and 305.

an announcement seeking donations for his *Jin Shishuo* as follows: "Materials and resources are scarce; all the publishing expenses have to depend on aficionados. If the elegant literati tilt their satchels and open their wallets to help my publishing, it will bring renown to obscure figures. Its virtue will not be inconsequential."[23]

During this period, the scope of sponsors often expanded beyond the private circles of coteries to encompass commercial publishers and bookshop owners as well. Since the Song dynasty, it had been common for writers to work with commercial booksellers,[24] but collaborations between private and commercial publishers were more widespread in the seventeenth century. Cooperation varied widely but generally took the form of a division of labor: the private publishers prepared the manuscript and, as long as their financial capacity allowed it, carved the blocks and printed a small number of copies, whereas the commercial publishers, with their relatively abundant finances and well-organized market network, took over carving and printing as needed and also handled marketing, selling, and transporting the imprints. For example, the early Qing literatus Zhang Fuxiang 張符驤 decided to publish the eminent writer Ai Nanying's 艾南英 (1583–1646) literary collection. After he finished editing the manuscript and carving it on the blocks, he passed his blocks on to a bookshop for printing and sale, likely to lessen his burden of labor and his financial outlay for distribution.[25]

Such cooperation was precipitated not only by the writers' need to find financial sponsors for their publishing projects but also by the booksellers' need to find new ways to survive in the severe competition of the rapidly growing book market. Beginning in the Ming Wanli 萬曆 period (1572–1620), commercial booksellers and publishers competitively invited qualified and competent writers to create manuscripts for them in order to meet the diversified and specialized demands of a widening readership.[26] The portrayals of the fictional

23. "物力艱難, 剞劂之資全賴好事。倘有高賢傾囊解橐, 以助棗梨, 則闡幽表微, 為德不淺。" Wang Zhuo, "*Jin Shishuo* liyan," in *Zhuye ting zaji; Jin Shishuo*, 141.

24. Inoue, *Chūgoku shuppan bunkashi*, 202–3.

25. *CDYS* 8.15b–16a.

26. See, for example, Xie Zhengguang and She Rufeng, *Qingchu ren xuan*, 66, 274.

examination candidates Chen Zhenhui 陳貞慧 and Wu Yingji 吳應箕 in the drama *Taohua shan* 桃花扇 (Peach Blossom Fan, 1699) and also of Master Ma'er 馬二先生 in the vernacular novel *Rulin waishi* 儒林外史 (The Scholars, 1750) being hired by commercial publishers to work on their books show how prevalent the practice of employing literati in the book market had become in this period.[27] The name of a renowned literatus often caused an imprint to gain popularity and market value because the scholar's reputation was believed to guarantee the book's quality.[28] For instance, Wang Guangcheng 王光承 (1606–77), a member of the renowned literary group Jishe 幾社 (Incipience Society), made several examination guides for commercial publishers in Suzhou and Nanjing, and those books to which his name was attached all became bestsellers. His contribution to commercial success was so immense that, despite his firm refusal, a Suzhou bookseller insisted on repaying Wang Guangcheng when he fell into poverty.[29]

As such collaborations between writer and publisher became more common, so, too, did disputes over the profits that the printed books earned. The printed books were traditionally the exclusive property of the publisher because his financial investment in making the woodblocks and printing the copies was perceived to be a direct exchange for the financial profit that the printed book brought in. In contrast, the notion of authorial property was not yet fully fledged because a writer's time and effort, as invisible intellectual labor, was not necessarily counted as something that merited material exchange.[30] Thus, when a commercial bookseller hired a writer and paid him for a manuscript, which is commonly called "selling off" (*maiduan* 賣斷), the bookseller was supposed to have the property rights to the manuscript.[31] This meant that the bookseller purchased the right not only to print the manuscript at will but also to its authorship. That is, the bookseller could erase the author's name and put his own name as the author on the printed book.

---

27. See act 29 in *Taohua shan* and chapter 18 in *Rulin waishi*.
28. Chow, *Publishing, Culture, and Power*, 111.
29. Li Yanshi, "Wang Jieyou" 王玠右, in *Nanwu jiuhua lu* 6.35a–b.
30. Suyoung Son, "Writing and Publishing Letters," 886–91.
31. *CDOC* 11.11b.

The increasingly frequent monetary transactions in the literary marketplace, however, raised the fundamental question of whether or not authorship was transferrable via contract. When Xu Wei 徐渭 (1521–93) worked as a ghostwriter, he displayed an obvious discomfort with his own status, particularly after his writing of a memorial won his employer accolades from the emperor himself. Xu Wei was afraid that reclaiming authorship of the memorial would subject him to mockery, since as a ghostwriter he had already been compensated with money, and, accordingly, his writing was officially credited to the person who had hired him. But he also believed that selling his writing did not nullify the fact that he was the author of the work. The work could be reclaimed, he argued, once the writer's employment was complete, because the alignment of an author with his products was inherently nonseverable.[32] The far-reaching contest over authorship, authorial property, and financial compensation was one of the newly emerging and debated issues in the literary marketplace in the seventeenth century along with the expansion of the commercial book market and the blurry boundaries between private and commercial publishing practices.

In short, the book market was no longer a discrete realm that individual writers might choose to enter in pursuit of personal gain or to ignore on the grounds of moral condemnation. Instead, it had become an indispensable milieu in which the printed book was created and circulated. Writers had to embrace the presence of the book market out of necessity, constantly accommodating and negotiating with the market rules of transaction. In the following sections, I reconstruct how economic considerations played a central role in creating and distributing the two compilations, *Tanji congshu* and *Zhaodai congshu*, that Zhang Chao and Wang Zhuo copublished.

Collaboration with Wang Zhuo

When Zhang Chao started by publishing his own collection of writings, he seems to have been comfortably well-off, if not staggeringly affluent, because his inheritance from his family was enough for him to live on

---

32. Xu Wei, "Chaoxiao ji zixu" 抄小集自序, in *Xu Wei ji*, 2:536–37.

and to invest in publishing. Zhang Chao's sound financial situation, however, did not blind him to the importance of financing. In particular, the expansion of his publishing beyond his own writings and those of his late father to make an anthology must have caused considerable emotional and financial anxiety, for he sought advice from his cousin Zhang Zhaoxuan, who had taken up printing as a profession. Zhang Zhaoxuan had carved and sold copies of the *Sanzi jing* 三字經 (Three-Character Classic), one of the most popular primers, after realizing that he lacked the talent to pass either the civil service or the military service exam.[33] After hearing from Zhang Chao, Zhang Zhaoxuan promptly urged him to embark on the project as planned because the publishing cost would be surely recouped: "As for the publishing expenses, you have the money to spare. At a cost of mere two or three hundred taels of silver, your name will be able to pass down from age to age without decaying."[34]

In order to lighten his financial burden, Zhang Chao chose to look for a collaborator. In the summer of 1694, he traveled to Hangzhou to meet Wang Zhuo, who was already an established writer-cum-publisher at the time, especially famous for his anthology of contemporary anecdotes *Jin Shishuo*, published in 1683.[35] Zhang Chao had not met Wang Zhuo in person before, though he was familiar with Wang Zhuo's publishing activities from his printed books.[36] In fact, Wang Zhuo had also planned to make a collection of contemporary prose pieces and collected manuscripts,[37] but he had been unable to execute

---

33. *Sanzi jing*, attributed to Wang Yinglin 王應麟 (1223–96) of the Song dynasty, was widely distributed and reprinted as a textbook for children in Ming and Qing times, along with *Baijia xing* 百家姓 and *Qianzi wen* 千字文. It seems that Zhang Zhaoxuan did not have any stable occupation after giving up studying. He learned swordsmanship but soon found that he was not good at that either. He eventually came back to his native town and took up publishing as a livelihood. The relationship between Zhang Chao and Zhang Zhaoxuan was so close that Zhang Zhaoxuan suggested that Zhang Chao take over the woodblocks of *Sanzi jing* and even sell them if necessary. *CDYS* 1.11b–12a.

34. "至於刻資，先生可優為之。所費不過二三百金，而可以垂不朽於千古。" *CDYS* 6.29a–b.

35. Zhang Chao, "Xu" 序, in *TJCS*, 1.

36. *CDOC* 2.26a–b.

37. *CDYS* 6.16b.

the publishing project by himself, since he was old and impecunious by then.[38] It is not certain whether Zhang Chao visited him because he had heard that Wang Zhuo had an unfinished anthology project or whether Wang Zhuo, as it happened, had something on hand when they met. In any case, the two men discovered that their needs perfectly complemented each other: Wang Zhuo had considerable experience in publishing an anthology and an almost complete draft, yet insufficient resources to incur the financial risk of publishing, whereas Zhang Chao, as a novice with little experience of gathering materials by himself, was able to finance cutting the woodblocks and printing and distributing the book. "I just blamed myself for lacking the capacity to transmit the book, but, having suddenly met you, I reinitiate it," Wang Zhuo wrote, not concealing his excitement about the partnership with Zhang Chao. "Once it is hung on a city gate [i.e., the book is advertised], it will be the manifestation of great virtue!"[39]

As Zhang Chao's senior by fourteen years, Wang Zhuo had experience and practical skills that became major resources for Zhang Chao in planning his large compilation project. Zhang Chao consulted Wang Zhuo in detail on numerous practical decisions, such as what materials to gather, how many prefaces to attach, who should write the prefaces, what the title page should look like, how the texts were edited, and the like.[40] Beyond everything else, the collaboration with Wang Zhuo also brought with it the support of the coterie network that Wang Zhuo had created over time. As discussed in chapter 1, Wang Zhuo's involvement resulted in the mobilization and participation of a large group of Hangzhou writers. In addition to their intellectual contributions, Wang Zhuo's coterie provided a reliable network whose members had a stake in mitigating the financial burden in completing and circulating the compilation by involving themselves in gathering, collating, proofreading, and distributing the printed book.

As it turned out, *Tanji congshu*, the first product of the collaboration between Zhang Chao and Wang Zhuo, enjoyed great success as

38. *CDYS* 11.22b.
39. "方恨無力不能傳布，忽得先生，起任其事。一旦懸之國門，已為表章莫大之德！" *CDYS* 6.16b.
40. *CDYS* 6.16a–17b, 6.36b–38a, 7.19a–b, 8.16a–17b, 9.12a–13a, 10.6b–7a.

soon as it came out in 1695. Zhang Chao and Wang Zhuo were swamped with requests from readers asking for more copies and from writers submitting their work in the hope of being selected to work on subsequent volumes of the compilation.[41] Just one year after the first collection (*chuji* 初集) of *Tanji congshu* was published, the first collection (*jiaji* 甲集) of *Zhaodai congshu* came out in 1697. And the publishing of the second collection (*erji* 二集) and the extra collection (*yuji* 餘集) of *Tanji congshu* in 1697 was subsequently followed by the second collection (*yiji* 乙集) of *Zhaodai congshu* in 1700, and the third collection (*bingji* 丙集) of *Zhaodai congshu* in 1703. Each collection contains fifty short prose pieces—except for the extra collection of *Tanji congshu*, which contains fifty-seven—for a total of 307 works by about 240 contemporary writers.

Dispute over Editorship

Beneath the smooth success of *Tanji congshu* and *Zhaodai congshu* lay a confrontation between Zhang Chao and Wang Zhuo over the profits from their compilation that eventually led them to end their collaboration. As soon as they completed the first installment of *Tanji congshu*, the issue of editorship surfaced, because it was difficult to determine which man's contribution ought to receive more weight. Was editorship owed to Wang Zhuo, who had gathered and edited the most manuscripts? Or was it rightfully due to Zhang Chao, who had financed the process of making the manuscript into a printed book? The line of demarcation was very thin, because, in addition to his financial backing, Zhang Chao had made editorial contributions to the shaping of the collection no less than Wang Zhuo. From the stage of initial conception, Zhang Chao had proposed detailed ideas about the physical shape, format, length, and contents of *Tanji congshu*, and he had also taken responsibility for a considerable amount of collation and proofreading at his printing studio.[42] Apparently, Zhang Chao had actively

41. Wang Zhuo, "Xu" 序, and Zhang Chao, "Xu," in *TJCS*, 203 and 204, respectively.

42. Zhang Chao had clear ideas for his compilation—the number of works to be included (fifty in each collection), their length (short length that did not exceed one

played the role of an editor rather than confining himself to that of a financial sponsor.

In the Chinese literary tradition, the question of editorship was important in claiming status and making reputation, as the editor was perceived to carry significant interpretive weight on a par with the author.[43] The issue of the editorship of the compilation was initially expressed in a gentle yet intense debate as to whose name should appear and in what order on the cover page of *Tanji congshu*. When the first collection of *Tanji congshu* was almost complete, Zhang Chao and Wang Zhuo exchanged several letters about the proper order in which their names should appear:

> In front of each work, the name should be put as so-and-so's editing and so-and-so's collating. Since the works were acquired from your studio, your name should be put first and mine would follow . . . It shows that both of us are working together in two places [Hangzhou and Yangzhou]. What do you think? (Zhang Chao to Wang Zhuo)
>
> 每種前署名處，一為某輯，一為某校。得自高齋者，台銜前列，僕附其次⋯⋯以見吾兩人兩地共事之意，何如何如？[44]

> As for the order of the names, only yours ought to appear since you have long won public respect. [But] you insist on putting my humble name together [with yours]. You are too insistent on modesty . . . In addition, several earlier anthologies named by one famous person have been easily transmitted later. [But] the books edited by two people are hard to remember, and it is often the case that both names are not transmitted. How could I bring trouble to you by including my name? (Wang Zhuo's reply to Zhang Chao)

thousand characters), topics (no limit to the genres), block size (the same as those for Wang Zhuo's *Xiaju tang ji*), and the number of lines and characters per page (nine lines of twenty characters each)—and successfully persuaded Wang Zhuo on these matters. See *CDOC* 3.9b–10a; *CDYS* 10.7a.

43. Since Confucius proclaimed himself not the creator but the transmitter of tradition (*shu er buzuo* 述而不作), the activities of reading, studying, copying, transmitting, editing, and creating texts did not form discrete categories, and authorship was flexibly understood as covering all activities that enacted the established lines of transmission. Connery, *Empire of the Text*, 15–16.

44. *CDOC* 3.10a.

但署名處, 先生久為人望, 所歸自當專列, 至必欲兼列賤名, 尊謙亦太
固矣……又況從來諸選本一人出名者, 日後易傳, 兩人共事者, 卒難省
記, 往往俱不傳。奈何以弟故而并累先生也?[45]

    In these letters couched in polite wording, both men clearly convey
their positions: Zhang Chao makes a yielding gesture, proposing that
Wang Zhuo's name be put first in recognition of the works having been
edited from Wang Zhuo's studio. This meant that if Wang Zhuo accepted Zhang Chao's offer, Zhang Chao would give up the credit for
his own editorial contributions to the first installment of *Tanji congshu*. Trivial as it might sound, in fact, the order of the names served as
a customary marker to distinguish an author from a financial sponsor
in this period. For example, in *Rulin waishi*, a novel known for its micro-
scopic description of literati culture, a scholar called Ju Gongsun 遽公孫
happens to see a complete collection of examination essays collated by
his fellow literatus Ma Chunshang 馬純上. Ju Gongsun asks whether
Ma Chunshang would be willing to add his name to the collection. Ma
Chunshang flatly declines, with the remark that publishing is "a question of profit and reputation," and adds, "if I put your name down after
mine, people will think that you finance the publication and that I am
working for money. On the other hand, if I put your name before mine,
that will mean that the little reputation I have enjoyed all these years
will seem false."[46] According to Ma Chunshang, Ju Gongsun is shamelessly trying to lay claim to the gain that the book will earn by asking
that his name be included on it at the last minute, even though he has
invested neither cultural capital (in which case his name would be put
before Ma Chunshang's) nor financial capital (in which case his name
would be put after Ma Chunshang's) in it. In light of this convention,
Zhang Chao's suggestion that his name be placed after Wang Zhuo's
indicates that he would not insist on having his editorial contribution
acknowledged but would endure being presented as no more than the
financial sponsor of the first collection.

45. *CDYS* 6.16b–17a.
46. Wu Jingzi, *Rulin waishi*, chapter 13; translation of Yang Hsien-yi and Gladys
Yang, *The Scholars*, 205.

On the surface, Wang Zhuo's reply gently declines this generous proposal by Zhang Chao and even proposes that Zhang Chao be acknowledged as the main editor. But his ostensibly modest refusal of "How could I bring trouble to you?" is only a rhetorical question. Wang Zhuo states that Zhang Chao's reputation would attract readers so that an anthology with Zhang Chao's name only would be much more marketable than one with the names of the two coeditors. But this belies his true intention: he was, in fact, much better known than Zhang Chao when they began working on the compilation. Thus, when Wang Zhuo insinuates he does not wish to be listed as one of two coeditors under the pretext that "one famous" editor will make the book successful in the market, he is firmly declaring his single editorship of the compilation.

It is not certain whether Zhang Chao read between the lines of Wang Zhuo's letter or whether he respected Wang Zhuo's experience and age, but the first collection of *Tanji congshu* printed Wang Zhuo's name before Zhang Chao's in the body of the text ("Wang Zhuo from Hangzhou compiled; Zhang Chao from Huangshan [Huizhou] collated"),[47] thus indicating their roles as the main editor and the supplementary collator, respectively. Wang Zhuo's editorial credit was further inscribed by the fact that his studio name, Xiaju tang, was carved under the centerfold (*banxin* 版心)—which has given rise to the misconception that *Tanji congshu* was to be a work by Wang Zhuo alone, despite the fact that the book was actually printed and completed in Zhang Chao's studio Yiqing tang in Yangzhou.[48] Wang Zhuo seems to acknowledge how unusual Zhang Chao's concession was. He repeatedly expressed his gratitude in terms such as these: "Seeing that my name is

47. "武林王晫丹麓輯; 天都張潮山來校。" The first page of the text proper of the first collection of *TJCS*, 8.

48. Zhang Chao mentioned that, "when I met Wang Zhuo in West Lake in the early summer of 1694, he took out the collected manuscripts of *Tanji congshu*. We burned incense and read them together. I brought this treasure back home and circulated it to the world after collating and carving it" 甲戌初夏晤王君丹麓于西子湖頭, 出所輯檀几叢書, 焚香共讀, 予也載寶而歸, 校梓行世. Zhang Chao clearly indicated that he brought the manuscripts back and printed the collection in his studio in Yangzhou. Wu Sugong also supported this claim, having seen the completion of *Tanji congshu* when he was staying in Yangzhou. See Zhang Chao, "Xu," in the first collection of *ZDCS*, 2, and Wu Sugong, "Xu," in the first collection of *TJCS*, 2.

wedged into your two compilations, my feelings of gratitude will not be forgotten until I am long in the tooth!"[49]

It is evident that this arrangement of editorship was not completely satisfactory to Zhang Chao because he started to compile a collection of his own, *Zhaodai congshu*, as soon as he finished publishing the first installment of *Tanji congshu* in 1695. Between 1696 and 1697, he published not only the second collection of *Tanji congshu*, which this time marked the two men as co-compilers ("Wang Zhuo from Hangzhou and Zhang Chao from Huangshan coedited"),[50] but also the first collection of *Zhaodai congshu*, which was credited to Zhang Chao alone. Wang Zhuo and Zhang Chao had had some initial disagreements on the format of *Tanji congshu*, which gave Zhang Chao a good excuse to launch a separate project of his own: he had wanted to include a short preface and a postscript to every work in *Tanji congshu* but had not been able to overcome Wang Zhuo's opposition for practical reasons.[51]

Compared to *Tanji congshu*, which merely selected works without any editorial introduction, every piece in *Zhaodai congshu* is preceded by Zhang Chao's preface and followed by his postscript, thus foregrounding his editorial presence. Although *Zhaodai congshu* turned out to be a series separate from but obviously connected to *Tanji congshu*, because of its identical format and content[52]—Wang Zhuo had therefore initially opposed giving it a title other than *Tanji congshu*[53]—and even though Wang Zhuo continued to contribute to gathering and collating the manuscripts for *Zhaodai congshu* as well as *Tanji congshu*,

49. "兩部尊選俱得厠名, 其中青雲之感, 沒齒不忘矣!" *CDYS* 11.10b.

50. "武林王晫丹麓; 天都張潮山來, 同輯。" The first page of the text proper of the second collection of *TJCS*, 208.

51. Wang Zhuo raised three objections to Zhang Chao's idea: first, the difficulty of cooperation due to the division of work in Hangzhou and Yangzhou; second, his slow speed of editing; and third, his poverty and illness. *CDYS* 6.37a–b.

52. Each collection of both *TJCS* and *ZDCS* consists of fifty short prose pieces, except that the extra collection of *TJCS* consists of fifty-seven, with each piece one *juan* long. Each page of both collections has nine lines with twenty characters per page. The same page format is also maintained, with white fore edge, no fishtail, and single borderline. The blocks are all approximately 18 by 13.5 cm, and prefaces and editorial principles are attached to the front of each collection.

53. *CDYS* 8.16b–17a.

this time the editorship belonged solely to Zhang Chao.[54] He hastily printed the first collection of *Zhaodai congshu* even before the second installment of *Tanji congshu* as though he intended to establish himself as the editor of this successful series before he would become known as a mere financial sponsor.

The competition over the editorship of *Tanji congshu* attests to the fact that the printed book in this period was not a transparent embodiment of a writer's intellectual achievement. Rather, it was a medium through which a literatus could earn a reputation that affirmed his literary eminence, cultural influence, and social status. When Zhang Chao excerpted works of contemporary writers for his compilations, therefore, the writers, instead of berating him for not asking their permission beforehand, usually expressed gratitude or often sent him gifts of appreciation for helping their works to become anthologized, publicized, and widely disseminated. For example, the Qing official Zhang Ying 張英 (*jinshi* 1667), whose work was selected by Zhang Chao for *Zhaodai congshu*, sent Zhang Chao rolls of silk and an inkstone to thank him for the publicity and fame that Zhang Chao's compilation would earn him.[55]

The rewards gained by being included in Zhang Chao's compilations even made some writers attempt to buy their way into print. The calligrapher Wang Shihong recommended the work of a friend for inclusion in the collection *Yimin shi* 遺民詩, which Zhang Chao was publishing on behalf of the editor Zhuo Erkan. Wang Shihong acknowledged that his friend did not yet possess sufficient reputation to have his work collected in *Yimin shi* with some of the leading writers of the time, so he proposed that he cover the entire expense of printing in return.[56] It seems that such arrangements were not rare at all, for Zhang Chao once complained that some writers were pushing to have their inferior works selected for his compilations simply because they had contributed to the publishing expenses.[57] When he was preparing to publish *Yu Chu xinzhi*, he even assured potential contributors of

54. *CDYS* 9.3b–4a.
55. *CDYS* 13.15a–b, 14.4b; *CDOC* 9.16a–b.
56. *CDYS* 14.29b–30a.
57. *CDOC* 4.30a–b.

manuscripts that, since he himself was covering the publishing expenses, they would not have to pay to be included in the collection.[58] The money invested in publishing was thus expected to be returned in the form of the enhanced reputation that the wide circulation of a printed book garnered. Publishing not merely mediated the translation from intangible symbolic to tangible financial capital but also testified to the increasing importance of money in generating a reputation in this period.

Cooperation with Commercial Bookshops

Zhang Chao's collaboration with Wang Zhuo earned widespread popularity that propelled the *Tanji congshu* compilation into a series of subsequent installments, but the series faced financial impediments midway. In April 1699 Zhang Chao's implication in a legal case put him in jail and appears to have driven him almost into bankruptcy. The details of the scandal are not known, but it appears that he was betrayed by one of his close friends and imprisoned on a false charge.[59] He was not jailed for long, but the incident cost him a great deal both emotionally and financially.[60] He even changed his cognomen (*hao* 號) to "Sanzai daoren" 三在道人 (The Master Left with Only Three Things) to express his anguish that he was left with only a farm, a house, and his own body.[61] His deteriorating financial situation affected several publishing projects that he was working on concurrently. He had undertaken the publishing of his friends' books and had even finished cutting two or three hundred blocks, but he could not complete them.[62] He also could not print his new collection of drinking games, *Xi'nang cunjin* 奚囊寸錦 (Bag of Small Gems of Poetry), and had to circulate it in manuscript until 1707, when he found money to print it.[63]

58. Zhang Chao, "Fanli shize" 凡例十則, in *Yu Chu xinzhi* (Guji chubanshe), 2.
59. Zhang Chao, "Zongba" 總跋, in ibid., 286.
60. See, for example, *CDOC* 7.8b, 7.13b, 7.20a, 9.30a.
61. *CDOC* 8.28b.
62. *CDOC* 9.30a.
63. *CDOC* 11.6b, 11.17a–b, 11.19a.

Zhang Chao's financial setback can also be discerned through the length of the interval between installments of the compilations. During the first years of publishing the compilations, beginning in 1695, Zhang Chao's ventures had been highly productive: the second collection and the extra collection of *Tanji congshu* plus the first collection of *Zhaodai congshu* all came out in 1697. But the second collection of *Zhaodai congshu* was published after one and a half years and the third collection took more time, two and a half years to complete.[64] Zhang Chao also indicated that he had barely managed to finish the third collection and hence had no plans for a fourth.[65] In fact, when he was preparing the second collection of *Zhaodai congshu* in 1700, the pressure had built up to such an extent that he publicly divulged his financial travails:

> My several compilations are only for praising good works, not designed for profit. But paper and printing particularly cost a lot of money. If everyone takes the copies and I give out the copies to everyone, it must

64. The second collection of *ZDCS* was compiled from the winter of 1698 to the summer of 1700, and the third collection was made from the winter of 1700 to the summer of 1703.

65. In the "Editorial Principles" to the third collection of *ZDCS*, Zhang Chao again reveals that his financial predicament has kept him from making another installment: "Since I faltered in 1699, I could scarcely make ends meet and was in straitened circumstances every day. Because I had already suffered financial difficulties when I made the second collection, I did not dare to make plans to produce another installment. But, since my younger brother Mushan [Zhang Jian] urged me to collect and edit the manuscripts and helped me to complete the book, I was able to resume this endeavor. If some friends have any works to send me, you may put them aside a while for a chance [to publish it] to come" 僕自己卯歲失足以來，生計蕭然，日就困憊。乙集已自拮据，故不復作鉛槧之想。緣舍弟木山力為慫恿搜輯，其襄厥成，是以復有是役。自後諸知交或有大著見貽，姑什襲珍藏，以待機緣之至. Zhang Chao, "Liyan," in *ZDCS*, 344. The present fourth collection of *ZDCS* was compiled by Yang Fuji seventy-three years after Zhang Chao died. Yang Fuji assembled the sequels, that is, the fourth to eighth collections, during 1777–1816, but he only managed to find money to have the blocks cut for the prefaces and postscripts to each work. These collections were published only with the financial support of Shen Maode 沈懋德, a fellow townsman, in 1833. Shen Maode published the eighth collection after replacing sixty works he thought were frivolous with his own selections and printed two more collections in 1844.

be contrary to moderation and kindness.[66] With the virtue of fair affection, I tell my coterie: If you have a penchant for this trivial book, you may send me some contribution toward expenses. Every copy costs 0.05 tael of silver per one hundred pages. Alternately, like-minded friends can gather money to print [my book] together or bring money to seek the book at bookstores.

種種拙選, 祇為揚芳, 匪圖射利。但紙張刷印, 殊費朱提。若人人如取如攜, 則在在傷廉傷惠。愛人以德, 告我同儕: 倘果癖嗜瘡痂, 何妨略償工價。每書百葉實銀五分。或同志醵金合印, 或攜貲轉覓坊間。[67]

In the announcement attached to the second collection of *Zhaodai congshu*, Zhang Chao specifically points to the cost of paper and printing as factors that have aggravated his financial burden. Unlike the onetime expense of purchasing blocks and having them cut, the recurring expenses of paper, ink, and printing escalated as an imprint gained popularity. Zhang Chao could not afford to pay all the paper and printing fees needed to meet the flood of requests from readers, so he suggested two alternative ways of obtaining printed copies: either paying him the book price or purchasing the book at a bookshop. That is, he decided to charge for his compilations instead of continuing to distribute them free of charge. As explained in chapter 1, Zhang Chao routinely circulated a limited number of printed copies among his close circle of friends as gifts.[68] But his pressing financial concerns combined with the enthusiastic response of readers caused him to adjust his distribution in the following way: he continued to give his close coterie printed copies without cost but had readers outside his

66. This phrase comes from "Lilou II" 離婁下, in *Mengzi*. The original text is "Mencius said: 'When it appears proper to take a thing, and afterwards not proper, to take it is contrary to moderation. When it appears proper to give a thing and afterwards not proper, to give it is contrary to kindness'" 孟子曰: 可以取, 可以無取, 取傷廉; 可以與, 可以無與, 與傷惠。James Legge's translation in *Four Books*, 749.

67. Zhang Chao, "Fanli," in *ZDCS*, 183.

68. It was conventional for books and paintings circulated within the coterie of a writer or an artist to be given as a gift without direct monetary transaction. See, for example, Clunas, *Elegant Debts*. Leon Jackson has also discussed the economy of gift exchange of books in Antebellum America. See his *Business of Letters*, 89–141.

group of friends pay for their copies so as to recompense him for the publishing expenses he had incurred.

In the small print in his announcement, Zhang Chao clearly specifies the price of a book based on the cost of paper as "0.05 tael of silver per one hundred sheets." This means that each collection might cost 0.5 tael of silver, because it usually contained fifty works in one thousand pages. The paper cost varied widely, but the cost of bamboo paper (*zhuzhi* 竹紙), commonly used for printing, ranged from 0.026 to 0.7 tael of silver per hundred sheets in the late Ming.[69] Considering the high quality of engraving, what Zhang Chao charged to print his compilations appears to have been reasonable, although he probably included the printing fee as well as the cost of the paper. A number of Zhang Chao's readers seem to have understood the selective distribution by responding favorably to his notice by paying him the book price because they were aware that publishing involved a substantial financial investment.[70] Taking into consideration the large size of the volumes of compilations, some friends had voluntarily sent money even before Zhang Chao made the cost of the book public, and those who could not afford to do so felt embarrassed to ask Zhang Chao for copies.[71]

Zhang Chao's other suggestion was for readers to purchase copies at bookshops. After printing a certain number of copies himself at his studio, he also sent printed copies to several bookshops for sale or entrusted his blocks to them. The commission of woodblocks had been a long-standing practice since the Song dynasty, and it was not uncommon for writers to entrust their carved woodblocks to bookshops, Buddhist temples, or *Guozi jian* 國子監 (imperial academies of learning), where readers could obtain copies of volumes they desired as long as they paid the cost of paper and ink.[72] Wang Zhuo had once lent the woodblocks of his *Suisheng ji* to the renowned temple in Hangzhou

---

69. Qian Hang and Cheng Zai, *Shiqi shiji jiangnan*, 135–45; Joseph Dennis argues that not many common farm families could easily afford a copy, but someone richer than common farmers, such as a modestly successful landlord, merchant, or artisan, probably could buy a book. Dennis, *Writing, Publishing, and Reading*, 229–47.

70. See, for example, *CDYS* 12.40a, 15.7b, 15.32a.

71. See, for example, *CDYS* 3.31a, 9.31b, 10.8a.

72. Ye Dehui, *Shulin qinghua; Shulin yuhua*, 120–21; Zhang Xiumin, *Zhongguo yinshua shi*, 1:71, 249.

Ma'nao si 瑪瑙寺 (Temple of Agate) so that readers could obtain copies easily since the book's theme was Buddhist retribution.[73] Because in this period most bookshops did not preprint copies but stored the woodblocks until readers sought out the books they wanted to purchase,[74] readers usually bought the paper needed for a desired book and paid the bookshop to have the book printed.

The bookshops to which Zhang Chao commissioned his blocks were Daibao lou 岱寶樓 and Baohan lou 寶翰樓 in Yangzhou. They were known for having a good business relationship with the writers of the time and worked with the budget-stricken ones on their publishing projects. Daibao lou was located in Xinsheng Street 新盛街, where most Yangzhou bookshops were lined up, and Zhang Chao had a close relationship with its owner, Wang Yuanchen 王元臣. Zhang Chao not only entrusted his blocks of *Tanji congshu* and *Zhaodai congshu* to Wang Yuanchen but also forwarded to him the carved blocks of the examination guide *Sishu zunzhu huiyi jie*, which he copublished with the Yangzhou publisher Zhang Yongde 張庸德 (fl. 1706) for their distribution and sale.[75] Daibao lou also established a business relationship with Zhang Chao's close friend Chen Ding,[76] not only publishing his collection of contemporary biographies, *Liuxi waizhuan*, but also gathering the manuscripts for its next installment.[77]

Baohan lou in Yangzhou seems to have been a branch store of Baohan lou in Suzhou, one of the most successful bookshops that operated from 1587 to 1853. It published a wide variety of books, ranging from canonical works of the Confucian classics, history, philosophy, and literature to popular novels and examination manuals. It also published the books of Zhang Chao's close friends, such as Cai Fangbing's

73. Ma'nao si had its own printing studio for Buddhist sutras. Wang Zhuo later reclaimed his woodblocks when he found out that they were becoming worn-out and worm-eaten owing to not having been cared for properly. He repaired the blocks and reprinted them in 1693. Wang Zhuo, "Congjiao Suisheng ji xu" 重校遂生集序, in *Congjiao Suisheng ji* 重校遂生集, in *Xiaju tang quanji dingben* 3.2a.

74. Brokaw, *Commerce in Culture*, 15–16.

75. Suyoung Son, "Between Writing and Publishing," 882.

76. *CDYS* 10.27b–28a; *CDOC* 6.12b–13a.

77. "Zheng jindai zhongxiao jieyi zhenlie haoxia yinyi gaoren shishi zuozhuan fake qi" 徵近代忠孝節義貞烈豪俠隱逸高人事實作傳發刻啟, in Chen Ding, *Liuxi waizhuan*, 30:518.

蔡方炳 (1626–1709) examination guides *Guangzhi pinglüe* 廣治平略 (General Outline of a Broad Government, 1664) and *Huian xiansheng Zhu Wengong wenji* 晦庵先生朱文公文集 (Huian's [Cai Fangbing's] Collected Works of Master Zhu Xi, 1688) and Dai Mingshi's *Nanshan ji ouchao* 南山集偶鈔 (Casual Manuscripts of Collected Works of Nanshan [Dai Mingshi], 1701).[78] Because of the interregional operation of Baohan lou, Zhang Chao's books appeared in Suzhou as soon as they were circulated in Yangzhou.[79]

It is unfortunate that there is not enough evidence to determine the details of how Zhang Chao made business contracts with these bookshops. Conventionally, when woodblocks were rented to a commercial bookshop, the owner of the blocks was paid a small fee called the woodblock fee (*bantou qian* 板頭錢) or block-renting fee (*linban qian* 賃板錢). Li Yu 李漁 (1610–80), one of the most popular writers and publishers of the early Qing, thus earned money not only by selling copies at his own bookshop but also by loaning his blocks to other bookshops.[80] It looks as though Zhang Chao also received a woodblock-renting fee from the bookshops because he once complained that Wang Yuanchen had delayed in sending him the fee.[81] Although how much fortune it brought him is not clear, it is undeniable that the cooperation between Zhang Chao and the commercial bookshops was mutually profitable: Zhang Chao was able to distribute his printed copies to a wider readership without the additional overhead cost of paper, ink, and labor, and the bookshops could turn a profit from the commission of printing and selling books that were in high demand.

In effect, the collaboration with bookshops contributed substantially to the commercial success of Zhang Chao's compilations. Because of their vigorous marketing strategy, commercial booksellers attracted more readers and distributed the printed copies more extensively than an individual writer-cum-publisher could do on his own. For example, the bookshops urged Zhang Chao to print more copies and send them

78. Kasai, "Gogun hōkanrō shomoku," 55. See chapter 4 for the details of publishing Dai Mingshi's *Nanshan ji ouchao*.

79. *CDOC* 3.1a–b

80. Ōki, "Chūgoku: Minmatsu no shuppan jijou," 163–64.

81. *CDOC* 11.13a.

to be ready at the time of the provincial examination so as to meet the expected rise in demand from the readers who flocked to Yangzhou to take the examination.[82] In addition, they asked Zhang Chao to send over a cover page so they could paste it on the front of their shop as an advertisement.[83] One of the cover pages of *Tanji congshu* advertised the book thus (fig. 3.1):[84]

Fifty [pieces of] casual short prose by famous masters of our dynasty
Wang Zhuo from Hangzhou and Zhang Chao from Huizhou coedited
Tanji congshu
The second collection will follow
Retention of the blocks
國朝名家小品五[十种]
武林王丹麓 新安張山來 同輯
檀几叢書
二集嗣出
本衙藏版

The conventional cover page of the book, published privately in the Qing dynasty, was blank except for the title (fig. 3.2). But this cover page—although it is not certain whether Zhang Chao himself designed it or the booksellers attached it at their will—displays the book's chief points of appeal. Sören Edgren points out that the use of a cover page (*fengmian ye* 封面葉) grew out of the commercial need for advertising.[85] Likewise, every line on this cover page effectively announces the book's marketing points, such as novelty, reliable quality, and authenticity:

82. *CDOC* 4.19b.
83. *CDOC* 6.13a. This was a popular way to advertise books. See, for example, act 29 in *Taohua shan*.
84. Because the description of the cover page of *TJCS* in *Zhejiang caiji yishu zonglu* is identical with this one attached to Library of Congress edition, it seems that the edition with this cover page had been widely distributed until the eighteenth century despite its lack of availability today. See Shen Chu et al., *Zhejiang caiji yishu zonglu* 58a, Yonsei University Library edition.
85. Edgren, "*Fengmianye*," 262.

Fig. 3.1 *(left)*. The cover page of the first installment of *Tanji congshu*. Library of Congress edition.
Fig. 3.2 *(right)*. The cover page of the first installment of *Tanji congshu*. Cornell University Library edition.

1. "Fifty pieces of short prose by famous masters of our dynasty" and "Tanji congshu" identify the book's title and indicate that its contents are the prose pieces of contemporary literary celebrities.
2. "Wang Zhuo from Hangzhou and Zhang Chao from Huizhou coedited" reveals the names of the editors, important not only for identification of the book's editorship but also for translatability of their reputation into market value. For example, Zhang Chao once sent printed copies of one of his books to his old friend Yu Huai's son Yu Lanshuo because he hoped to help Yu Lanshuo overcome financial trouble with profits from the sale of his books. But Yu Lanshuo later told Zhang Chao that, when he had brought Zhang Chao's imprints to a bookshop called Lüyin tang 綠蔭堂 in Suzhou,

the owner declined to buy Zhang Chao's books because he had not heard of Zhang Chao before.[86] This anecdote exemplifies the centrality of reputation and its marketing appeal to the commercial book market and explains why the proper display of names became such an important part of the conflict between Wang Zhuo and Zhang Chao.

3. "Retention of the blocks" is the customary phrase indicating the property rights of the woodblocks,[87] and it also claims the authenticity of the copies in that they were made from the publisher's original woodblocks and hence not an unauthorized reprint or pirated edition.

4. "The second collection will follow" indicates that the first collection of *Tanji congshu* was part of a serial publication and advertises the coming of subsequent installments. The second collection of *Tanji congshu* also announced its forthcoming installment with the words "the extra collection will follow" (*yuji sichu* 餘集嗣出), thus drawing the attention of intended buyers.[88]

The commercial bookstores' marketing strategies, along with their widespread and organized network of distribution, precipitated the success of Zhang Chao's compilations, and provided them with wide circulation. Zhang Chao received requests for his printed copies from booksellers beyond Yangzhou and Suzhou and established relationships with bookshops in Hangzhou and Nanjing.[89] In addition, a letter written by Zhang Chao's friend Gu Cai reveals that the bookshops in Beijing also showed great interest in Zhang Chao's books,[90] and it appears that most of Zhang Chao's books became available in the Liuli chang 琉璃廠 book market district in Beijing by the early eighteenth century at the latest.[91] Zhang Chao's books also crossed borders, circulating in Chosŏn Korea

86. *CDYS* 9.30a–b.

87. Brokaw, *Commerce in Culture*, 178–79.

88. Cover page of the second collection of *TJCS* in the Library of Congress. See chapter 4 for details of the marketing strategy of installment publication.

89. *CDYS* 10.27b, 11.22a; *CDOC* 3.1a–b.

90. *CDYS* 3.5b–6a; *CDOC* 5.18b.

91. Pak Chi-wŏn, "Togangnok" 渡江錄, in *Yŏrha ilgi*, 1:97.

via the tribute book trade between Beijing and Seoul,[92] and in Edo Japan through the sea trade between Nagasaki and the Jiangnan area.[93]

Translation of Elite Taste into Market Appeal

The funds needed to sustain a publishing venture inevitably entangled the production and circulation of Zhang Chao's compilations with the expanding commercial book market. Yet the wide popularity and broad appeal of his compilations in the book market drew, paradoxically, upon their ostensible distance from it. Far from following the marketing strategies that commercial publishers often adopted, Zhang Chao did not sacrifice the physical quality of his books to lower production costs or attune their content to a less-educated audience at a relatively low level of literary competence. Instead, Zhang Chao presented his books as reading material for high elites by faithfully following the format and the content traditionally produced for elite interests. The success and wide popularity of Zhang Chao's compilations show that the prestige attached to an uncompromised elite product ironically served as a highly effective marketing strategy in the increasingly diversified and differentiated book market in this period.

When Zhang Chao first launched the compilation project, he expressed his dissatisfaction with commercial imprints several times. He pointed to their cramped spacing, frequent errors, blurry print, and shabby illustrations,[94] and was proud of his own efforts to make his books meet the high standards of the finest editions, such as the renowned Song editions (*songban* 宋板), treasured for their neat carving and

92. See chapter 5 for details of the transmission of Zhang Chao's imprints to Chosŏn Korea.

93. Edo Japan imported Chinese books from the Jiangnan region to Nagasaki via trade ships. The import of books was tightly controlled, but it is owing to the strict rules of the Bakufu that we have detailed lists of some books and the dates of their import. The books imported were called *hakusai sho* 舶載書, and the lists of them were preserved as *hakusai shomoku* 舶載書目. This is the reason why some rare editions of Zhang Chao's imprints of *TJCS*, *ZDCS*, *Xinzhai liaofu ji*, *Yu Chu xinzhi*, and *Xi'nang cunjin* are extant today in the Naikaku Bunko. See appendix for the details of Zhang Chao's books that are extant in Japan.

94. *CDOC* 1.16b–17a, 8.12b–13a; Zhang Chao, "Fanli," in *Xi'nang cunjin*.

ample spacing.[95] Therefore, the first thing that he discussed with Wang Zhuo, as soon as their collaboration began, was such details of format as the width of the blocks and the number of lines and characters per page. Each leaf had nine lines with twenty characters per line to give ample space because he knew that the dense arrangement of the text often found in commercial imprints made reading difficult.[96] He even considered adopting five-color printing (*wuse taoban* 五色套板), the new printing technology developed in the late Ming period, to make an effective division of the content but abandoned this idea because he was afraid that the colors would fade over time.[97] He also put the title of the compilations and the individual work in the centerfold of every leaf for the convenience of readers so that they would not mix them up with the pages of other books when they bound them.[98] All this scrupulous concern for the minutiae of the physical text contributed to distinguishing his imprints from other similar slipshod imprints mass-produced by the commercial publishers at the time.

95. Zhang Chao particularly complimented the imprints of Gu Sili in Suzhou, noting that his edition was better than the finest Song edition. *CDOC* 10.22a. In fact, Gu Sili's edition was one of the best editions in the early Qing. Gu Sili took special care with the physical quality of his printed books and even engraved the names of the carvers on each page in the centerfold. See his *Yuanshi xuan* 元詩選 (1694) and *Changli xiansheng shiji* 昌黎先生詩集 (1699). Both books are in the National Library of China. But instead of blindly praising the Song editions, Zhang Chao criticized one particular physical characteristic, a black line in the centerfold (*heikou* 黑口) that spoiled the neatness of the page: "[Song editions] left about a 1 *cun* [1.3 inch] vertical black bar or black line in the centerfold. But this space touches the fingers of binders, so the line easily stains the book. I do not understand what the ancient people [of the Song dynasty] did with this black line" 板心上下，各留黑條，或黑線寸許。裝釘家手指抹處，必至污書。竟不知古人此黑條，何所取義. *CDOC* 4.18a.
96. *CDOC* 3.9b–10a, 4.18a.
97. Zhang Chao, "Fanli," in *Xi'nang cunjin*. Zhang Chao must have been familiar with the multicolor printing technology not only because his hometown of Huizhou was famous for its technology but also because he was a friend of Hu Qiyi 胡其毅 (ca. 1650–1700), the son of Hu Zhengyan 胡正言 (1584–1674), who published the painting manuals, *Shizhu zhai shuhua pu* 十竹齋書畫譜 and *Shizhu zhai jianpu* 十竹齋箋譜, two of the best multicolor woodcut imprints in the period.
98. Zhang Chao, "Fanli," in *ZDCS*, 183; *CDOC* 9.25a. Zhang Chao put the phrase "[Original] woodblocks of Yiqing tang" (*Yiqing tang cangban* 詒清堂藏板) on every cover page and carved the name of his printing studio below the centerfold on every leaf of his imprints.

In addition, Zhang Chao's compilations followed the traditional format of the compendium for the transmission of scholarly and intellectual achievement. Unlike the perennially bestselling almanacs, literacy primers, encyclopedias, and the fashionable book items in the seventeenth-century book market, such as the vernacular novels, drama miscellanies, and songbooks,[99] Zhang Chao's books fit into the category of books traditionally perused by the literati. His compilation brought together in print a number of independent self-contained works by different writers in a single edition, which resembled the format of the *leishu* 類書, a topically arranged reference work, or the *congshu* 叢書, a reissue of a number of rare works in a uniform format. The compilation format of *leishu* and *congshu* had originated in the Song dynasty as a response to the loss of works, especially monographs too small to circulate independently, or to reprint rare books as well as short works of scholarship and newly collated versions of previous published texts to achieve the scholarly aim of preservation and transmission of knowledge.[100]

While Zhang Chao's compilations were similar in format to books of the established compendium tradition, they exhibited the adaptation of the format that had begun in the late Ming book market. The traditional compendia were limited to reprints of old and eminent works, whereas the late Ming book market witnessed the abundant production and circulation of compendia in varied forms and genres, often encompassing miscellaneous and less esteemed genres (*xiaopin*). Ever since Chen Jiru's *Baoyan tang miji* 寶顏堂秘笈 (Secret Satchel of the Hall of Precious Colors)—a helter-skelter collection of diverse genres of writings that revealed the elites' highly sophisticated cultural tastes, cultivated lifestyle, and private leisure activities—gained huge commercial success in the market, similar competitive collections had come out, targeted not only to elite readers but also to a widening pool of elites-to-be and would-be-elites.[101]

---

99. See Lowry, *Tapestry of Popular Songs*; and Yuming He, *Home and the World*.

100. Xie Guozhen, "Congshu kanke yuanliu kao" 叢書刊刻源流考, in *Ming Qing biji tancong*, 202; Elman, "Collecting and Classifying," 141.

101. See, for example, Greenbaum, *Chen Jiru*; Clunas, *Superfluous Things*; Wai-yee Li, "The Collector, the Connoisseur"; and idem, "Shibian yu wanwu."

With such heated competition among published compilations, it was difficult to ensure survival and success.[102] When planning his first collection, Zhang Chao was primarily looking for a niche that would keep his publication from falling into neglect. He initially had a collection of classical prose in mind because he estimated that the popularity of poetry anthologies had already reached its peak. But when he ran this idea by his relatives Zhang Zhaoxuan and Zhang Yu'an, who were experienced publishers,[103] he realized that he needed to make a more radical change. Zhang Zhaoxuan's involvement in book commerce gave him access to information about ongoing publishing projects, and he soon discovered that Sun Cong's 孫琮 (fl. 1692) Shanxiao ge 山曉閣 (Pavilion of Mountain Dawn) in Zhejiang province had already produced a book similar to the one that Zhang Chao had in mind.[104] Hence Zhang Zhaoxuan suggested that, instead of making a collection of famous prose pieces from all historical periods, Zhang Chao produce a collection of prose of the recent period. Once again, they learned that they had already fallen behind the competition because a new prose collection of the Ming and Qing periods had been printed by another publisher, Zhang Xiazhong 張夏鍾, from Fujian province.[105] This forced Zhang Chao to revise his plans once more, and eventually he decided to produce a collection of prose pieces by contemporaries. Wang Zhuo and Zhang Chao monitored the formats of several popular compilations on the market and agreed to imitate the format of one of the popular compilations in the late Ming, *Kuaishu wushi zhong* 快書五十鍾 (Fifty Delightful Books), made by Min Jingxian 閔景賢 in 1626 and later He Weiran 何偉然, which was a collection of fifty prose pieces.[106]

The choice of contemporary prose turned out to reflect the current demands of elite readers. The newly written yet not easily available works of the literary celebrities whom members of Zhang Chao's wide

---

102. See, for example, Tao Xuan 陶煊, "Fanli," in *Guochao shidi* 國朝詩的, in *Qingchu ren xuan*, 303.

103. *CDYS* 6.29a–b; *CDOC* 3.27b–28a.

104. *CDYS* 1.11a. As for Sun Cong, see Zheng Weizhang, *Wenxian jia tongkao*, 1:164.

105. *CDYS* 6.29a.

106. *CDYS* 6.1b–2a; *CDOC* 3.9b.

coterie network were able to enlist met the literati's desire to keep up with the most recent cultural, intellectual, and political trends and information. Zhang Chao mentions several times in his individual prefaces and postscripts in *Zhaodai congshu* that it was the fervent requests of his coterie for the recent literary news and information that drove his publishing. Examples include the following excerpts, from his preface to the work of the contemporary celebrity Wang Shizhen 王士禛 (1634–1711) and from his postscript to the work of Kong Shang-ren, respectively:

> I had already obtained a copy of Mr. Wang's work [*Long Shu yuwen*], but I do not store it selfishly but want to share it with my friends. My friends are eager to read Mr. Wang's copy but have not been able to obtain it so they often borrow it from me. Judging from this, I am sure that this com-pilation must be read with pleasure by my friends.
>
> 予既獲聞先生之所聞, 不敢私為枕秘, 願與吾之友共聞之。蓋吾之友欲讀先生之書而不可得者, 往往假閱于予, 以是知此編必為吾友之所樂聞者也。[107]

> As my coterie have retreated to lonely cottages, how can we witness this kind of event [the imperial ritual for Confucius]? Now Mr. Kong Shang-ren records the particular details of how he basked in imperial favor from the beginning to the end. By reading his account and envisioning what he describes, aren't all of us as readers endowed with this grandeur? It is not merely Mr. Kong Shangren alone who receives the grace of the emperor, but, in fact, we all also receive the grace of the emperor.
>
> 吾輩伏處蓽蘆, 亦何從得見之乎? 今東塘先生自以其所躬被之恩, 特詳記其始末。俾讀書衡泌者, 咸不啻躬逢其盛? 此非獨先生一己之異數, 實吾道之異數也。[108]

The two works of Wang Shizhen and Kong Shangren that Zhang Chao included in his compendium were disparate in their genre and theme, but they were alike in appealing to Zhang Chao's intended

---

107. Zhang Chao's preface to "Long Shu yuwen" 隴蜀餘聞 by Wang Shizhen, in *ZDCS*, 239.

108. Zhang Chao's postscript to "Chushan yishu ji" 出山異數記 by Kong Shang-ren, in *ZDCS*, 232.

audience, whom he often referred to as "like-minded friends" (*tongzhi* 同志), "coterie" (*tongren* 同人), and "companions" (*zhijiao* 知交)."[109] Wang Shizhen, one of the most influential poets and critics of the time, had recorded his trip to and information about the Long and Shu regions, which were bleak and remote areas few people were able to visit at that time. And Kong Shangren's piece recounted his attending a ritual for Confucius performed by the emperor. Kong Shangren was not only an eminent writer, dramatist, and official of the time but a direct descendant of Confucius who was therefore entitled to attend the imperial ritual. In other words, Wang Shizhen and Kong Shangren were contemporary luminaries whom most of Zhang Chao's readers wished to become close to and emulate. Moreover, their works also recorded events and contained information of great interest to elite readers not otherwise easily accessible to them. These readers were so eager to read such works that they not only made Zhang Chao lend the manuscript to them but also pushed him to start carving the woodblocks for the compendium even before the manuscript was complete.[110]

Both *Tanji congshu* and *Zhaodai congshu* boasted of their comprehensive gathering, but access to the most up-to-date accounts of various subjects by contemporary writers was one of the major selection principles for the compilations. Zhang Chao mentioned several times that, whereas the collections published from bookshops were nothing but reprints of old and already-known works, his compilation contained the most novel and most recent works created by contemporary writers of repute.[111] Each installment indeed included an array of works in diverse genres by contemporary writers on a number of subjects. Selected less for their literary merit than for the information in them, many of these works dealt with contemporary topics of elite concern, such as ongoing and wide-ranging discussions about current political events, especially news related to the reigning Kangxi 康熙 emperor (r.

109. Zhang Chao, "Xu," in the first collection of *ZDCS*, 2; "Liyan," in the second collection of *ZDCS*, 183; and "Liyan," in the third collection of *ZDCS*, 343–44. Zhang Chao in fact clearly distinguished his inside group of readers from the readers beyond his coterie by using the term *gong zhu hainei* 公諸海內. *CDYS* 8.35b.

110. Zhang Chao's postscript in "Long Shu yuwen," in *ZDCS*, 245.

111. Zhang Chao, "Xu," in the first collection of *TJCS*, 1; "Fanli," in the second collection of *ZDCS*, 183; Wang Zhuo, "Xu," in the first collection of *TJCS*, 3.

1661–1722);[112] recent cultural activities, fashion, and hobbies of fellow literati;[113] opinions about manners and rules;[114] scholarly findings and treatises that reflected new research;[115] and literati games and game manuals popular at the time.[116] In sum, Zhang Chao's compilations were characterized by works about contemporary elites as well as works by

112. See, for example, a list of books received from the emperor ("Yinsi yushu ji" 恩賜御書紀); travel accounts of authors accompanying Kangxi's tours ("Hucong xixun rilu" 扈從西巡日錄, "Feng Changbai shan ji" 封長白山記, "Jien lu" 紀恩錄, and "Songting xingji" 松亭行紀); and a record of a court audience with the emperor ("Qianqing men zoudui ji" 乾清門奏對記).

113. See, for example, rules for elite society gatherings ("Doufu jie" 豆腐戒, "Jushe yue" 菊社約, and "Fangshenghui yue" 放生會約); a record of taking the highest level of civil examinations ("Changchun yuan yushi gongji" 暢春苑御試恭紀); travel records ("Guangzhou youlan xiaozhi" 廣州遊覽小志, "Liuqiu ru taixue shimo" 琉球入太學始末, "Long Shu yuwen," and "Miaosu jiwen" 苗俗紀聞); anecdotes about friends ("Zhiwo lu" 知我錄); a record of the pen names of renowned writers of the time ("Wenyuan yicheng" 文宛異稱); a list of people who lived a long life in the contemporary period ("Renrui lu" 人瑞錄); reading notes ("Dushi guanjian" 讀史管見); essays on literati hobbies, such as rock collecting ("Xuanshi ji" 選石記, "Guanshi lu" 觀石錄, "Guanshi houlu" 觀石後錄, and "Guaishi zan" 怪石贊), inkstone collecting ("Mantang mopin" 漫堂墨品, "Xuetang mopin" 雪堂墨品, and "Yanlin" 硯林), painting ("Huajue" 畫訣), and garden making ("Jiangjiu yuan ji" 將就園記); and records of objects and subjects of personal interest, such as a history of bound feet and women's socks ("Furen xiewa kao" 婦人鞋襪考), a history of women's cosmetics ("Daishi" 黛史), and manuals on different kinds of snakes ("Shepu" 蛇譜), bamboo ("Zhupu" 竹譜), and pigeons ("Gejing" 鴿經).

114. See, for example, conduct manuals such as family precepts ("Jiaxun" 家訓); rules for a young man ("Youxun" 幼訓) and a married daughter ("Xinfu pu" 新婦譜); and aphorisms of life and wisdom ("Jingyuan xiaoyu" 荊園小語, "Oushu" 偶書, "Rilu guoyan" 日錄裏言).

115. See, for example, records of rubbings ("Jiaoshan guding kao" 焦山古鼎考, "Yiheming bian" 瘞鶴銘辨, "Zhaoling liujuntu bian" 昭陵六駿圖辨, and "Ganquan gongwa kao" 甘泉宮瓦考); research on chronologies ("Mengzi kao" 孟子考, "Xie Gaoyu nianpu" 謝皋羽年譜, and "Shiliu guo nianbiao" 十六國年表); Western knowledge introduced by a missionary ("Xifang yaoji" 西方要紀); studies on the Confucian classics ("Chunqiu sanzhuan yitong kao" 春秋三傳異同考 and "Sanbai pian niaoshou caomu ji" 三百篇鳥獸草木記); and a study of astronomy ("Jiangnan xingye kao" 江南星野考).

116. See, for example, drinking games ("Yinzhong baxian ling" 飲中八仙令, "Jiulü" 酒律, and "Shangzheng" 觴政), a board game ("Lansheng tu" 攬勝圖), word games ("Lianwen shiyi" 連文釋義 and "Qiezi shiyi" 切字釋義), and card games ("Tongjie fumo" 桐階副墨 and "Sishi zhang zhipai shuo" 四十張紙牌說). On the games selected in *TJCS* and *ZDCS*, see Lo, "Amusement Literature."

them and were therefore a cultural commodity embodying a prestigious brand of elite interest. Although they may not have circulated quickly and regularly enough to serve the role that modern scholarly journals do in updating recent knowledge and news,[117] Zhang Chao's collections of the novel and fresh accounts by living renowned writers must have instantly attracted the attention of elite readers of the early Qing. Zhang Chao's friend Jiang Zhilan amusingly compared Zhang Chao's compilations to similar anthologies published at the time, remarking that "the anthologies these days are like bringing out a hot pan that everybody uses and baking just another cake with it. But you are able to make this type of cake with a distinct taste with no sign of imitation. It is just a marvelous skill!"[118]

It is also likely that the aura of elite prestige that Zhang Chao's books carried served to increase their popularity and market value. For example, the imperial ritual for Confucius that Kong Shangren recorded was open to attendance only by a privileged few, such as Kong Shangren himself as a direct descendant of Confucius. As Zhang Chao sighed, "How can we [common literati] witness this kind of event?" But by reading Kong Shangren's account in Zhang Chao's compilation, readers were able to share this exclusive experience: "By reading his account and envisioning what he describes, aren't all of us as readers endowed with this grandeur?" Highlighting the prerogatives that demarcated members of the inner circles of literati from the widening pool of readers, Zhang Chao's compilations in effect enhanced their appeal to readers who aspired to acquire a semblance of insider knowledge and information.

As high-end books that served as a depository of the most recent elite taste and information, Zhang Chao's compilations purported to be a cultural authority that readers could pride themselves on being familiar with. In this respect, they challenge the prevailing perception that commercialization necessarily entailed popularization for wider

117. Arthur Hummel argued that collectanea played a role comparable to modern periodical literature in which authors could print short articles, papers, or monographs. Hummel, "Ts'ung Shu," 40–41.
118. "今之輯書者, 總是取大家熱鐺子, 再作一餅耳。但能將此餅做得別些, 不見雷同之跡, 便是妙手!" CDYS 7.32a.

consumption. Instead, Zhang Chao's books appealed to the highest stratum of supply and demand in the market, a stratum that was formed by the prestige built by the sociability of exclusive elites, and, in turn, their aura of cultural and social prestige of elite taste conferred popularity and high market value. Conversely, this high market value was also translated as the credentials to verify the cultural eminence and social influence of the imprint. Zhang Chao once confessed that one of his wishes was to "have time to write books that booksellers want to buy and print,"[119] books whose high value was confirmed by none other than their contemporary commercial appeal. This bespeaks how Zhang Chao's compilations calibrated themselves to the intricate enmeshment of the socially embedded economy of prestige with the impersonal economy of the book market, thus maximizing their symbolic and economic capital.

---

119. "有暇著書, 坊人購梓." Zhang Chao, "Sishi ba yuan" 四十八願, in *Xinzhai zazu* 1.33a.

PART II

*Transregional Impact
in the Eighteenth Century*

CHAPTER 4

Censorship of Installment Publication in Qing China

In the fiftieth year of the Kangxi emperor's reign (1711), the president of the Censorate, Zhao Shenqiao 趙申喬 (1644–1720), proposed that the book *Nanshan ji ouchao* published by eminent early Qing scholar Dai Mingshi be censored. In his first memorial to the throne about this book, Zhao Shenqiao claimed:

> [Dai Mingshi] fancied himself to be a literary celebrity. Relying on his talent, he was wild and unbridled. When he was a government student, he privately published his literary collections, which discussed rumors without restraint, replaced right with wrong, and spoke many reckless and erroneous words. This book caused a serious disruption of morals by flaunting his personal opinions at any given moment. His goal was that commercial bookshops reprint and sell them so that he would profit and make a living.
> 妄竊文名, 恃才放蕩。前為諸生時, 私刻文集, 肆口游談, 倒置是非, 語多狂悖。逞一時之私見, 為不輕之亂道, 徒使市井書坊, 翻刻貿鬻, 射利營生。[1]

This memorial, written ten years after *Nanshan ji ouchao* was published, reveals the reason for recommending censorship: the collection contained contentious works that "discussed rumors without

---

1. *Ji Tongcheng Fang Dai liangjia shu'an* 4a, reprinted in *Congshu jicheng xubian*, 25:226.

restraint," "replaced right with wrong," and "spoke many reckless and erroneous words." The specific bases for these accusations are not clear because most of Dai Mingshi's works in the *Nanshan ji ouchao* did not explicitly express his political views.[2] However, the matter turned into one of the most serious political censorship cases during the Kangxi period after the inquisition found a quote from the work of Fang Xiaobiao 方孝標 (b. 1617) in the book. Because Fang Xiaobiao's *Dian Qian jiwen* 滇黔紀聞 (Records about Yunnan and Guizhou) designated the Southern Ming (Nanming 南明) dynasty and its emperor as the legitimate successor of the Ming, it was considered a serious act of rebellion against Manchu rule. The simple fact that Dai Mingshi quoted the work of Fang Xiaobiao identified *Nanshan ji ouchao*, too, as a rebellious work.[3]

Of interest here is the 1711 memorial's description of the production of Dai Mingshi's *Nanshan ji ouchao*: the book was privately published by the writer and then circulated by commercial bookshops in order to make a profit from the sales. As the memorial contends, the book was initially carved by Dai Mingshi, and the revised edition by his disciple You Yun'e 尤雲鶚 was published by the Suzhou bookshop Baohan lou in 1701.[4] Baohan lou was the bookshop that distributed Zhang Chao's copies in Suzhou (see chapter 3), and Dai Mingshi also worked with Baohan lou in publishing his several other books.[5] Further, he also conducted business with the commercial bookshop Daibao lou in Yangzhou. For instance, when Dai Mingshi was preparing to publish the examination guide *Youming lichao xiaotiwen xuan* in 1699, he personally asked the Daibao lou's owner, Wang Yuanchen, to contact Zhang Chao for financial help because he knew that Wang Yuanchen worked closely with Zhang Chao. Zhang Chao agreed to print

2. Guo Chengkang and Lin Tiejun, *Qingchao wenziyu*, 127–28; and Okamoto, *Shindai kinsho no kenkyū*, 35.

3. Guo Chengkang and Lin Tiejun, *Qingchao wenziyu*, 130; Wang Bin, *Jinshu wenziyu*, 86.

4. Dai Tingjie, *Dai Mingshi nianpu*, 505–6, 561–64. Also see the cover page of Dai Mingshi, *Nanshan ji ouchao*, reprinted in *Xuxiu Siku quanshu*, 1418:565.

5. Dai Mingshi's other books, such as *Jieyi lu* 孑遺錄 (1695), *Dai Tianyou guwen ouchao* 戴田有古文偶鈔, and *Sishu zhuzi daquan* 四書朱子大全 (1708), were all published by Baohan lou.

the book on behalf of Dai Mingshi, and they established a close relationship after that.[6] It appears that Dai Mingshi's established fame together with the collaboration of commercial bookshops made his *Nanshan ji ouchao* an enormous commercial success. One of the memorials mentioned that Suzhou bookshops had printed about three thousand copies—a huge hit by the standards of the day.[7]

The publishing of the *Nanshan ji ouchao* followed a pattern typical of seventeenth-century writers, as the preceding chapters have described: the writer wrote a manuscript and then, with the help of his coterie, managed to forward either his printed copies or woodblocks to commercial bookshops for wider circulation and financial profit. To the censors, however, this practice was a sign of the writer's moral degeneration, for they saw self-publishing as a case of a writer's self-aggrandizement: "fancying himself to be a literary celebrity" and being "wild and unbridled, relying on his talent." Moreover, collaborating with commercial bookshops was also considered morally problematic because it was at odds with the traditional ideal of literati noninvolvement in monetary transactions. Lurking behind the moral reproach in the censorship of *Nanshan ji ouchao*, however, was the state's increasing awareness not merely of the ideas that the book expressed but also of the conduit of its circulation, since the widespread practice of literati publishing, aligned with the well-developed network of the book market, could transmit texts that contained dangerous ideas throughout the empire.

The censorship of *Nanshan ji ouchao* presaged the upcoming large-scale censorship that accompanied the Qianlong emperor's compilation of *Siku quanshu*, which began in 1772 and lasted nearly twenty years. As Timothy Brook astutely points out, this spate of censorship cannot be explained solely by the political conflict between the Manchu state and

---

6. *CDOC* 7.11a, 7.16b. Also see Dai Tingjie, *Dai Mingshi nianpu*, 463–64. Zhang Chao and Dai Mingshi exchanged help in their respective publishing endeavors. For example, Dai Mingshi added comments to *Youmengying*, and Zhang Chao sent his work to the anthology called *Jiangshang jinwen* 江上今文 that Dai Mingshi compiled with Cheng Yuanyu 程元愈. *CDOC* 10.18a–b. Zhang Chao also added a comment to Dai Mingshi's *Dai Tianyou ziding shiwen quanji* 戴田有自定時文全集, printed in 1704. Dai Tingjie, *Dai Mingshi nianpu*, 606.

7. Guo Chengkang and Lin Tiejun, *Qingchao wenziyu*, 133.

Han elites. "Rather than dwelling exclusively on Manchu ideological vigilance or projecting onto Qianlong an excessive paranoia about his regime's legitimacy," he contends, "we should also view the inquisition in terms of the book trade and consider the context of book production and organizational control within which the inquisition took place."[8] Besides weeding out works that challenged Qing rule, censorship reflected the state's response toward the expansion of literati publishing. The publishing activities of the growing numbers of elites who were readily associated with the rapidly developing book market newly raised questions of who was responsible for determining what kind of texts were worthy of transmittal to posterity, and the state responded by trying to regain the position of authority in the competition with the literati community and the commercial book market. As a result, privately published seventeenth-century imprints were mostly excluded from *Siku quanshu*, and many of these works were also censored, resulting in neglect by modern scholars despite the continuing popularity of the seventeenth-century imprints in the eighteenth century.

This chapter follows the censorship of *Yu Chu xinzhi* 虞初新志 (The Magician's New Records), one of Zhang Chao's most successful imprints, in order to examine the state response to literati publishing in the seventeenth century. *Yu Chu xinzhi* was a collection of classical tales printed in a series of installments, a compilation format that was popular with late Ming and early Qing writers. The collection gained wide success and extensive circulation while Zhang Chao was alive and even after his death, into the eighteenth century. But, during the compilation of *Siku quanshu*, *Yu Chu xinzhi* was not only excluded from *Siku quanshu* but also banned. Although most scholars suggest that its censorship was due to its display of Zhang Chao's anti-Qing sentiment, this chapter demonstrates that the censorship of *Yu Chu xinzhi* was related less to the state's suppression of anti-Manchu ideas than to its anxiety about the impact of literati publishing—particularly the installment publication, which brought about a collective, malleable, and often uncontrollable product dependent on a process of private and commercial transmission that could go easily beyond state control.

8. Brook, "Censorship," 195. Also see idem, *Chinese State in Ming Society*, 125–36.

Creating *Yu Chu xinzhi*
as an Installment Publication

One of Zhang Chao's most popular imprints, *Yu Chu xinzhi* is a collection of about 150 classical tales in twenty *juan*,[9] exemplifying the typical pattern of compiling, publishing, and circulating an installment publication in the seventeenth century. It gathered supposedly true stories of extraordinary events and figures in a wide variety of highly flexible genres, such as biography (*zhuan* 傳), record (*ji* 記), preface (*xu* 序), inscription (*ming* 銘), and memorial (*shu* 疏). Its entries range in length from a couple of pages to a few dozen and feature figures ranging from top officials and scholars to commoners, women, and animals. As its title indicates, *Yu Chu xinzhi* was intended as a successor to the popular Ming dynasty *Yu Chu zhi* 虞初志 (The Magician's Records), a collection of classical tales that had already inspired a number of sequels.[10] Yet, instead of reprinting stories of the past, as many sequels did, *Yu Chu xinzhi*—as the word "new" (*xin* 新) announced in its title— brought together works "mostly set in recent times largely by contemporary admirable writers."[11] All the stories collected in *Yu Chu xinzhi* were, therefore, about recent events and figures in the late Ming and early Qing periods and were written by contemporaries of Zhang Chao.

In fact, *Yu Chu xinzhi* is a series of separately published installments, rather than being a single book—as is implied by its title and unanimously indicated by all modern library catalogs. All the extant

9. Depending on the edition of *Yu Chu xinzhi*, the number of tales included varies from 146 to 153. See the appendix for details of various extant editions of *Yu Chu xinzhi*.

10. It was popular to repackage earlier materials and reprint them in the late Ming. Following this trend, *Yu Chu zhi* reprinted extraordinary accounts of the Tang dynasty that modern scholars usually categorize as the narrative genre called *chuanqi* 傳奇 (tales of the marvelous). The instant and immense success of *Yu Chu zhi*, mostly due to the fame of literary celebrities who attached comments, such as Yuan Hongdao, Tu Long 屠隆 (1542–1605), and Li Zhi 李贄 (1527–1602), inspired publication of several sequels in the late Ming, including *Xu Yu Chu zhi* 續虞初志 (Sequel to the *Magician's Records*) and *Guang Yu Chu zhi* 廣虞初志 (Expanded *Magician's Records*). Zhang Chao was clearly aware of the popularity of the *Yu Chu* series, particularly comparing his collection with *Xu Yu Chu zhi*. See his "Zixu" 自序 and "Fanli shize," in *Yu Chu xinzhi* (Guji chubanshe), 1.

11. "其事多近代也, 其文多時賢也。" Zhang Chao, "Zixu," in *Yu Chu xinzhi*.

editions and modern reprints consider the twenty-*juan* edition to be the complete compilation, which has led bibliographers to assume that editions containing fewer than twenty *juan* are "incomplete" (*que* 闕) or "impaired" (*can* 殘). But, far from being damaged or incomplete remnants of the process of transmission of an original twenty-*juan* text, these shorter editions are actually the remnants of installment publication as an evolving entity—in this case, a book that grew in stages over a period of two decades, from 1684 to 1704. The modern scholar Deng Changfeng's pioneering study shows that the twenty-*juan Yu Chu xinzhi* was made up of four installments: the first installment consisted of *juan* 1 to 8 (61 stories); the second installment presented *juan* 9 to 12 (38 stories); the third installment covered *juan* 13 to 16 (33 stories); and the final installment spanned *juan* 17 to 20 (17 stories).[12] As they all shared the same title, each installment circulated not as a separate volume but in a larger, expanded volume every time a new installment came out. For instance, Zhang Chao wrote in a letter to his friend around 1683: "I initially completed *Yu Chu xinzhi* as eight *juan*, and I heard that it will be sold by a bookseller. I think that you can purchase it in Suzhou next spring as well. I continue to make a second installment."[13] A letter sent much later, around 1704, apparently refers to the second and fourth installments: "The *Yu Chu xinzhi* that I had mailed to you earlier must have been twelve *juan*. I have added eight more *juan*, and it is now twenty *juan* in total."[14] Thus it appears that four *juan* were added whenever a new installment was printed, with the first edition (eight *juan*) printed soon after the preface was

---

12. Deng Changfeng, *Ming Qing xiqujia*, 157–60. Allan Barr modifies Deng's observation and argues that *Yu Chu xinzhi* was amassed in three installments: the first installment in eight *juan* (1684), the second installment in twelve *juan* (1700), and the third installment in twenty *juan* (1704). See his "Novelty, Character, and Community," 284–85. But Zhang Chao's letters indicate that the third and the fourth installments were made separately, which supports Deng Changfeng's original observation. See *CDOC* 1.28a; *CDYS* 15.14b.

13. "茲先以八卷成書，聽坊人發兌。想明春吳門亦可購矣。嗣有二集之役。" *CDOC* 3.1a–b.

14. "虞初新志前所奉寄者，似是一十二卷。今又續成八卷，共二十卷。" *CDOC* 10.13a. For more examples of the process of making installments, see *CDOC* 7.18a; *CDYS* 10.37a, 13.3b–4a, 15.14b.

written in 1683, an enlarged second edition (twelve *juan*) published in 1700 with the postscript, the expanded third edition (sixteen *juan*) appearing not too long thereafter, and the final edition (twenty *juan*) completed in 1704.

It was not unprecedented to publish installments that expanded the volume format in this way. The famous Song dynasty anthology of classical tales *Yijian zhi* 夷堅志 (Record of the Listener), for example, grew from its inception in 1143 to a final length of 420 *juan* in 1202 in twelve installments.[15] Since the sixteenth century, however, installment publication had become a pervasive form of anthology in the thriving commercial book market.[16] Collections of vernacular stories such as *Sanyan* 三言 (Three Collections of Stories), *Paian jingqi* 拍案驚奇 (Slap the Table in Amazement), and *Wusheng xi* 無聲戲 (Silent Operas) appeared in volume format for continuous sequels, as did numerous anthologies of poetry, prose, correspondence, scholarly treatises, and painting albums published in uniform series of installments, typically numbered or dated.[17] For example, Chu Renhuo's enormous collection of classical tales, *Jianhu ji* 堅瓠集 (Useless Gourd Collection), many of which were selected for *Yu Chu xinzhi*, consisted of sixty-six *juan* in its final form, after being serially published in fifteen separate installments every one to three years from 1690 to 1703, with each installment adding four to six *juan* of new material. Such installment publications varied in length and frequency of appearance, but they usually took the form of large, multivolume sets of anthology that gathered a large number of self-contained works organized by the same literary genre, subject, or locality of writers.

15. Inglis, "Textual History," 288–89.

16. Lowry, *Tapestry of Popular Songs*, 200.

17. See, for just a few examples, Zhou Lianggong's 周亮工, *Chidu xinchao* 尺牘新鈔 (three installments); Wang Qi, *Chidu xinyu* (three installments in 1663, 1667, and 1668); Chen Jiru's *Baoyan tang miji* 寶顏堂秘笈 (five installments); Deng Hanyi's *Shiguan* 詩觀 (three installments); Niu Xiu's 鈕琇 *Gusheng* 觚賸 (two installments in 1700 and 1702); Zhang Chao and Wang Zhuo's *Tanji congshu* (three installments in 1695, 1697, and 1697); and Zhang Chao's *Zhaodai congshu* (three installments in 1697, 1700, and 1703).

What factors contributed to the widespread popularity of install-ment publications in the seventeenth century? An obvious one was cost. Given the expense of carving, printing, and storing a large set of woodblocks, serial publication was a business strategy that enabled publishers to gauge market viability with a smaller financial investment before committing to a large print run. Gu Shizhen 顧施禎 (fl. 1687), the compiler of the 1689 *Shengchao shixuan chuji* 盛朝詩選初集 (Selec-tion of Poetry of the Prosperous Dynasty, First Collection), explained that "a large number of volumes is regarded highly. But the difficulty of carving, in particular, renders the selection of some works over other works inevitable. Therefore, I have first published a few *juan*. I will widely collect several poems and gradually add more volumes so that the full grandeur of the edition will be realized."[18] Another example is the 1639 *Huang Ming jingshi wenbian* 皇明經世文編 (Col-lection of Essays on Statecraft in the Ming), attributed to Chen Zilong 陳子龍 (1608–47). A collection of essays and memorials on political and economic problems by leading scholar-officials of earlier Ming reigns, its huge volume would have caused delays in publishing and difficulty in transportation. At the demand of the bookseller, the man-uscript was eventually divided into two installments, reducing the size of each volume.[19] A bulky volume was less affordable for buyers as well. Zhang Chao acknowledged that, "as for the huge size of the book, printers suffer because engraving is difficult; buyers also sigh because the book price is high."[20] The format of installment publication for a large compilation was therefore an economically beneficial choice for both publishers and customers.

Moreover, installment publication was advantageous in marketing. When Zhang Chao discussed the format of *Zhaodai congshu* with Wang Zhuo, the two men recognized that a sequential series would catch the at-tention of buyers over a longer period of time. Wang Zhuo thus insisted:

18. "卷帙貴乎大備，特以剞劂維艱，不無棄取。茲先數卷問世，禎將廣輯諸詩，逐漸增刊，以備大觀云。" Gu Shizhen, "Fanli," in *Shengchao shixuan chuji*, in Xie Zheng-guang and She Rufeng, *Qingchu ren xuan*, 245.
19. Song Weibi 宋微璧, "Fanli," in Chen Zilong, *Huang Ming jingshi wenbian*, 55.
20. "大部之書，刻者既苦，剞劂維艱，購者復歎，朱提不易。" Zhang Chao, "Xuanli," in the first collection of *ZDCS*, 3.

When people see a compilation, they will surely think that there is a second installment. Therefore, anyone who had bought the first installment with the old title will want to buy the second one [of the same title], in order to have a complete set, when he hears that the second installment is coming out. Or those who have bought the second installment will also surely want to buy the first one, because they would like to make the two halves of a piece of jade into a single perfect one [i.e., make a complete set].

夫人見叢書, 必思有二集。若仍舊名買初集者, 聞有二集, 必買成全書。或先買二集者, 亦必求初集, 買為合璧。[21]

It was thus often the case that the cover page of an imprint, usually attached for advertising purposes during this period, announced upcoming installments. For example, the cover page of the first installment of the poetry collection *Guochao shixuan* 國朝詩選 (Selection of Poetry of Our Dynasty), published in Nanjing in 1749, included the promotional phrase "the second installment will continue to come out" (*erbian xuchu* 二編續出) right next to the book title.[22] The owner of Yisheng tang 翼聖堂, who published *Liweng yijiayan chuji* 笠翁一家言初集 (Liweng's [Li Yu] School of Thought, First Collection), also declared on the cover page of that collection: "Because of the immense number of volumes, I am afraid that buyers will be reluctant to purchase it. So I have divided it into several installments and will publish them in order. This is the first volume [of the serial]" (fig. 4.1).[23]

The announcement of upcoming installments was not driven entirely by marketing needs, however, but was also aimed at soliciting manuscripts from readers. A large number of literary anthologies in the seventeenth century, regardless of genre, called on readers to submit manuscripts for further installments in their "editorial principles" (*fanli*

---

21. *CDYS* 8.16b–17a.

22. Reprinted in *Qingchu ren xuan*. For more examples, see the cover page of *TJCS* in the Library of Congress (fig. 3.1) and the cover page of *Xinzhai liaofu ji*, in *Siku jinhuishu congkan bubian*, 85:222.

23. "又恐篇帙浩繁, 購者不易, 分為數集, 次第刊行。此其發端者也。" Cover page of Li Yu, *Liweng yijiayan chuji*, 2.

Fig. 4.1. The cover page of Li Yu's *Liweng yijiayan chuji*. Reprinted in *Siku jinhuishu congkan bubian*, vol. 85.

凡例 or *xuanli* 選例)[24] or attached an announcement of solicitation (*zhengqi* 徵啓) on a separate page.[25] Some even put such an announcement on the cover page (fig. 4.2):

> Announcement: A selection of tales has been made into a book in each dynasty. Only the current dynasty has not witnessed such a collection. This casual project simply shares the manuscripts that my old friends have sent me with my coterie. If several gentlemen have old manuscripts put aside on your bookshelves or newly created works at a cloudy pavilion, I hope that you will mail them to [two illegible characters] for this refined collection.
>
> 歷代說部, 各有成書。唯本朝未見彙輯。茲偶舉年昔知交投增先公同好。諸君子鄴架舊藏雲亭新著, 望祈郵□□雅集謹啟。[26]

Following this widespread practice, Zhang Chao also solicited manuscripts at the front of the first installment of *Yu Chu xinzhi*,[27] and, consequently, the second, third, and fourth installments consisted of manuscripts submitted by contemporary writers.[28] Whether it was the solicitation itself or the instant popularity of *Yu Chu xinzhi* that inspired the submission of manuscripts, it appears that works sent in by Zhang Chao's readers were more than sufficient to make up the second and subsequent installments.[29] The table of contents of one of the extant editions of *Yu Chu xinzhi* (fig. 4.3) showed the original

24. Wang Zhuo solicited submission of manuscripts and published the second installment of *Lanyan ji*, which is not extant. See Qian Churi 錢礎日, "Wenjin erji xu" 文津二集序, in Wang Zhuo, *Lanyan ji* 12.1a–b. Also see Meyer-Fong, "Packaging the Men," 33–35.

25. See, for example, Li Yu's "Zheng chidu qi" 徵尺牘啓 at the front of his collection of letters *Chidu chuzheng*. He announced that, as long as the manuscripts kept coming, he would continue to develop installments. See *Chidu chuzheng*, 502; and more examples in Chow, *Publishing, Culture, and Power*, 75–76.

26. Cover page of the Qing compendium of stories *Shuoling*, compiled by Wu Zhenfang.

27. Zhang Chao, "Fanli shize," in *Yu Chu xinzhi*, 2. See the translation on p. 34 of this book.

28. This explains why the first installment of *Yu Chu xinzhi* in eight *juan* included both living and dead authors of the late Ming, whereas the subsequent installments consisted only of works of contemporaries of Zhang Chao who were still alive.

29. *CDYS* 3.34a, 4.30b–31a, 5.9a–b, 9.10b, 12.23b.

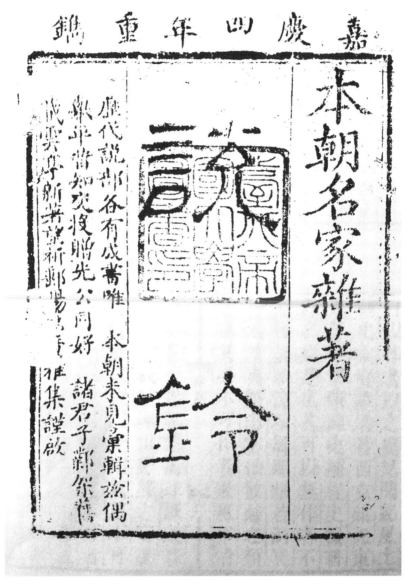

Fig. 4.2. The cover page of *Shuoling*, compiled by Wu Zhenfang. Reprinted in *Congshu jicheng xubian, zibu*, vol. 96.

sources of the stories selected in the form of a line of acknowledgment such as "manuscript submitted in person" (*shoushou chaoben* 手授 抄本) or "manuscript submitted by mail" (*youji chaoben* 郵寄抄本), thus attesting to direct submission of newly created works by the writers themselves. It was also often the case that a member of a writer's close coterie submitted a manuscript on behalf of the writer in response to the solicitation. For example, Nie Xian recommended another friend to Zhang Chao for inclusion in *Yu Chu xinzhi*, writing to Zhang Chao that "his works are so abundant as to stack up to his height, and their popularity momentarily raises the price of paper. A number of works in his literary collection are good enough to be selected for *Yu Chu xinzhi* and the compilations. I especially searched for copies and mailed them to you."[30]

The response from and participation by writers played a decisive role in the final shape of *Yu Chu xinzhi*. Zhang Chao did not originally plan to make an anthology that consisted of four installments. He considered the second installment to be the last one, as indicated by the fact that he attached the "postscript to the whole collection" (*zongba* 總跋) to the second installment. But continuing submissions and enthusiastic demand for copies drove him to compile the third and fourth installments. Zhang Chao was constantly pestered with requests for more copies of the book.[31] For instance, Chen Ding wrote to Zhang Chao that he had been hounded by acquaintances who searched for the book. He even mentioned a rumor that was widespread in Nanjing: "There is talk around Nanjing that Mr. Zhang Chao holds the treasures in his possession and does not circulate the copies from his woodblocks, so that several members of the coterie cannot taste their extraordinary flavor together. Aren't you afraid of this?"[32]

Just as the expansion of *Yu Chu xinzhi* was not premeditated, the ending of the installments appears to have been unexpected as well. In 1704, the fourth installment was published, but its quality was

30. "所著等身, 書籍紙貴一時。其文集中多有足供尊選虞初叢書之取裁者。特索一部奉寄。" *CDYS* 9.31a.

31. See *CDYS* 2.30a–b, 3.6a, 3.23a, 3.32a, 4.16b, 4.25b, 4.36a–b, 5.29a, 8.20b, 9.22a, 11.36a, 14.18a.

32. "張山來先生懷寶迷邦, 藏板不行, 俾諸同人不得共嘗異味。此言已遍金陵矣, 先生能無懼乎？" *CDYS* 10.20b.

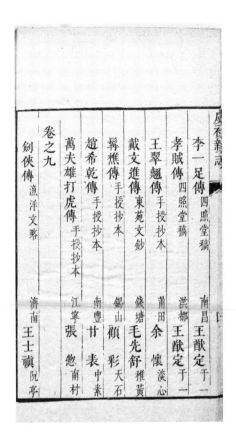

Fig. 4.3. The table of contents of
Yu Chu xinzhi, 5a. Courtesy of the
Institute for Advanced Studies on
Asia Library, University of Tokyo.

degenerated. For example, eight out of nineteen stories in the fourth installment were excerpted from Niu Xiu's *Gusheng* alone.[33] Moreover, the last *juan* of the fourth installment contained only two works, whereas the preceding three installments contained seven to eleven stories per *juan* on average. It was common for installment publication to cease midway for various reasons such as financial difficulty, lack of popularity, or deterioration of the health of an editor; for *Yu Chu xinzhi*, Zhang Chao's implication in a legal case in 1699 and subsequent financial downturn may have been decisive factors. Indeed, the relatively inferior quality of the fourth installment—its repeated use of the

33. For a discussion of *Gusheng*, see Barr, "Novelty, Character, and Community," 299–309.

same sources for stories and the limited number of stories collected—pointed toward an unforeseen, hasty conclusion to the series. Both the unplanned continuation and the sudden termination of *Yu Chu xinzhi* imply that Zhang Chao did not design *Yu Chu xinzhi* as a finite unity but rather allowed it to evolve naturally, depending on whether or not sufficient materials had been gathered, the demands of readers had been accurately gauged, and sufficient financial support had been procured.

Organizing *Yu Chu xinzhi*

The contingent nature of installment publication inevitably made the organization of *Yu Chu xinzhi* loose and desultory, for the unpredictability of submissions rendered the consistent and tight implementation of an editorial frame difficult at best. Despite the fact that *Yu Chu xinzhi* was a series with a single uniform format—with each installment sharing the same title and consisting of self-contained units of classical tales followed by Zhang Chao's short comments—it suffered from a general lack of stability and editorial coherence. Zhang Chao himself acknowledged that "the works in this anthology are mixed up without order."[34] Indeed, the works included in *Yu Chu xinzhi* were arranged not by any unifying theme or category but by the order in which they had been received: "what arrives first is commented on first and sent to the block carvers."[35] The installment publication that relies heavily on the voluntary and composite accumulation of submissions from readers thus resists the modern notion of an anthology as a "collection of texts guided by an editorial, authorial, scribal, or patronal aegis"[36] and instead directs our focus to the multiplicity of meanings and interpretations that textual fluidity and malleability generated.

Zhang Chao had stipulated his editorial position at the outset. In the front of the first installment, he suggested two main selection criteria:

---

34. "今茲選，錯綜無次。" Zhang Chao, "Fanli shize," in *Yu Chu xinzhi*, 1.
35. "隨到隨評，即付剞劂之手。" Ibid. It was common for anthologies and miscellanies in this period to be arranged in the order in which they were submitted. See Meyer-Fong, "Packaging the Men," 26–27.
36. Lerer, "Medieval English Literature," 1265, n. 8.

first, that the stories should be new works written by contemporary writers and, second, that the stories should be extraordinary but authentic, in the sense that they ought to be rooted in actual lived experience.[37] In other words, he attempted to make *Yu Chu xinzhi* the most recent collection available with authentic records about remarkable events and figures. But, as the compilation proceeded, his implementation of these editorial principles was often hindered by requests from readers. In the early stages, Zhang Chao firmly refused to accept any work that was not up to his standard of selection,[38] but, when close friends or influential celebrities asked him to include their works, he could not refuse them. For example, when Wang Zhuo importuned Zhang Chao to include his fictional piece "Kanhua shuyi ji" in *Yu Chu xinzhi*, Zhang Chao was hesitant. But Wang Zhuo insisted on his bending the rule, saying that "my work 'Kanhua shuyi ji' was created by expounding a dream that I accidentally dreamed. I have long hoped that it would be selected for your anthology *Yu Chu xinzhi*. But because you dislike false [fictional] stories, I had stopped asking. But Niu Sengru's 'Zhou Qin xingji,' which the people in the past had faulted for false attribution, has been selected to be part of anthologies and transmitted to the present. Please break the editorial principles and accept my clumsy work."[39] Overruling his own guidelines, Zhang Chao eventually included "Kanhua shuyi ji," thus tempering the identity of *Yu Chu xinzhi* as an assembly of historically factual accounts that he initially intended.[40]

Not only did readers of *Yu Chu xinzhi* alter the original design of Zhang Chao, but Zhang Chao's own editorial intentions also shifted over the course of the four installments. In the preface attached to the first installment in 1684, Zhang Chao reveals that he sees *Yu Chu xinzhi* as providing readers with amusing pieces of superb writing skill and novel content. He claims that, "if scholar-officials have this book in their hands and glance at it during the leisure time that remains after they have had guests over and have studied books, not only will the

37. Zhang Chao, "Fanli shize," in *Yu Chu xinzhi*, 1.
38. See, for example, *CDOC* 2.13a–b.
39. "拙作看花述異記，偶因一夢數衍成文。久欲附入虞初尊選，因先生曾有假文之嫌，遂爾中止。然牛奇章周秦行記，昔人亦有疑其假托者，而各選相傳至今，則拙記先生破例收之。" *CDYS* 10.37a–b.
40. *CDYS* 11.13a.

vexations of life be dispersed and their boredom relieved, but their spirits will also be unconstrained immediately."[41] Accordingly, Zhang Chao's comments attached at the end of each work are short and casual, highlighting the literary skills of the writer in question and the remarkable events that the text portrays: "This is one of the most pleasant matters in a hundred years! After reading, I pour wine in a big cup"[42] or "In describing the details of this event, the beard and eyebrows are rendered in lifelike fashion. Indeed, it even captures the soft hairs on the cheek."[43] In the first installment, thus, Zhang Chao's comments mainly express his excitement in reading the pieces he has selected and urge readers to share this reading pleasure with him.[44] When he selected a work for inclusion, he did not even delete earlier comments attached to the original text. Instead, he added his own comment after others' comments or even commented on an earlier comment,[45] positioning himself as a fellow reader of the work rather than the presiding editorial authority.

As subsequent installments came out, however, the tone of Zhang Chao's comments changes to one of self-vindication. It appears that the change was initiated by the personal calamity he suffered in 1699, costing him a great deal of money and emotional stress. In the postscript that he attached to the end of the second installment, he wrote: "Unfortunately, I by accident tumbled into a pitfall in 1699. A close friend was like the wolf of Zhongshan,[46] and, instead of pardoning me for the trouble, he constantly extorted me. . . . At that time, had I not found one or two extraordinary books to spend time with, how could I have endured such a situation?"[47] In contrast to the carefree and relaxed manner that he had voiced in the first installment, he redefined the

41. "學士大夫酬應之餘, 伊吾之暇, 取是篇而瀏覽之, 匪惟滌煩祛倦, 抑且縱橫俯仰。" Zhang Chao, "Zixu," in *Yu Chu xinzhi.*
42. "此百年來第一快心事也, 讀竟, 浮一大白。" Ibid., 75.
43. "敘瑣屑事, 鬚眉活現, 是煩上添毫手也。" Ibid., 47.
44. Zhang Chao, "Fanli shize," in *Yu Chu xinzhi,* 2.
45. See, for example, *Yu Chu xinzhi* (Guji chubanshe), 67, 92–93, 95, 100, 122.
46. Deriving from a popular legend, the wolf of Zhongshan is a reference to the ingratitude of a creature after being saved. For a version of the story, see Idema, *Personal Salvation,* 35–37.
47. "予不幸, 於己卯歲誤墮坑阱中, 而肺腑中山, 不以其困也而貰之, 猶時時相噉嚙……苟非得一二奇書, 消磨歲月, 其殆將何以處此乎？" Zhang Chao, "Zongba" 總跋, in *Yu Chu xinzhi.*

meaning of *Yu Chu xinzhi* as an outlet for his frustration at having been wronged: "I attach this record [to my anthology] because I also intend to make readers of my book understand my situation and feel sympathy for me."[48] As if he himself had authored the story to divulge his exasperation, his comments move into expressing resentment toward evil people, a corrupt society, and the degenerate order of the world:

> I encountered the wolf of Zhongshan and deplored that there was no knight-errant I could go and appeal to. After reading this piece, I understand that there is still such an extraordinary person. But I am not sure if the extraordinary person and I are strangers or not.
>
> 予嘗遇中山狼, 恨今世無劍俠, 一往訴之, 讀此乃知尚有異人, 第不識於我有緣否也。[49]
>
> If I met the person [the knight-errant], I would earnestly ask the blue-faced one with the red beard to release frustrations for me. What would there be to be afraid of?
>
> 若我遇其人, 當即懇靛面赤髭者為我泄憤矣, 尚何所畏耶?[50]

It is not clear whether Zhang Chao changed his selection criteria after the second installment, but, by writing about his own predicament, he shifted the second installment toward the serious undertaking of a frustrated literatus. By appropriating the long-standing image of the author in the Chinese literary tradition, the persona who has no way to express his frustration and anger except in his writing,[51] Zhang Chao transformed *Yu Chu xinzhi* from light reading material for scholarly leisure into a self-conscious literary construct that deserved to be carefully read and closely commented on.

48. "因附記於此, 俾世之讀我書者, 兼有以知我之境遇而憫之。" Ibid.
49. Zhang Chao's comment to "Jianxia zhuan" 劍俠傳, in *Yu Chu xinzhi*, 106.
50. Zhang Chao's comment to "Yinshuwu shuying" 因樹屋書影, in ibid., 190.
51. Beginning with Sima Qian's image as the prototype of an author "writing from righteous indignation" (*fafen zhushu* 發憤著書) and including Han Yu 韓愈 (768–824), Ouyang Xiu 歐陽修 (1007–72), Li Zhi, and Jin Shengtan 金聖歎 (ca. 1610–61), the author as a frustrated and alienated literatus who could not realize his ideals in political service and had to find an alternative in his writing became one of the popular personas after which the writers routinely fashioned themselves. See, for example, Martin Huang, *Literati and Self-Re/Presentation*, 17–19.

Zhang Chao's reconstruction of the meaning of *Yu Chu xinzhi* combined with his accommodation of the needs of readers made *Yu Chu xinzhi* a variable that was constantly shaped, expanded, and reinterpreted. *Yu Chu xinzhi* as an installment publication thus defies all modern scholarly attempts to confine it to a fixed identity. Rather than being an enclosed unity in terms of a defining genre (such as *xiaoshuo* 小說), a unifying theme (such as the collective sensibility of writers troubled by the new Qing rule), or authorial intention (such as Zhang Chao's political affinity for the late Ming), the installments of *Yu Chu xinzhi* became more a cluster of potential meanings, readings, and interpretations that sought to coordinate the changes in the editor, readers, and writers in the conditions of its textual production and reception.

Censoring *Yu Chu xinzhi*

Yu Chu xinzhi enjoyed great popularity not only during Zhang Chao's lifetime but after his death as well. In 1802 Zheng Shuruo 鄭澍若, who made a sequel titled *Yu Chu xuzhi* 虞初續志 (The Continued *Magician's Records*), observed that "almost every household owns *Yu Chu xinzhi* edited by Zhang Chao."[52] It enjoyed broad circulation in Yangzhou, Suzhou, Nanjing, and Beijing, propelling the creation of a number of sequels up until the Republican period.[53] In addition, it soon crossed national borders to Edo Japan and Chosŏn Korea. In the preface of a Japanese reprint edition of *Yu Chu xinzhi* in 1823, Arai Kimiyasu 荒井公訓 mentioned that, although the book had been transmitted to Japan a long time before, he had decided to reprint it because it had become rare and more expensive owing to its explosive popularity.[54] It was also well received by the literati of Chosŏn Korea, and the eminent officials Kim Ryŏ 金鑢 (1766–1821) and Kim Cho-sun 金祖淳 (1765–1832) wrote their own sequel titled *Yu Chu xuzhi* 虞初續志 in 1792.[55]

52. "山來張先生輯虞初新志, 幾於家有其書矣。" Zheng Shuruo, *Yu Chu xuzhi*, 1.
53. These sequels include *Guang Yu Chu xinzhi* 廣虞初新志 (1803), *Yu Chu xu xinzhi* 虞初續新志, *Yu Chu jinzhi* 虞初近志 (1913), *Yu Chu guangzhi* 虞初廣志 (1915), and *Yu Chu zhizhi* 虞初支志 (1921).
54. Song Lihua, *Ming Qing shiqi de xiaoshuo chuanbo*, 341–44.
55. Unfortunately, this sequel titled *Yu Chu xuzhi* is not extant.

After sixty-four years, when the final installment of *Yu Chu xinzhi* came out, however, it was subject to inspection and expurgation during the Qianlong emperor's large-scale censorship in the late eighteenth century. Beginning in 1772, Qianlong ordered provincial and local officials to conduct a thorough search for rare books in every part of the empire with the aim of preserving rare books and the most standard editions for the benefit of scholarship. In the campaign, which lasted more than twenty years, a total of 13,254 titles of books were collected and forwarded to the capital for examination, transcription, and preservation. Under the scrutiny of the commission specifically appointed to supervise them, 3,461 of the most important books were eventually made into *Siku quanshu*.

The compilation process was, however, also accompanied by the destruction of what was disapproved of during the sorting and selecting of texts for inclusion. Initially, the books collected were classified and ranked according to the imperial principles of compilation. In 1774 Qianlong issued an edict establishing the imperial catalog and mandating the classification of books into three main categories: "those that should be engraved" (*yingke* 應刻), "those that should be copied" (*yingchao* 應抄), and "those whose table of contents alone should be preserved" (*yingcun shumu* 應存書目). More detailed classifications soon followed as the compilation proceeded. The most important 138 books were designated "those that should be printed in movable type," and a category of "books that should be banned" was added at the other end of the spectrum. The latter category was also subdivided by the degree of infraction—into "books that are offensive but not to be banned" (*weiai* 違礙), "books for which some of whose contents should be banned" (*chouhui* 抽燬), and "books that should be banned in their entirety" (*yinghui* 應燬). As a consequence, about 3,100 titles were censored, amounting to 151,000 copies in total, and more than 80,000 woodblocks were destroyed, although the numbers varied in different records.[56]

The simultaneous preservation and destruction involved in the compilation of *Siku quanshu* have been discussed mainly in terms of

56. Huang Aiping, *Siku quanshu zuanxiu yanjiu*, 72–78.

the Qing dynasty's brutal crackdown on political dissidents.[57] Revising this monolithic understanding of the Qianlong emperor's censorship as a literary inquisition imposed by the Manchus on the Han Chinese, however, scholars such as Kent Guy and Timothy Brook have explored the effect of the Qianlong era censorship on bureaucratic and ideological systems. For example, Kent Guy claims that the *Siku quanshu* compilation resulted not in a political separation between the Manchu emperor and the Han elite but in an ideological consolidation between them. Highlighting the system of collaboration between the Qianlong emperor and Han scholar-officials, he demonstrates how successfully the *Siku quanshu* project achieved a reconciliation between the two by establishing official sanction for evidential scholarship (*kaozheng xue* 考證學).[58] Timothy Brook argues that Qianlong's pursuit of censorship sought to rectify the bureaucratic system and was a kind of litmus test for determining how effectively the bureaucracy was in serving Qing interests in whatever way the emperor deemed necessary. The focus of the inquisition, therefore, fell more on the men responsible for removing the books from circulation than on those who actually wrote and published the censored books.[59]

Indeed, the censorship of Zhang Chao's books was not necessarily related to the suppression of anti-Manchu ideas. Although most of Zhang Chao's books were censored, none of Zhang Chao's books explicitly dealt with Ming loyalism. As part of the generation born after the Manchu takeover, Zhang Chao did not position himself in a simple dichotomy between Ming loyalism and Qing assimilation.[60] Though some works collected in Zhang Chao's compilations reflected hindsight and

57. See, for example, Ren Songru, *Siku quanshu dawen*; Wang Bin, *Jinshu wenziyu* and *Qingdai jinshu zongshu*; Wu Zhefu, *Qingdai jinhui shumu yanjiu*; Goodrich, *Literary Inquisition*; and Hok-lam Chan, *Control of Publishing*.

58. Guy, *Emperor's Four Treasuries*.

59. Brook, "Censorship," 177–96; and "State Censorship and the Book Trade," in *Chinese State*, 125–26.

60. On the political position of early Qing literati, see Wakeman, "Romantics, Stoics, and Martyrs." Tobie Meyer-Fong and Zhang Ying emphasize that the porous political orientations among early Qing literati groups cannot be neatly relegated to such dichotomized identities as officials who surrendered to the Qing and Ming loyalists. See Meyer-Fong, *Building Culture*; and Zhang Ying, *Confucian Image Politics*.

nostalgia commonly shared by the early Qing literati who experienced the traumatic dynastic transition,[61] he himself seems to have accepted the rule of the Qing as part of a perpetual cycle of dynastic rise and fall and gone on to pursue his political career under the Qing. *Xinzhai liaofu ji*, a collection of Zhang Chao's early writings in a variety of genres that were probably written as examination exercises, printed several of his mock memorials and eulogies on the Kangxi emperor's southern tour celebrating the prosperity of Qing rule.[62] He was also cautious about not offending Qing authorities when he published books. For example, he initially considered Dai Mingshi's *Jieyi lu* 子遺錄 (Record of the Survi-vors) for his *Zhaodai congshu*, but he eventually decided not to include it because it was a record about Ming loyalists.[63] He also declined to publish several works that had been submitted for his compilations be-cause they touched on the matter of the frontier and hence might include disparaging references to Manchu ancestry or might not properly main-tain the taboos concerning the use of emperors' names (*bihui* 避諱).[64]

Nonetheless, the emphatically apolitical nature of Zhang Chao's books did not keep them from being excluded from *Siku quanshu*; further, most of his original editions were expurgated as a result of the censorship. Zhang Chao's books, such as the collection of northern plays and popular songs *Bige* 筆歌 (Song of Brush), the collection of Zhang Chao's early writings *Xinzhai liaofu ji*, the collection of riddles *Xi'nang cunjin*, and the civil service examination guide, *Sishu zunzhu huiyi jie*, were all classified as "books to be banned in their entirety" in 1781; *Yu Chu xinzhi* and *Zhaodai congshu* were categorized as "books to be banned in part" in 1769 and 1781, respectively; and *Chidu yousheng* and *Chidu oucun* were also banned, although it is not clear whether they were completely or only partially banned. Because the censors supplied few explanations as to why they censored a particular book, the reasons for the censorship of Zhang Chao's imprints are not clear. For example, extant records show that *Zhaodai congshu* was initially

61. See, for example, Idema, Li, and Widmer, eds., *Trauma and Transcendence*; and Wai-yee Li's *Women and National Trauma*.

62. Zhang Chao, *Xinzhai liaofu ji* 50a–75b, 115a–117a. Also see his compliments on Qing rule in ZDCS, 217 and 219.

63. CDOC 9.11b.

64. CDOC 5.28b.

sought out and sent to Beijing for inclusion in *Siku quanshu*,[65] but it ended up being excluded and assigned to the category of "books whose table of contents alone should be preserved." And, as the censorship proceeded, it was reclassified in the category of "books to be banned in part" in 1781.[66] Some records point to the inclusion of works of politically ostracized figures such as Lü Liuliang 呂留良 (1629–83) and Qian Qianyi 錢謙益 (1582–1664) as the reason for the censorship of *Zhaodai congshu* along with *Sishu zunzhu huiyi jie*.[67] But it is not clear why *Sishu zunzhu huiyi jie* was classified among "books to be banned in their entirety," whereas *Zhaodai congshu* was allowed to circulate after the problematic works were deleted.

There are, however, material vestiges pointing to the reason behind the censorship of *Yu Chu xinzhi*. Among Zhang Chao's imprints, *Yu Chu xinzhi* was the first book to be classified as to be censored, in 1769. It was categorized as a book to be banned in part,[68] which resulted in the loss of the original edition of *Yu Chu xinzhi*. Instead, it remains in four separate reprint editions whose tables of contents are not identical. The earliest reprint edition that is extant is the reprint made by Zhang Chao's grandnephew Zhang Yi 張繹 in 1760 (fig. 4.4). Zhang Yi was proud of possessing the original blocks that Zhang Chao had left as a token of his family's legacy and decided to reprint *Yu Chu xinzhi* because the original edition had become scattered as time went by.[69] It appears that Zhang Yi also had a financial motive, considering that the reprint, with its small size as a sleeve edition (*xiuzhen ben* 袖珍本), was circulated

65. Wu Weizu, *Siku caijin shumu*, 136.

66. Lei Mengchen, *Qingdai gesheng jinshu*, 68, 79; and Wu Zhefu, *Qingdai jinhui shumu*, 322.

67. There were no official guidelines for the censorship, but general rules of censorship can be conjectured from scattered records. The censorship of the writings of Lü Liuliang and Qian Qianyi is among one of the obvious ones. See Sima Chaojun, *Siku quanshu zongmu yanjiu*, 48–49; Wu Zhefu, *Qingdai jinhui shumu*, 86–88; and Okamoto, *Shindai kinsho*, 54–55.

68. According to Yao Jinyuan and Sun Dianqi, *Qingdai jinshu*, *Yu Chu xinzhi* was censored in 1779. But the Korean bibliophile Yu Man-ju (1755–88) mentioned that he had seen the edition, whose preface stated that the text had already been censored in 1769. See his diary, *Hŭmyŏng*, 5:166–67 (March 23, 1784).

69. Zhang Yi, "Ba" 跋, in Zhang Chao, *Yu Chu xinzhi*, Taiwan University Library edition.

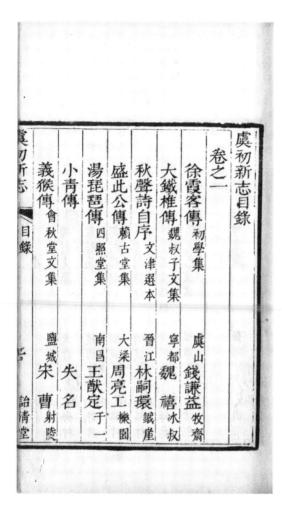

Fig. 4.4. The table of contents of *Yu Chu xinzhi*, 1a. Reprint by Zhang Yi of 1760. Courtesy of National Taiwan University Library.

in collaboration with the commercial bookshop Guhuan lou 古歡樓, located in Dingjia Bay 丁家灣 in Yangzhou. The warning on the cover page "pirates will be prosecuted even from a thousand *li* away" (*fanke qianli bijiu* 翻刻千里必究) clearly indicates the publisher's intention to protect his property rights from unauthorized pirated editions.

After nine years, however, this reprint edition of *Yu Chu xinzhi* caught the eye of the censors. The mark of censorship is evident in the table of contents, where two works by Qian Qianyi—the biography of

the renowned traveler Xu Xiake (1587–1641), "Xu Xiake zhuan" 徐霞
客傳 (Biography of Xu Xiake), and the story of an extraordinary for-
tuneteller, "Shu Zheng Yangtian shi" 書鄭仰田事 (Narrating the Story
of Zheng Yangtian)—have been torn away (fig. 4.5) or blotted out (fig.
4.6). Traces of censorship are also revealed in the main body of the
book. For example, copies of *Yu Chu xinzhi* in the National Library of
China and Ewha Womans University in Korea reveal that the first
work of the first installment, "Xu Xiake zhuan," has been extracted
from the main body. The page number of the first page is listed as "from
one to six" (*yi zhi liu* 一至六), but the style of the carved characters
"from one to" (*yi zhi* 一至) is radically different from the style of the
carved character "six" (*liu* 六). This indicates that "from one to" was
added right before the original character "six" after "Xu Xiake zhuan"
was removed. It is likely that the censorship was executed in a hasty
and inconsistent manner because, unlike the case of "Xu Xiake zhuan,"
the title of "Shu Zheng Yangtian shi" was taken out of the table of contents, whereas the text proper remains in the body of the book.

As the censorship campaign proceeded, the Qianlong emperor suggested in 1780 that blackened or blank spaces caused by censorship be
replaced with texts that were acceptable.[70] As a result, in later reprint
editions of *Yu Chu xinzhi* the marks of censorship were removed by completely erasing the titles of problematic works from the table of contents,
as if to suggest that they had never existed (fig. 4.7), or, alternatively, other
works were inserted in the space where the censored works had
originally been located. For instance, the Chosŏn bibliophile Yu Man-ju
俞晚柱 (1755–88) left a record to the effect that he had seen an edition
with a preface mentioning that, following the imperial edict, Qian
Qianyi's "Xu Xiake zhuan" in *juan* 1 and "Shu Zheng Yangtian shi" in
juan 6 had been omitted and that "Jiang Zhenyi zhuan" 姜貞毅傳 (Biography of Jiang Zhenyi) and "Sun Wenzheng shi" 孫文正事 (Story of
Sun Wenzheng) had been added instead.[71] In fact, other copies of this

70. See, for example, the edict on the twentieth day, eleventh month, forty-fifth
year, in Wang Zhongmin, *Bianli Siku quanshu*, 1:71.

71. In 1784, Yu Man-ju mentioned that "this book is a new edition that the emis-
sary to Beijing acquired. It is twenty *juan*. The new preface said that, 'following the

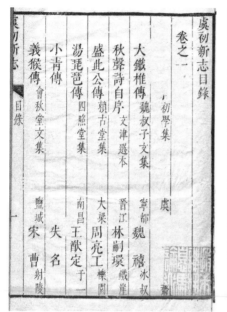

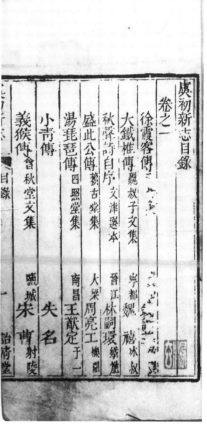

Fig. 4.5 *(left)*. The table of contents of *Yu Chu xinzhi*, 1a. Courtesy of the Institute for Advanced Studies on Asia Library, University of Tokyo.
Fig. 4.6 *(right)*. The table of contents of *Yu Chu xinzhi*, 1a. Reprint by Zhang Yi after 1769. Courtesy of Ewha Womans University Library, Seoul.

edition bear direct traces of censorship, such as a censor's red stamp on the cover page stating: "Special Announcement: according to the catalog of banned books, the blocks of three writings by Qian Qianyi

imperial edict in autumn 1769, the woodblocks of Qian Qianyi's *Chuxue ji* and *Youxue ji* were destroyed. And 'Xu Xiake zhuan' in *juan* 1 and 'Zheng Yangtian shi' in *juan* 6 of *Yu Chu xinzhi* were culled and eliminated and instead replaced by 'Jiang Zhenyi zhuan' and 'Sun Wenzheng shi.'" 是謝恩使所得新本也, 凡二十卷。其新序云: 己丑秋奉詔, 銷燬錢謙益初學有學二集, 而新志第一卷中徐霞客傳、第六卷中鄭仰田事, 皆從刪去, 以姜貞毅傳、孫文正事補刊云。*Hŭmyŏng*, 5:166–67.

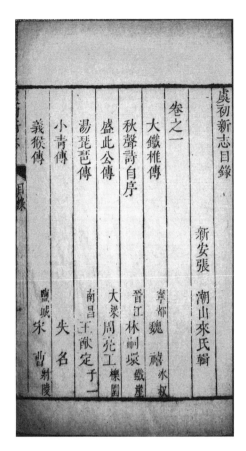

Fig. 4.7. The table of contents of *Yu Chu xinzhi*, 1a. Qianlong reprint. Courtesy of the University of Chicago Library.

were extracted and sent to the Book Service of Zhejiang Province, where they were destroyed" (fig. 4.8).[72]

Owing to the complex process of censorship, the total number of pieces included in several reprint editions of *Yu Chu xinzhi* varies, ranging from 146 to 153. Apart from Qian Qianyi's works, later reprints also show that two more works were removed: Xu Fang's 徐芳 "Liu furen xiaozhuan" 柳夫人小傳 (Short Biography of Lady Liu) in *juan* 5

72. "謹遵飭禁書目, 將錢謙益文三篇, 抽板送浙江書局銷毀, 記特白。" Cover page of the reprint edition of Zhang Chao, *Yu Chu xinzhi*, reprinted in *Siku jinhuishu congkan*. Only the editions in the Naikaku Bunko and the National Library of China contain the stamp.

Fig. 4.8. The cover page of *Yu Chu xinzhi*. Reprinted in *Siku jin-huishu congkan*, *zibu* vol. 38.

and Yu Huai's "Banqiao zaji" 板橋雜記 (Miscellaneous Records of Plank Bridge) in *juan* 20. Instead of those omitted works, it seems that Hou Fangyu's 侯方域 (1618–55) "Gusheng zhuan" 賈生傳 (Biography of Mr. Gu) and Lu Ciyun's 陸次雲 (1636–ca. 1702) "Ji Zhou Shiyu shi" 紀周侍御事 (Recording the Story of Censor Zhou) were inserted. The distinction between the original works included by Zhang Chao and the works added after the censorship is clear because the comments to the added works were not by Zhang Chao but by Jin Zhaoyan 金兆燕 (1718–ca.1789, *hao* Zongting 棕亭), who worked as the head of the

Confucian school at Yangzhou prefecture from 1768 to 1779.[73] It is not certain whether Jin Zhaoyan added the comments at the direction of the Qing state or by his own volition. Considering Jin Zhaoyan's close connection with the bookshops in Yangzhou,[74] it is also possible that a bookshop initiated the request to help counter or disguise the marring of *Yu Chu xinzhi* and to make it look like an intact whole.

Censorship of the Installment Publication

What caused *Yu Chu xinzhi* to be excluded from *Siku quanshu* and censored? Considering the material traces of the censorship, it must have been censored for its inclusion of two pieces by Qian Qianyi in the first place. During the period of censorship, Qian Qianyi was represented as the epitome of opportunism, a typical example of twice-serving ministers (*erchen* 二臣) who had served both the Ming and Qing regimes. In fact, the literary inquisition directed against Qian Qianyi began not when he was alive but one century after he died, and the censorship was caused not by any particular writing of his having touched on political issues but by a reevaluation of his career. As several scholars have pointed out, the historical evaluation of Qian Qianyi's life changed drastically over time:[75] in the early Qing, Qian Qianyi had prospered as an outstanding poet and writer. His writing exerted a deep influence on the contemporary literati, and he was even a favorite writer of the Shunzhi 順治 emperor (r. 1643–61). Although there were some ambivalent responses to his having served two regimes in the early Qing, not until Qianlong declared him a turncoat official was the harsh reevaluation of his career firmly established. The emperor's redefinition of loyalism and his rewriting of the political history of the late Ming led

73. See the biography of Jin Zhaoyan in Zhou Miaozhong, *Qingdai xiqu shi*, 243–45.

74. Jin Zhaoyan was the one who printed the first edition of the novel *Rulin waishi* in a Yangzhou bookshop. Jin He 金和, "Rulin waishi ba" 儒林外史跋, in the Qunyu zhai 群玉齋 edition of *Rulin waishi* of 1869, reprinted in Zhu Yixuan and Liu Yuchen, *Rulin waishi ziliao*, 279.

75. See Goodrich, *Literary Inquisition*, 25–26, 154–55; Xie Zhengguang, "Tanlun Qingchu shiwen."

him to see Qian Qianyi as a symbol of villainy for violating the universal principle of loyalty. The emperor even ordered a new section, "Erchen zhuan" 二臣傳 (Biography of Turncoat Officials), to be placed in the official history and put Qian Qianyi at the front of it.[76] Because of the emblematic significance of the reevaluation of Qian Qianyi, which began in 1769 and continued through the completion of *Siku quanshu*, every work that he had written was removed from the shelves of bibliophiles and bookshop and transported to Beijing to be destroyed. Moreover, all books that contained works by Qian Qianyi, whether his poetry, prose, or even a preface, were subject to censorship.

This explains why the two works written by Qian Qianyi that appeared in the first installment of *Yu Chu xinzhi*—namely, "Xu Xiake Zhuan" and "Shu Zheng Yangtian shi"—were censored. It also reveals why Yu Huai's "Banqiao zaji" and Xu Fang's "Liu furen xiaozhuan" were later targeted as well. Yu Huai's "Banqiao zaji" quoted a poem by Qian Qianyi in the middle of the text, even though the poem merely extolled the beauty of Nanjing; Xu Fang's "Liu furen zhuan" was censored not because it contained any passages by Qian Qianyi but because it was a biography of none other than Liu Rushi 柳如是 (1616–64), Qian Qianyi's beloved concubine, who was imagined as a patriotic poet of the Ming in the popular imagination.[77]

The censorship of Qian Qianyi's works appears to indicate that the censorship of *Yu Chu xinzhi* resulted from the political nature of its content. A majority of modern scholars assume that *Yu Chu xinzhi* was filled with anti-Manchu sentiment, and, in fact, it contains many works that celebrate the uncompromising integrity and loyalty of figures in the tumultuous Ming-Qing dynastic transition. For example, "Jiang Zhenyi zhuan," which was printed as the first work of *Yu Chu xinzhi* in the Qianlong reprint editions, lauds the courage of the poet Jiang Cai 姜埰 (1607–73), who was brutally tortured on a false charge prior to the fall of the Ming regime yet remained loyal to the

76. See Crossley, *Translucent Mirror*, 291–96, for the general background of making "Erchen zhuan."

77. Liu Rushi enjoyed a reputation as a courtesan, poet, and lover of Qian Qianyi. It was believed that she urged Qian Qianyi to commit suicide to resist Manchu rule during the dynastic transition. For the relationship between the courtesan and her loyalty, see, for example, Chang, *Late Ming Poet*; and Wai-yee Li, "Late-Ming Courtesan."

dynasty by choosing to become a recluse when the new regime took power. Modern scholars often cite this story as an indication of Zhang Chao's political loyalty to the fallen Ming dynasty and hence as a contributing factor to the censorship of *Yu Chu xinzhi*.[78] However, "Jiang Zhenyi zhuan" was not selected by Zhang Chao—it was, in fact, one of the works added to distract from the deletion of Qian Qianyi's pieces by the censors. That is, the characterization of *Yu Chu xinzhi* as an anti-Manchu work is, far from historical reality, projected by a simplistic definition of the censorship as the political conflict between Han and Manchus.

Instead of viewing *Yu Chu xinzhi* as the political expression of Ming loyalists, the censors seem to have understood *Yu Chu xinzhi* mainly as a typical anthology of fictional accounts. Although the voices of the censors were seldom consistent and never univocal, it is reasonably safe to conclude that they considered *Yu Chu xinzhi* to be a work lacking in veracity. Despite Zhang Chao's initial emphasis on the factuality of the tales, the censors doubted the authenticity of the stories and perceived none of the works as worthy of being included in *Siku quanshu*, even though they were all written by seventeenth-century writers of some renown.[79] The collections from which the stories in *Yu Chu xinzhi* were excerpted—such as Niu Xiu's *Gusheng*, Zhao Jishi's 趙吉士 (1628–1706) *Jiyuan ji suoji* 寄園寄所寄 (Tales from Temporary Garden), Song Luo's 宋犖 (1634–1714) *Yunlang oubi* 筠廊偶筆 (Casual Writing from the Green Bamboo Hall), and Wang Mingde's 王明德 *Dulü peixi* 讀律佩觿 (Reading the Laws Close at Hand)—were all denigrated as "petty talk" (*xiaoshuo* 小説) and assigned to the category of "books whose tables of contents alone should be preserved." The wordings for the disqualification varied, such as "true and false are mixed,"[80] "mentioning the medical miracles of gods and

---

78. See, for example, Li Mengsheng, *Zhongguo jinhui xiaoshuo*, 308; and Lu Lin, "Sheren Zhang Chao," 99–100.

79. Because of the paradoxical function of the *Siku quanshu* compilation as both preservation and destruction of books, the compilers and commentators also played a role as censors. For the members of the commission, see Guy, *Emperor's Four Treasuries*, 67–120.

80. Comment on *Jiyuan ji suoji*, in Yong Long et al., *Siku quanshu zongmu*, 1:1131.

ghosts,"[81] "no evidence to verify,"[82] and "fabricated events with embellishment,"[83] but they all indicate a perceived lack of gravity and credibility. These remarks were common criticisms of *xiaoshuo* in terms of the orthodox Confucian literary tradition, which valued historicity over fictionality. For the compilers of *Siku quanshu*, who were particularly influenced by evidential scholarship prevalent during the mid-Qing dynasty,[84] the lack of veracity of the stories by no means satisfied the standard that they set. Their rigorous expectation of authentic and verifiable evidence even caused them to dismiss not only the scholarly pieces of the great classicist of the early Qing Yan Ruoqu 閻若璩 (1638–1704), but also the Jesuit missionary Ferdinand Verbiest's (1623–88) *Kunyu tushuo* 坤輿圖說 (Illustrated Discussion of the Geography of the World) about Western knowledge of the geography of the world on the grounds that they failed to provide reliable evidence and verifiable information.[85]

What is striking is that some of the censors' comments ascribed the lack of reliability of *Yu Chu xinzhi* to the ways in which the anthology was compiled in the seventeenth century. The censors felt that reliance on the voluntary submission of manuscripts inevitably compromised the quality of such installment works. For instance, their comments on *Liuxi waizhuan*, from which *Yu Chu xinzhi* excerpted eleven stories—the largest number from a single book—clearly reveal their association of lack of veracity with the installment publication. *Liuxi waizhuan* was a collection of 354 biographies of exceptional late Ming and early Qing figures published in 1698 by Zhang Chao's close friend Chen Ding. Faithfully following the installment publication practice of the era, Chen Ding not only relied on the assistance and participation of his 131 friends, who included Dai Mingshi, You Yun'e,

---

81. Comment on *Dulü peixi*, in ibid., 1:851.

82. Comment on *Yunlang oubi*, in ibid., 1:1109.

83. Comment on *Gusheng*, in ibid., 2:1232.

84. Guy, *Emperor's Four Treasuries*, 121–56.

85. See the criticism of Yan Ruoqu's works "Mao Zhu shishuo" 毛朱詩說 and "Mengzi kao" 孟子考, in Yong Long et al., *Siku quanshu zongmu*, 1:146, 534; and the criticism of Ferdinand Verbiest's work in ibid., 1:634.

and Zhang Chao,[86] but also solicited manuscripts for subsequent installments of *Liuxi waizhuan* from readers with the assistance of bookshops.[87] The book was initially submitted to Beijing to be included in *Siku quanshu*,[88] but it was evaluated as a book not worthy of being included. The *Siku quanshu* compilers presented their reasons as follows:

> What is recorded comprises events during the late Ming and early Qing period. The extraordinary chastity and remarkable actions in the book are enough to garner praise for the hidden hermits. But the events [selected in the book] are all gathered from submissions. If you see the last two sentences of the announcement of solicitation at the head of the volume, it says: "If you have any true stories, please send them to the carver Cai Danjing's residence in front of Cheng'en Temple in Nanjing or to the bookshop Daibao lou on Xinsheng Street in Yangzhou. Then they will deliver them to me." In other words, since this book follows the vogue of collecting poetry and prose by submission to adulate his coterie, the recorded events cannot be believed to be true. For example, [this book includes] biographies of some people, such as Zhang Chao, even though they were still alive. In particular, it violates the principle that a person's life should not be judged until after the person's death. And several eccentric events in the book even more resemble the accounts of the school of petty talk. They are not worth discussing.
>
> 所紀皆明末國初之事。其閒畸節卓行, 頗足以闡揚幽隱。然其事蹟由於微送。觀卷首徵事啓末附載二行云: 凡有事實, 可寄至江寧承恩寺前刻匠蔡丹敬家, 或揚州新盛街岱寶樓書坊轉付云云。則仍然徵選詩文, 標枋聲氣之風, 未可據為實錄。如張潮諸人, 生而立傳, 殊非蓋棺論定之義。其閒怪異諸事, 尤近於小說家言, 不足道也。[89]

86. Because Chen Ding was such a close friend of Zhang Chao, many of the members of Zhang Chao's coterie were also members of Chen Ding's coterie. They wrote prefaces, added comments, and proofread the manuscript. See the list of participants in *Liuxi waizhuan*, in Dai Tingjie, *Dai Mingshi nianpu*, 410–11.

87. "Zheng jindai zhongxiao jieyi zhenlie haoxia yinyi gaoren shishi zuozhuan fake qi" 徵近代忠孝節義貞烈豪俠隱逸高人事實作傳發刻啟, in Chen Ding, *Liuxi waizhuan*, 518.

88. Huang Lie, *Jiangsu caiji yishu mulu*, 4:268.

89. Yong Long et al., *Siku quanshu zongmu*, 1:567.

The censors' criticism points directly to conventions of publishing installments: the solicitation of manuscripts from readers, close association with commercial bookshops, and the inclusion of contemporary works by living writers—the very way in which *Yu Chu xinzhi* and other compilations in the seventeenth century were compiled. This comment on *Liuxi waizhuan* even specifically cites the example of the inclusion of Zhang Chao's biography in Chen Ding's collection in order to criticize the convention of publishing work during the writer's lifetime. According to the *Siku quanshu* compilers, the late Ming and early Qing literati installment publications were far from serious literary undertakings. Instead, they were denigrated as shameful acts of fame seeking for members of the writer-cum-publisher's coterie—as expressed in the set phrase "vogue of adulating his coterie" (*biaobang shengqi zhi feng* 標榜聲氣之風), which frequently appears in the comments of censors as the key criticism of seventeenth-century imprints. This must be one of the major reasons most of the early Qing Jiangnan literati who directly or indirectly engaged in publishing as a form of coterie enterprise became targets of censorship. Not only were the compilations published by Zhang Chao banned; those of his fellow literati publishers suffered a similar fate. The compilations of Wu Ai 吳藹, Sun Hong 孫鋐, Wei Xian 魏憲, Sun Cong, Zhu Guan, Deng Hanyi, Zhuo Erkan, and Nie Xian were all censored. As one commentator put it succinctly, "[The collection's] discussion is not unreasonable. But the selected pieces are made for keeping company with a coterie and cultivating affinities among them."[90] In effect, most of the installment publications were excluded from *Siku quanshu* for no stated reason.

On the surface, the comments by eighteenth-century censors echoed the critical attitude toward the self-publishing boom in the seventeenth century as described in chapter 2. They reiterated the conservative view of the growing practice of self-publishing by literati— that it was used not necessarily to promote deserving works but to obtain groundless literary reputation. Behind this seemingly apolitical concern about the separation of merit from reputation, however, lay

---

90. "其持論未為不當。然其所選，則皆為交游聲氣之地。" Yong Long et al., *Siku quanshu zongmu*, 2:1771.

the political anxiety of ensuring that the privately printed books of literati remained under the state's control. In fact, as early as 1653, a decade before this wave of censorship began, the state had issued an order that intended to check the growth of publishing by literati groups, specifically the circulation of privately printed books as a coterie enterprise.[91] Although a dearth of evidence makes it impossible to accurately gauge the outcome of this order, the order does testify to the state's apprehension about the collective enterprise of publishing by the Jiangnan literati and its potential conversion to political factionalism. For instance, one of the most active political groups of literati in the late Ming, the Fushe 復社 (Restoration Society), was established initially as a small coterie group based in Suzhou in 1630 yet grew into an empirewide literati organization through its publishing of compilations as a collective enterprise.[92] Although their publishing was driven mainly by the desire for success in the examinations, the group's wide social network and authority in the field of cultural production were swiftly redirected into a collective voice amid the political struggles in the late Ming. The censorship of installment publications as a coterie enterprise thus must be associated with the Qing state's vigilance for the slightest possibility of the transformation of the collective, malleable, and contingent nature inherent in the installment publication into a channel of political communication for the literati at large. The anxiety of the state regarding the control of literati publishing was also echoed across the national border in the literary inquisition in late eighteenth-century Chosŏn Korea.

91. *Da Qing huidian* 大清會典, Kangxi edition, 51.20a. Cited from Guy, *Emperor's Four Treasuries*, 18–19.
92. Xie Guozhen, *Ming Qing zhiji dangshe yundong*, 145–71.

CHAPTER 5

Transnational Circulation of Tanji congshu *and Censorship in Chosŏn Korea*

As one of the most talented and erudite rulers of the Chosŏn dynasty, King Chŏngjo 正祖 (r. 1776–1800) had been a voracious reader and collector of Chinese books since his days as crown prince. Once enthroned, he built the Royal Library, known as Kyujanggak 奎章閣, in 1776. One of its two buildings was dedicated to the storage of Chinese books he frequently asked envoys to search for. For instance, in 1781, Chŏngjo compiled a list of Chinese books whose titles he found intriguing after looking through *Zhejiang caiji yishu zonglu* 浙江採集 遺書總錄 (A Comprehensive List of Books Omitted from Collecting in Zhejiang Province)—a list made for collecting books for inclusion in *Siku quanshu*, which was imported to Chosŏn Korea in 1778.[1] As *Zhejiang caiji yishu zonglu* listed the books circulated in Zhejiang province, Chŏngjo's wish list of Chinese books titled *Naegak pang-sŏrok* 內閣訪書錄 (List of Books for Which the Court Searches) accordingly contained a number of books that enjoyed broad circulation in the Jiangnan area in eighteenth-century China.

What is noteworthy is that King Chŏngjo's 1781 list catalogued the compilations of Zhang Chao and Wang Zhuo, *Tanji congshu* and *Zhaodai congshu*. The entries for *Tanji congshu* and *Zhaodai congshu* are as follows:

1. Chŏngjo 5/6/29, in *Chŏngjo sillok*, in *Chosŏn wangjo sillok*. Following convention, references to texts are by monarch title and reign year/month/day.

The second collection of *Tanji congshu*, fifty *juan*
  Co-compiled by Wang Zhuo from Hangzhou and Zhang Chao from Hui-
zhou during the Qing dynasty. On the brow of the cover page appears
"Fifty pieces of casual short prose by famous masters of our dynasty."

檀几叢書二集五十卷
國朝錢塘王晫、新安張潮同輯。顏其額曰國朝名家小品五十種。[2]

Zhaodai congshu
  Compiled by Zhang Chao from Huizhou during the Qing dynasty. Its
"Editorial Principles" mentions, "This collection endeavors to remove
worn-out words and only collects short prose pieces. It only intends to
continue the excellent enterprise of Wang Zhuo [i.e., *Tanji congshu*] and
not to follow the grand model of *Wenxuan* (Selections of Great Literature). Some are solemn works, others humorous, yet you can read them
all together. Some are hortatory, others cautionary, yet no ambivalence is
allowed [on the part of the reader]. Teachers can make good use of it."

昭代叢書
清新安張潮輯。凡例以為"是集務去陳言，專取小品。祗以繼松溪之勝
舉，原非續文選之鴻裁。為莊為謔，自可同觀；或勸或規，無容二視。在
講書者善會之"云。[3]

Most entries in *Naegak pangsŏrok* are exact copies of those in *Zhejiang caiji yishu zonglu*, and that is the case here for the entry for *Tanji
congshu*.[4] But the entry for *Zhaodai congshu* is not merely different but
more detailed than the one in *Zhejiang caiji yishu zonglu*. In addition
to the names of two editors, it also records the first item of the "Editorial Principles" (*fanli*) of *Zhaodai congshu*.[5] We do not know the exact
circumstances in which Chŏngjo's book list was made, but the difference between his *Naegak pangsŏrok* and the earlier *Zhejiang caiji yishu
zonglu* indicates that the Chosŏn compilers' knowledge of *Zhaodai*

2. *Naegak pangsŏrok*, 104.
3. Ibid., 105.
4. Shen Chu et al., *Zhejiang caiji yishu zonglu*, 2:467. The edition mentioned appears
to have had the cover page as shown in fig. 3.1.
5. Ibid., 2:807. There is a difference in one character: where the original "Editorial
Principles" of *Zhaodai congshu* says "readers" 讀書者, *Naegak pangsŏrok* has "teachers" 講書者. It is not known whether this is a typo or an intentional alteration.

congshu was obtained from somewhere other than *Zhejiang caiji yishu zonglu* itself. It suggests that copies of *Zhaodai congshu* had already been circulating among Korean officials before Chŏngjo saw the *Zhejiang caiji yishu zonglu*.[6] In addition, the insertion of the first item of the "Editorial Principles" that highlights the wide selection of *Zhaodai congshu* reveals what attracted the attention of King Chŏngjo in the first place, namely, its encyclopedic comprehensiveness.[7] Indeed, Chŏngjo seems to have acquired *Tanji congshu* and *Zhaodai congshu* quickly because they appeared in the book catalog of his library of Chinese books called *Yŏlgogwan sŏmok* 閱古館書目 made in 1781.

Eleven years later, however, King Chŏngjo's view of *Tanji congshu* and *Zhaodai congshu* had changed dramatically. Beginning in 1792, Chŏngjo started a literary inquisition campaign, in which he attacked what he considered aberrant forms of writing and located the main cause of the degeneration of literati writings in the flood of books pouring into Chosŏn from Qing China. In this censorship campaign, often called the "Rectification of Literary Style" (Munch'e panchŏng 文體反正),[8] Chŏngjo not only criticized most of the imprints of seventeenth-century Chinese writers that I have discussed in the previous chapters, but also specifically cited *Tanji congshu* as a typical Chinese book that exerted a corrupting influence on the writings of Chosŏn literati because of its broad inclusion of "trivial and superfluous" works.

What caused the radical shift in King Chŏngjo's perception of *Tanji congshu* from appreciation of its all-inclusive breadth to criticism of its superfluous erudition? Why did he particularly single out *Tanji congshu* as an example of a book that should be removed from the bookshelves of the Chosŏn literati? The motivations for the literary inquisition have been variously discussed, but most scholarly discussions are

---

6. It appears that *Zhaodai congshu* was imported to Chosŏn Korea before 1756 at the latest, considering that the copy of *Zhaodai congshu* in Changsŏgak 藏書閣 Library bears the stamp of the official Pak Mun-su 朴文秀 (1691–1756). See Kim Yŏngjin, "U Ch'o sinji," 205, n. 9.

7. *Tanji congshu* also made comprehensive selection its main feature. Wang Zhuo, "Fanli," in the first collection of *TJCS*, 4. See the appendix for the translation.

8. For the debate on the title and the exact dating of the censorship, see Yun Chaemin, "Munch'e panchŏng."

dominated by a concern with national politics internal to Chosŏn Korea, particularly, the relationship of censorship to the consolidation of King Chŏngjo's monarchial power. For example, historians have insisted that the literary inquisition was part of Chŏngjo's political strategy to strengthen royal power by controlling political factions. Censorship is thus understood to have been a means to attain royal dominance over the bureaucracy in order to pave the way to a strong and centralized nation-state based on absolute sovereignty.[9] In contrast, most literary historians have highlighted the cultural and ideological suppression that the censorship brought about. They argue that the king's rigid cultural conservatism prevented the expression of diverse perspectives that created new genres and themes inspired by the reading of imported Chinese books. For this reason, some insist that the censorship served as a hindrance to the dynasty's movement toward modernization.[10]

Despite the opposing views on censorship and its relationship with Chosŏn's indigenous modernity, however, current scholarship has commonly overlooked the fact that Chŏngjo's literary inquisition itself sprang from the thriving transnational transmission of books,[11] a newly emerging channel of communication that separated itself from the long-standing state-dominated one. Chosŏn Korea had developed highly advanced printing technology, but, unlike in Ming and Qing China, the innovation in printing technology was mainly initiated by the government. The invention of metal movable type in the thirteenth century, considered the first use of metal movable type in the world,[12]

9. See, for example, Chŏng Ok-cha, *Chŏngjo ŭi munye sasang* and *Chosŏn hugi munhwa undong sa*; Ma Chung-rak, "Chŏngjo cho komun puhŭng undong." For a more recent and nuanced comparative approach, see Yŏksa hakhoe, ed., *Chŏngjo wa 18 segi*.

10. See, for example, Kang Myŏng-gwan, "Munch'e wa kukka changch'i."

11. A few recent studies discuss the role that the flow of the Chinese books played in the literary, intellectual, and political transformation of eighteenth-century Chosŏn Korea. See Kang Myŏng-gwan, *Chosŏn sidae ch'aek*, 27–28, and Evon, "Tobacco, God, and Books."

12. Ever since the impact of the so-called printing revolution that followed the invention of movable-type printing by Johannes Gutenberg (1398–1468) in Germany, the question of who first invented movable-type printing has been intensely debated among scholars. It is generally accepted that movable-type printing was first invented in Song China by the eleventh century. Whereas the Chinese initially used only clay

led the Chosŏn court to continue its adaptation and to use it for official purposes.[13] At the same time, woodblock printing remained useful owing to its capacity for large print runs and its low cost.[14] In effect, the Chosŏn dynasty maintained a dual structure of official printing: the court would first issue a work in movable type through the Central Bureau of Printing (Kyosŏgwan 校書館) in the capital, and this movable-type edition would then be reproduced by local officials in woodblock facsimile (*pokkak* 覆刻) for wide transmission.[15] The great efficacy of this dual structure along with the relatively belated development of a commercial book market—which did not appear until the beginning of the nineteenth century[16]—provided literati with a stable supply of books through official printing and thereby made book production and circulation almost a state monopoly.[17]

The large and diverse number of books from Qing China that flooded into Chosŏn Korea in the eighteenth century, however, indicates that the state monopoly in the circulation of books was challenged by private circuits of communication among the literati community. The imported Chinese books moved mainly within the tight-knit coterie network and family relationships of the Seoul literati, and their reading of Chinese books brought about the production and circulation of writings in imitation and parody. Given that most private publishing in Chosŏn Korea had been limited to posthumous family publications,[18] the importation and circulation of Chinese books

and wood movable type, use of metal movable type was pioneered in Korea by the thirteenth century.

13. On the innovations of cast type and the history of Korean typography, see Ch'ŏn Hye-bong, *Han'guk sŏjihak*, 188–294; and idem, *Ko inswae*.

14. See Heijdra, "Technology, Culture and Economics," for the comparison between xylography and movable-type printing in terms of economic considerations.

15. Chŏng Sang-gi, "Kwang sŏjŏk" 廣書籍, in *Nongp'o mundap*, 162–63.

16. Scholars are in agreement that, despite the emergence of book-lending stores in the eighteenth century, bookshops in the modern sense did not appear until the nineteenth century. See, for example, Yi Min-hŭi, *16–19 segi sŏjŏk chunggaesang*, 55–60.

17. Yi Chae-jŏng, *Chosŏn ch'ulp'an chusik hoesa*, 10–15; Kang Myŏng-gwan, *Ch'aek p'olledŭl Chosŏn ŭl mandŭlda*, 123.

18. See, for example, Sin Sang-mok, Chang Chae-sŏk, and Cho Ch'ŏl-lae, *Kanyŏksi ilgi*.

emerged as an alternative channel of communication among elites, setting itself apart from the state-dominated one. The executions and punishments carried out during King Chŏngjo's literary inquisition thus clearly indicated that king's concern was not merely with the allegedly heterodox ideas conveyed by the imported Chinese books. More important, he was concerned with restraining the private circuits of circulation among the literati community that were beyond the state's full control. By reconstructing the way in which *Tanji congshu* was imported, read, and censored in eighteenth-century Chosŏn Korea, this chapter sheds light on one of the major aspects of King Chŏngjo's censorship, which is not limited to national politics but relates to the larger flow of books on the transregional scale in the eighteenth century. In other words, the impact of the flourishing practice of private publishing among seventeenth-century Chinese writers did not stop at the national borders; rather, it exemplified the close interconnection between Qing China and Chosŏn Korea by contributing to the growth of diverse venues for the transmission of books, ideas, and knowledge in eighteenth-century Chosŏn Korea—venues that Chŏngjo's literary inquisition attempted to deter but did not fully succeed in discouraging.

Importing *Tanji congshu* to Chosŏn Korea

It is difficult to track down the details of the importation of a specific Chinese book into Chosŏn Korea, but there remains a brief yet concrete record about Zhang Chao's *Tanji congshu* and the circumstance of its transmission. A scion of a distinguished family in Seoul and bibliophile, Yu Man-ju, kept a diary for thirteen years from 1775 to 1787, titled *Hŭmyŏng* 欽英 (Admiration of the Talented), and most of its entries are related to his reading of imported books of the Ming and Qing dynasties. On December 1, 1778, he wrote: "I heard that *Tanji congshu* and *Zhejiang [caiji yishu] shumu* were all new books by Qing people and that they were brought by the tribute mission this time."[19]

---

19. "聞檀几叢書、浙江書目, 皆清人新書。今番使行所出來者云." Yu Man-ju, *Hŭmyŏng*, 2:291.

This brief record provides specific information on the importation of Zhang Chao's *Tanji congshu*: it was transmitted through the tribute book trade when the Korean mission went to Beijing to pay tribute to the Qianlong emperor in 1778. This mission, which lasted from March 17 to July 2, is well known because some members of the mission, such as Yi Tŏng-mu 李德懋 (1741–93) and Pak Che-ga 朴齊家 (1750–1805), talented young scholars who were full of intellectual curiosity, left records of their experience in Beijing. Their vivid and detailed travel accounts conveyed information about the most recent cultural, intellectual, and political atmosphere of Qing China—details that were not otherwise accessible to Chosŏn literati after the fall of the Ming dynasty and that eventually sparked a newly emerging boom of learning about Qing China (known as *pukhak* 北學, or Northern Learning) in the eighteenth century.[20]

Although there was a direct official channel through which the Chinese court would bestow books on Korea or the Korean court would ask the Chinese court to send the books it needed, it was rarely used and the books granted were limited to the Confucian classics and histories.[21] Instead, most Chinese books were purchased as a part of the tribute trade. The tributary relationship between China and Korea required Korea to send tribute missions to Beijing one to four times a year, and this official visit to China provided a legitimate opportunity for trade.[22] The Korean missions usually brought goods such as

20. In the highly charged political milieu of the eighteenth century, any particular political and cultural movement was inseparable from a certain position toward the Manchu's replacement of Ming. Northern Learning is often considered to represent a critical shift of the literati from renunciation of the Qing as the center of Sino-centric civilization to accommodation of the presiding Qing power. But this position was not necessarily in stark contrast to the emerging political consciousness of independence of Chosŏn from the China-centered relationship, often called "Small Central Efflorescence" (*So Chunghwa* 小中華) or "Chosŏn Sinocentrism" (*Chosŏn Chunghwa chuŭi* 朝鮮中華主義). On the complex relationship between Northern Learning and Chosŏn's repositioning in the Sinocentric order, see, for example, Kim Yŏngmin, "Chosŏn Chunghwa chuŭi," and Kye Sŭng-bŏm, "Chosŏn ŭi 18 segi."
21. For the list of books that the Chinese courts gave Korea, see, for example, Yi Tŏng-mu, "Chungguk sŏjŏk i urinarae tŭlŏon kŏstŭl," in *Kugyŏk Ch'ŏngjanggwan chŏnsŏ*, 9:105–6.
22. Ledyard, "Korean Travelers," 4.

ginseng, paper, hemp, and horses, and traded them for silk, cotton, medicine, and such luxury goods as hats, ivory, face powder, and jewelry. Books were among the most important items sought by the Koreans.

There are two ways that *Tanji congshu* may have been procured in the tribute trade. First, the May–July 1778 tribute mission might have been officially instructed to purchase the book by the king. But, if this had been the case, news of its importation might not have reached Yu Man-ju by December 1778 because it would have immediately been placed in the royal collection. Although high officials had relatively easy access to the royal library—there is a famous episode of the prime minister Yi Sang-hwang 李相璜 (1763–1840) being caught and reproached by Chŏngjo for reading imported Chinese novels from the royal library during his night duty in the palace[23]—Yu Man-ju did not hold any official position and so would probably not have been able to obtain the newly imported *Tanji congshu* so fast. In addition, the fact that King Chŏngjo included *Tanji congshu* on his 1781 wish list, *Naegak pangsŏrok*, indicates that it had not been added to the royal collection when the tribute mission came back with the book in 1778.

The second, more plausible possibility is that *Tanji congshu* was purchased for personal use by one of the members of the 1778 mission. An average mission consisted of hundreds of people, including higher-ranking officials such as the chief ambassador (*chŏngsa* 正使), deputy ambassador (*pusa* 副使), and secretary (*sŏjanggwan* 書將官), and minor posts such as protocol officers, military aides, interpreters, servants, cooks, and guides. The envoys not only conducted official duties but also purchased books, typically in large numbers, for private reasons for themselves and their friends. Since the missions provided Chosŏn literati with a rare and exciting opportunity to visit Beijing and buy books for their own needs, there was usually competition to be included in the delegations. It was also common that literati who were not selected for the missions but needed specific books would ask members of the tribute missions to purchase the books for them. The sixteenth-century bibliophile Yu Hŭi-ch'un 柳希春 (1513–77), for example, asked a friend who was about to depart for China as an envoy to

---

23. Chŏngjo 16/10/24, in *Chŏngjo sillok*, in *Chosŏn wangjo sillok*.

buy him some books.[24] The Chosŏn envoy's passion for book shopping in Beijing was so well known that the Ming writer Chen Jiru described it as follows:

> The people from Chosŏn love books very much. Their missions coming to China are usually limited to fifty to sixty people. They look for old canonical works, new books, or fiction and miscellaneous records. In order to find the books that they are short of [in Chosŏn], all fifty or sixty people go to the market during the day. Each one of them copies the book catalog and separately seeks out the books by asking around. Without hesitation, they purchase books at high prices and take them back to their country. As a result, their country possesses extraordinary books and collectible editions to the contrary [of our expectation].
>
> 朝鮮人極好書, 凡使臣到中土, 或限五六十人。或舊典、或新書、稗官小說, 在彼所缺者, 五六十人日出市中, 各寫書目, 分頭遇人遍問, 不惜重值購回, 故彼國反有異書藏本也。[25]

During their visits to China, the Korean envoys were required to stay in an official hostel, called Yühe guan 玉河館 (Jade River Lodge), in the southeastern part of Beijing, and their movements within the city were restricted to a designated area.[26] As a consequence, the Korean missions usually did business with minor officials called *xuban* 序班. The *xuban* was an usher on the staff of the Court of State Ceremonial (*Honglu si* 鴻臚寺) in charge of greeting officials and guests and preparing them for court audiences and other important ceremonies.

---

24. See, for example, Chŏng Ch'ang-gwŏn, *Hollo pyŏsŭl hamyŏ*, 98–99. Yu Hŭich'un also asked an interpreter close to him to buy him books from China, giving him ginseng as currency in exchange for the books because, in addition to the official envoys, official interpreters (*yŏkkwan* 譯官) also played a major role as book traders, using their knowledge of the Chinese language. The tribute trade usually guaranteed large profits, and the Chosŏn court consequently did not cover the travel expenses of official interpreters but instead conferred on them the right to trade. Song Chae-yong, *Chosŏn sidae sŏnbi iyagi*, 92.

25. Chen Jiru, *Taiping qinghua*, 1097.

26. The lodge was under the firm control of a Manchu director who managed all local affairs of the embassy: he not only supervised movements inside and outside the gate but also controlled the distribution of all the food and other supplies assigned for the support of the embassy. Hong Tae-yong, "Yŏn'gi," 56.

When a Korean mission arrived in Beijing, the Ministry of Rites (*Libu* 禮部) selected ten ushers and deputized them to serve the envoys. As their salary was meager, the ministry allowed them to earn extra income by granting them exclusive rights to engage in the luxury goods trade, including books, paintings, brushes, ink sticks, and tea.[27] Although the ushers were supposed to be selected from every province, most of them hailed from the southern part of China, and it was easy for them to acquire books from the Jiangnan area.[28] If a Korean envoy had certain books in mind, he would first ask an official interpreter to engage an usher, who would search for the books and bargain with the envoy over the price. But since it was common for the ushers to make substantial profits from the use of their exclusive trade privileges, the Korean envoys often begrudged them the exorbitant prices. The scholar-official Hong Tae-yong 洪大容 (1731–83) recorded an anecdote about an usher who followed him wherever he went because he wanted to see whether Hong would try to buy books without permission. Hong attempted to dissuade the usher from following him, but it was not until Hong left the book market that the usher eventually stopped following him.[29]

Beginning in the mid-seventeenth century, however, the restrictions on movement within the city had been loosened, and Korean envoys who had been disgruntled with the ushers' monopoly over the book trade would go outside the designated area to look for books by themselves. By this time, the book market in Beijing had expanded and was well developed. At the beginning of the seventeenth century, the book stalls were clustered inside Zhengyang Gate 正陽門 around the old Ministry of Punishment Street (Xingbu jie 刑部街) and inside Xuanwu Gate 玄武門, but, by the beginning of the eighteenth century, the market had moved to an area around Longfu Temple 隆福寺 and Liuli chang to the west of Zhengyang Gate. Liuli chang, which had once been the site of kilns where decorative and glazed bricks were made, had grown rapidly into a major emporium for books and antiques. Its heyday was during the reign of Qianlong, at the time of the compilation of the *Siku quanshu*. The officials entrusted with gathering books from all over

27. Ibid., 74; Pak Chi-wŏn, "Kuoe yimun" 口外異聞, in *Yŏrha ilgi*, 2:167.
28. Yi Ŭi-hyŏn, "Kyŏngja yŏnhaeng chapchi," 88.
29. Hong Tae-yong, "Yŏn'gi," 267.

China often stayed in the vicinity of Liuli chang, and the compilers of *Siku quanshu* would regularly visit Liuli chang to look for books and to collect information.[30]

The thriving book market of Liuli chang captivated the visiting Korean intellectuals. Fascinated by the market's scale and diversity, they were eager to make as many pilgrimages as possible to the bookshops during their stay. Their admiration and awe were rendered in lively and colorful language rarely found in Chinese records:[31]

The main street of the Liuli chang market is about 5 *li* [1.5 miles] long. Although the glamor of its pavilions and balustrades is less than that of other markets, rare and precious things are abundantly displayed and amassed, and its arrangement is quaint and beautiful. If one takes a slow walk along the street, one feels as though one is entering a treasure market in Persia. One can only see the enchantment and glitter, and cannot examine thoroughly enough even a single thing even if one spends an entire day. There are seven bookshops.[32] On three walls are mounted bookcases with ten shelves. The books with ivory clasps are neatly arranged, and each book case has a paper label attached. If one counts the total number of books in a bookshop, there cannot be less than several tens of thousands. No matter how long one keeps looking up, one cannot read all of the labels without becoming dizzy.

蓋一市長可五里, 雖其樓欄之豪侈不及他市, 珍怪奇巧, 充溢羅積, 位置古雅, 遵道徐步, 如入波斯寶市, 只見其瑰然爛然而已, 終日行不能鑑賞一物也。書肆有七, 三壁周設懸架十樓層, 牙籤整秩, 每套有標紙, 量一肆之書, 已不下數萬卷, 仰而良久, 不能遍省其標號, 而眼已眩昏矣。[33]

30. Sima Chaojun, *Siku quanshu zongmu bianzuan kao*, 192–93.

31. For more records on Liuli chang by Chosŏn envoys, see Pak Hyŏn-gyu, "Chosŏn sasintŭl," and Chŏng Min, *Pukkyŏng Yurich'ang*.

32. Hong Tae-yong recorded that "there are seven bookshops," but, according to Li Wenzao's "Liuli chang shusi ji," which was written three years after Hong Tae-yong's record, there were twenty-nine bookshops in Liuli chang. It is hard to believe that the number of bookshops could have increased more than fourfold in an interval of only three years. Pak Hyŏn-gyu therefore suspects that Hong Tae-yong may have mistakenly written "seven bookshops" when he meant to write "seventeen." See Pak Hyŏn-gyu, "Chosŏn sasintŭl," 239–40.

33. Hong Tae-yong, "Yŏn'gi," 271. I have modified Gari Ledyard's translation in "Korean Travelers," 25.

The bookshops are located outside Zhengyang Gate, and there are more than one. The method by which the books are arranged is [as follows]: a bookshop building has about thirty rooms, and on all four walls of each room are mounted bookcases in which the books are nicely arranged and stacked in layers. A label with the title is attached to each book case. Since the books are too numerous, it is impossible to count. But the front pavilion has a big table on which tens of folding book cases or more are placed. They are catalogs of the books. The customer sits in a chair, and, if he wants to buy a book, he raises his hand. It is very convenient and easy to take a book out and put it back. I looked through the catalog, and it listed large volumes of books such as *Siku quanshu*,[34] *Wenzhang dacheng, Cefu yuangui, Yuanjian leihan, Feiwen yunfu, Ershisi shi, Shisan jing zhushu, Kangxi zidian, Wanguo huitong, Dacang jing*, and more. Other than that, there are also Confucian classics, histories, all kinds of philosophy, books of medicine, divination, botany, fiction, miscellaneous records, the four marvelous novels, historical novels, and other genres. The number [of books] is unimaginable, and I have never heard of most of the titles.

冊肆在正陽門外，非止一處。其畜書之法，設堂數三十間，每間四壁設閒架，層層井井，排列積峙，每套付籤曰某冊。故充棟溢宇，不可計量。而前閣置一大桌，桌上置十餘卷冊匣，乃冊名目錄也。人坐椅上欲買某冊，則一舉手，抽給抽插，甚便易也。閱其目錄，則其大帙有四庫全書、文章大成、冊府元龜、淵鑑類函、佩文韻府、全史、十三經註疏、康熙字典、萬國會通、大藏經等，而外經史、諸子百家、醫藥、卜筮、種樹之類、稗官雜記、四大奇書、演義等書，其數亦不億，多有不知其名目者。[35]

The books in Liuli chang came from all over China, but books from the Jiangnan area made up a large proportion of them. Many bookshop owners were failed examination candidates from Jiangnan and were quick to catch up with information about books recently published there.[36] For instance, the owners of the bookstores Wuliu ju 五柳居 and Wencui tang 文粹堂, both from Suzhou, were able to use their Jiangnan connections to transport about four thousand books at a time by ship from Suzhou to Beijing.[37] Owing to the development of an interregional

34. This must be a misprint or a misunderstanding because *Siku quanshu* was produced only in seven manuscript copies and was not available for sale in bookshops.
35. Pak Sa-ho, *Simjŏn ko*, 175.
36. Hong Tae-yong, "Yŏn'gi," 271.
37. Li Wenzao, "Liuli chang shusi ji," 100–102.

network of book markets, Zhang Chao's books, which initially circulated in the Jiangnan area, were also sold in Liuli chang. For example, when the eminent writer Pak Chi-wŏn 朴趾源 (1737–1805) was on his way to Beijing as a member of a tribute mission, he encountered a Manchu school teacher. The teacher showed Pak the list of books that his father had sold when he managed a bookshop called Mingsheng tang 名盛堂 in Liuli chang. The book catalog listed more than seventy recently published books, including not only some of Zhang Chao's most popular works, such as *Tanji congshu*, *Yu Chu xinzhi*, and *Youmengying*, but also his relatively obscure book *Yichan lu* 亦禪錄 (Record of Dhyana at All Times).[38] It also listed a number of imprints by members of Zhang Chao's coterie in Jiangnan, such as Wang Qi's *Chidu xinyu*, You Tong's *Gonggui xiaoming lu* 宮閨小名錄 (Short Record of Royal Consorts), Song Luo's *Yunlang oubi*, and Mao Xiang's 冒襄 *Yingmeian yiyu* 影梅庵憶語 (Reminiscences of the Convent of Shadowy Plum Blossoms).[39]

Given the widespread sales of the imprints of Zhang Chao and his coterie in eighteenth-century Liuli chang, it is highly likely that a member of a Chosŏn tribute mission purchased *Tanji congshu* in one of the bookshops in Liuli chang. In fact, Yi Tŏng-mu and Pak Che-ga, in their travel records of the 1778 tribute mission, indicated several visits to Liuli chang, and Yi Tŏng-mu even stated that he purchased *Zhejiang caiji yishu zongmu* in Liuli chang.[40] Since Yu Man-ju mentioned that *Zhejiang caiji yishu zongmu* was imported along with *Tanji congshu* in his 1778 diary entry, *Tanji congshu* might have been acquired then.

Because the Chosŏn envoys usually purchased large numbers of books at a time, the bookshops in Liuli chang customarily prepared for the arrival of Chosŏn missions by stocking up on books in advance and placing announcements about them in the front of the bookshops.[41] The Chosŏn envoys' frequent visits not only made them

38. Pak Chi-wŏn, "Togangnok" 渡江錄, in *Yŏrha ilgi*, 1:97. According to Li Wenzao's record, however, the bookshop was called Mingsheng tang 鳴盛堂. It is not certain whether these names referred to the same bookshop and one of the records was a mistake. Li Wenzao, "Liuli chang shusi ji," 100.

39. Pak Chi-wŏn, "Togangnok," in *Yŏrha ilgi*, 1:96–98.

40. Yi Tŏng-mu, entry on Chŏngjo 2/5/25, in "Yipyŏn'gi ha" 入燕記下, in *Ch'ŏngjanggwan chŏnsŏ, juan* 27.

41. Kim Sŏng-jin, "Yŏng-Chŏng yŏn'gan," 100.

friends with the bookstore owners,[42] but also established relationships with some Qing literati who happened to shop for books in Liuli chang. For instance, Pak Che-ga visited Beijing three more times as an envoy after his first visit in 1778 and was able to become friends with the eminent painter Luo Pin 羅聘 (1733–99), the renowned bibliophile Huang Pilie 黃丕烈 (1763–1825), and the esteemed scholars and compilers of *Siku quanshu*, Ji Yun 紀昀 (1724–1805) and Weng Fanggang 翁方綱 (1733–1818). Pak Che-ga exchanged correspondence with all four men after returning to Korea. From these Chinese contemporaries and their coterie, he received more than seventy letters and poems, which were later collected in a book titled *Hojŏ jip* 縞紵集 (Collection of Friendship of Silk and Ramie).[43] The interactions with contemporary Qing scholars received intense attention from Chosŏn literati, and the scholars who participated in subsequent missions paid visits to the same Qing literati in order to maintain their transnational friendship.[44] For Korean intellectuals in the eighteenth century, tribute mission travel and book shopping thus provided a valuable opportunity not only to acquire the books they needed but also to experience the intellectual, cultural, and political atmosphere of the contemporary Qing not as a distant image but as a concrete reality.

Circulating and Reading *Tanji congshu*

The books imported to Chosŏn Korea from Qing China were distributed through official, commercial, and private routes. Because the official channel was usually limited to certain genres of books, such as the Confucian classics, histories, and practical books on legal codes,

42. For example, the Chosŏn envoys established a relationship with Tao Zhengxiang 陶正祥, the owner of Wuliu ju, and this friendship was admired by Chosŏn intellectuals. Henceforth, envoys dropped by Tao's bookshop every time they visited Beijing. See Pak Chi-wŏn, "Kwannae chŏngsa" 關內程史, in *Yŏrha ilgi*, 1:406.

43. "Friendship of silk and ramie" (*gaozhu zhi jiao* 縞紵之交) was a set phrase indicating deep and intimate friendship. Pak Hyŏn-kyu, "Chosŏn Pak Che-ga Yu Tŭk-kong"; and Kim Kwan-ung et al., "Hojŏ ŭi chŏng."

44. On the interaction between Pak Che-ga and the Qing intellectuals, and their sustained friendship, see, for example, Chŏng Min, *18 segi hanchung chisigin*.

medicine, and geography,[45] *Tanji congshu* must have been distributed mainly through either commercial or private channels. Yu Man-ju who left a diary record about *Tanji congshu* also mentioned the two frequent means of Chinese book acquisition he used: he either bought them from book brokers or obtained them from fellow literati with whom he was connected via family relationships or his coterie network.

Book brokers, called *sŏk'wae* 書儈 or *ch'aekk'wae* 冊儈, provided a major commercial channel of book circulation in Chosŏn until the beginning of the nineteenth century, when a full-fledged commercial book market eventually emerged.[46] The book brokers usually made house calls in the areas of the capital where officials, scholars, and writers gathered, and supplied the books that the elites wanted. One of the famous brokers active in this period was Cho Sin-sŏn 曹神仙, who specialized in selling a variety of Chinese books, including the Confucian classics, histories, works on phonology, encyclopedias, and novels. He was depicted—often in popular rumors—as going everywhere, through markets, alleys, and public offices, and meeting everyone, irrespective of rank or age, in order to sell books. In addition, he was known for his extensive knowledge of books and for having memorized the names of the author and number of volumes of each book.[47] According to the eminent scholar Chŏng Yag-yong 丁若鏞 (1762–1836), Cho Sin-sŏn spoke about the Confucian classics as though he were an erudite scholar himself, although Chŏng adds that Cho

---

45. The Central Bureau of Printing reprinted some imported Chinese books and provided ample copies of Chinese books to the literati who held official posts in the Seoul area. High officials often received such reprints as a royal gift from the king (*pansa* 頒賜), or they would request the Central Bureau of Printing to reprint a book using the official's own supply of paper. Sometimes officials with good connections or strong influence would make requests to local offices where the woodblocks of the Chinese reprint were stored, hoping to be able to print copies of the books they needed themselves. Yi Chon-hŭi, "Chosŏn chŏn'gi," 71–75.

46. Yi Min-hŭi, *16–19 segi sŏjŏk chunggaesang*, 287.

47. Because Cho Sin-sŏn was well known among elites of the time, there are several records about him by scholars, including Cho Su-sam's "Chuksŏ chosaeng chŏn," in *Ch'ujae chip, juan* 8, reprinted in *Yŏhang munhak ch'ongsŏ*, 3:691–94; and Cho Hŭi-ryong's "Cho sinsŏn chŏn," in *Hosan oegi*, in *Yŏhang munhak ch'ongsŏ*, 9:60.

was a profit-driven merchant by nature who would buy books from orphans or widows for a low price and then sell them for twice what he had paid.[48]

Given the sporadic nature of the work of book brokers and their lack of organization, the second, more reliable way for Chosŏn literati like Yu Man-ju to obtain Chinese books was through their personal networks. Once a mission returned to Korea, its members who had purchased Chinese books were highly sought after in elite circles, as they usually returned with a large number of books. For instance, the renowned scholar and novelist Hŏ Kyun 許筠 (1569–1618) brought back about four thousand books from Beijing in 1614 and 1615, but he was far from exceptional in doing so.[49] Those who had acquired books in China would loan the books to their close friends, give them as presents, or exchange them for personal favors. Instead of woodblock printing, the imported Chinese books were mostly reproduced by hand by the literati who wished to read them. The scribes whom they hired for this purpose could be friends known for the high quality of their calligraphy, official transcribers (sŏsagwan 書寫官), commercial transcribers, or impoverished literati trying to eke out a living.[50] By convention, the paper was provided to the scribe by the work's commissioner, who would also pay for the transcription in advance.[51]

Through this interpersonal transmission, imported Chinese books tended to circulate along the branching networks of literati coteries — that is, among men whose social status enabled them to establish and maintain friendships with the envoys to China, particularly the ones residing in or near Seoul. In fact, in terms of access to Chinese books, the gap between Seoul and provincial localities widened during this period. One record notes that a scholar would instantly become a celebrity in a province if he brought with him the imported Chinese encyclopedia Shiwen leiju 事文類聚 (Classified Historical Facts and

---

48. Chŏng Yag-yong, "Cho sinsŏn chŏn," in Kugyŏk Tasan simunjip, 7:279–80.

49. Kim Yŏng-jin mentions other records of literati importing books to Korea by the thousands. Kim Yŏng-jin, "Chosŏn hugi chungguk sahaeng," 595–98.

50. For example, before Yi Tŏng-mu held an official post, he eked out a living by copying books, such as You Tong's Ni Mingshi yuefu 擬明史樂府. Ibid., 622, n. 71.

51. Yu Chae-yŏp, "Chosŏn chunggi," 91–92.

Literature), which was commonly acquired in the Seoul area.[52] In contrast, the emerging bibliophiles in the eighteenth century who collected volumes numbering in the tens of thousands, such as Ch'oe Sŏk-jŏng 崔錫鼎 (1646–1715), Yi Ha-gon 李夏坤 (1677–1724), Sŏ Yu-gu 徐有榘 (1764–1845), Wŏn In-son 元仁孫 (1721–74), and the brothers Yu Myŏng-ch'ŏn 柳命天 and Yu Myŏng-hyŏn 柳命賢 (1643–1703), were all from the "distinguished clans of Seoul" (kyŏnghwa sejok 京華世族), scholar-official families that had lived in Seoul for generations.[53] For example, the modern scholar Kim Yŏng-jin discovered three transcribed copies of Yu Chu xinzhi, one of which had been transcribed by the grandson of Yu Myŏng-hyŏn along with his family members connected by blood and marriage and a friend of elite social standing.[54]

It is not known from whom Yu Man-ju heard about the importation of Tanji congshu, but he must have heard the news via a close-knit elite network. The bibliophiles built exclusive social networks, undergirded by friendships and family relationships clustered in the Seoul area, which made it easy to exchange information about newly imported Chinese books and to trade books in their collections with each other. For instance, Yu Man-ju was a close friend of Min Kyŏng-sŏk 閔景涑, the descendant of the prime minister and famous bibliophile Min Sŏng-hwi 閔聖徽 (1581–1647), and they often borrowed from and lent books to each other. Once, they exchanged lists of the books in their libraries, and Yu Man-ju was impressed by Min's list of books, which contained 580 titles in more than ten thousand volumes of Chinese books.[55]

The importation of large numbers of Chinese books accompanied a widespread boom in reading Chinese books in the eighteenth century.

52. Yi Hak-kyu, "Yŏ" 與, in "Yinsuok chip" 因樹屋集, in Nakhasaeng chip, juan 10.
53. Kang Myŏng-gwan, Chosŏn sidae munhak yesul, 253–76 and 279–88. For the distinct identity of kyŏnghwa sejok, see Yu Pong-hak, Chosŏn hugi hakkye, 95–202.
54. The record indicates that Yu Chu xinzhi was transcribed by Yu Kyŏng-jong 柳慶種 (1714–84), the grandson of Yu Myŏng-hyŏn, along with his nephew; his brother-in-law Kang Se-hwang 姜世晃 (1713–91) and his three sons; and Yi Yong-hyu 李用休 (1708–82). All of them were high officials and respected scholars of the time. See Kim Yŏng-jin, "U Ch'o sinji," 227.
55. Yu Man-ju, Ilgi rŭl ssŭda, 1:208–9.

Aside from perennially imported items, such as the Confucian classics and histories, eighteenth-century Chosŏn readers were able to access an unprecedentedly diverse range of books through the book trade. Particularly, a large number of less canonical works enjoyed broad circulation such as novels; literary collections; and anthologies of prose, miscellanies, letters, and tales, often called *sop'um* (小品), that were published in the late Ming and early Qing periods.[56] Zhang Chao's books, such as *Tanji congshu, Zhaodai congshu, Yu Chu xinzhi*, and *Youmengying*, as depositories of miscellanies, were among the most popular books among elite readers—for this reason, some extant editions that remain in Korean libraries today are original editions printed by Zhang Chao and imported before Qianlong's censorship. For example, Yu Man-ju purchased two different editions of *Yu Chu xinzhi* in 1775 and 1784, respectively.[57] The renowned scholar-official Yu Tŭk-kong 柳得恭 (1748–1807) also specifically asked his uncle, who was leaving for Beijing on a diplomatic mission, to buy him a copy of *Yu Chu xinzhi*.[58] Moreover, the books of Zhang Chao's coterie that Zhang Chao had excerpted and included in his *Tanji congshu* and *Zhaodai congshu* circulated widely as well. These books included Wang Zhuo's *Jin Shishuo*,[59] Chen Ding's *Liuxi waizhuan*,[60] Zhao Jishi's *Jiyuan ji suoji*,[61] Song Luo's *Yunlang oubi*,[62] Zhou Lianggong's *Yinshuwu shuying* 因樹屋書影 (Shadows of Books from the House Founded on

56. For a list of Chinese books that members of the Chosŏn literati read, see, for example, Hong Sŏn-p'yo et al., *17–18 segi Chosŏn*.

57. Yu Man-ju, *Hŭmyŏng*, 1:26 (March 4, 1775) and 5:166–7 (March 23, 1784). See Kim Yŏng-jin, "U Ch'o sinji," 209–13, for more records on the Chosŏn literati's reading of *Yu Chu xinzhi*.

58. Yu Tŭk-kong, "Songin puyŏn ku U Ch'o sinji" 送人赴燕求虞初新志, in *Yŏngjae chip, juan 2*.

59. See, for example, Yi Tŏng-mu, *Noeroe nangnak sŏ* 磊磊落落書, in *Ch'ŏngjanggwan chŏnsŏ, juan 39, 40*.

60. See, for example, Pak Chi-wŏn, "T'aehak yukwallok" 太學留館錄, in *Yŏrha ilgi*; Chŏng Yag-yong, "Yŏlpuron" 烈婦論, in *Tasan simun chip, juan 11*; and Yi Kyu-gyŏng, "Koesang" 乖常, in *Oju yŏnmun changjŏn san'go, juan 5*.

61. See, for example, Yi Kyu-gyŏng, "Kyŏngchŏn ch'ongsŏl" 經典總說, in *Oju yŏnmun changjŏn san'go, juan 58*.

62. See, for example, Yi Tŏng-mu, "Yongsin" 龍身, in "Angyŏp gi" 盎葉記, in *Ch'ŏngjanggwan chŏnsŏ, juan 56*. For more examples, see An Tae-hoe, Yi Ch'ŏr-hŭi, Yi Hyŏn-il et al., *Chosŏn hugi Myŏng-Ch'ŏng munhak*, 1:495–500.

Table 5.1. Partial list of works by Chosŏn literati that mention works collected in Zhang Chao's imprints

Name of Chinese writer	Title of Chinese work collected by Zhang Chao	Title of Zhang Chao's collection in which the work appears	Name of Korean writer	Title of Korean work in which mention appears
Zhang Chao	Qiliao 七療 (Seven Remedies)	Tanji congshu	Yi Ok 李鈺 (1760–1815)	Chiliyŏl 七物 (Seven Fervors)
Huang Zhouxing 黃周星 (1611–80)	Jiangjiu yuan ji 將就園記 (Account of the Approximate Garden)	Zhaodai congshu	Chŏng Yag-yong 丁若鏞 (1762–1836)	Che Hwang Sang yuin ch'ŏp 題黃裳幽人帖 (Endorsement of the Calligraphy of the Recluse Hwang Sang)[1]
			Sŏ Yu-gu 徐有榘 (1764–1845)	Yiunji 怡雲志 (Record of the Solitary Enjoyment of Clouds)
			Hong Kil-ju 洪吉周 (1786–1841)	Wŏngŏ nyŏm 爰居念 (Thoughts of Moving)[2]
			Hong Hyŏn-ju 洪顯周 (1793–1865)	"Wŏrya ch'ŏnghŭng to" 月夜清興圖 (Painting of a Leisurely Night under the Moon)
Zhang Wanzhong 張萬鍾 (1592–1644)	Gejing 鴿經 (Classic of Pigeons)	Tanji congshu	Yu Tŭk-kong 柳得恭 (1748–1807)	Palhapgyŏng 鴶鴿經 (Classic of Domestic Pigeons)[3]
Chen Ding 陳鼎 (b. 1650)	Shepu 蛇譜 (Register of Snakes)	Zhaodai congshu	Hong Nak-sun 洪樂純 (b. 1723)	Sapo chan 蛇譜讚 (Endorsement of the Register of Snakes)

Yu Huai 余懷 (1616–96)	Banqiao zaji	Yu Chu xinzhi and Zhaodai congshu	Han Chae-rak 韓在洛 (1775–ca. 1833)	Nokp'a chapki 綠波雜記 (Miscellaneous Records of Green Waves)[4]

1. Chŏng Yag-yong, "Che Hwang Sang yuin ch'ŏp," in Yŏyudang chŏnsŏ, juan 14.

2. Hong Kil-ju stated, "I had wanted to write this kind of piece for a long time, but after I read Jiangjiu yuan ji, I further gained some ideas about the overall arrangement and structure" 蓋余欲著是書, 厥惟久矣。而至讀粋排鋪匠搆之大略。孟有所得粋排鋪匠搆之大略. Hong Kil-ju, "Suyŏ nanp'il" 睡餘瀾筆, in Hanghae pyŏngham, 2:14–15.

3. Yi Kyu-gyŏng 李圭景 (1788–1856) specifically stated: "Zhang Chao's Tanji congshu contained 'Gejing.' Our country's Yu Tŭk-kong also wrote 'Palhap-gyŏng'" 張潮山采檀几叢書, 有鴿經。我束柳冷齋得恭, 亦撰鵠鴿經. See his "Palhap pyŏnjŭng sŏl" 鵠鴿辨證說, in Oju yŏnmun changjŏn san'go, 532.

4. Sin Wi 申緯 (1769–1845) mentioned: "When I read Nokp'a chapki that followed Banqiao zaji, I realize that Yu Huai is the Old Master of Lotus Root of today [the author of Nokp'a chapki]; he is better than Yu Huai since he took pains in depicting the spring of the prosperous era" 按橋記後綠波記, 余潑心今藕老人。更比潑心君又勝, 盡情事窵太平春. Sin Wi, "Preface to Nokp'a chapki," in Han Chae-rak, Nokp'a chapki, 3.

Trees),[63] Zhuo Erkan's *Yimin shi*,[64] Yu Huai's "Banqiao zaji,"[65] Ferdinand Verbiest's *Kunyu tushuo*,[66] and so forth.

The popularity of Zhang Chao's imprints was also evidenced in a considerable number of sequels and imitative works that directly reference the format and themes of works that appeared in Zhang Chao's compilations (table 5.1). One such example is Huang Zhouxing's account of his imaginary garden, "Jiangjiu yuan ji" 將就園記 (Account of the Approximate Garden), which Zhang Chao had selected for his *Zhaodai congshu*. It inspired a number of writings by Chosŏn literati about their idealized gardens—a genre of sorts that accompanied the popularity of gardening as an elite hobby in the eighteenth century.[67] Huang Zhouxing's account further gave rise to a series of three paintings by Hong Hyŏn-ju 洪顯周 (1793–1865), the royal son-in-law of King Chŏngjo. On one of the paintings, Hong Hyŏn-ju specifically mentions Jiangjiu yuan in a colophon at the left side: "The painting on the right imitates the meaning of Jiangjiu yuan that is left behind" (fig. 5.1).[68]

The mobility of Zhang Chao's imprints across the national border was not one of direct spatial transposition from one culture to the other; rather it involved the proliferation of multiple interpretations of the text and took on new meanings by reference to its local context. In spite of the heterogeneous and disparate nature of the texts included, Zhang Chao's compilations overall were considered as creating reading pleasure out of adroit literary play in the jocular pursuit of erudition or cultural sophistication as was popular in the late Ming and early Qing literati culture.[69] But Chosŏn readers' readings and reinterpretations tended to treat them more as scholarly investigations of ordinary things

63. See, for example, Yi Tŏng-mu, "Noeroe nangnak sŏ yinyong sŏmok" 磊磊落落書引用書目, in "Noeroe nangnak sŏ," in *Ch'ŏngjanggwan chŏnsŏ, juan* 36.

64. See, for example, Yu Tŭk-kong, "Sŏlch'i chip sŏ" 雪痴集序, in *Yŏngjae chip, juan* 7.

65. See, for example, Yi Kyu-gyŏng, "Nonsa" 論史, in *Oju yŏnmun changjŏn san'go, juan* 43; Yi Ok, "Yuriwŏn ch'ŏng'ak gi" 游梨園聽樂記, in *Yŏkchu Yi Ok chŏnjip*, 1:236; and Yu Man-ju, *Hŭmyŏng*, 5:135 (February 3, 1784).

66. See, for example, Yi Ik, "Ilil ch'iljo" 一日七潮, in *Sŏngho sasŏl, juan* 1.

67. See Widmer, "Between Worlds," 249–81, for a discussion of "Jiangjiu yuan ji." For further examples of writings by Chosŏn literati on their imaginary gardens, see An Tae-hoe, "18–19 segi ŭi chugŏ munhwa," 914–48.

68. "右仿將就園遺意。"

69. Yong Long et al., *Siku quanshu zongmu*, 1:1140.

Fig. 5.1. Hong Hyŏn-ju's *Wŏrya chŏnghŭng to* 月夜清興圖. Courtesy of Kansong Art Museum, Seoul.

and practical knowledge. The imitations and sequels created by Chosŏn literati, though seemingly similar to the original, led Chosŏn writers not only to experiment with new prose styles, which departed from the entrenched classical prose style, but also to pursue themes and topics hitherto unexplored in its minute depictions of everyday objects and things. For example, some prose pieces included in *Zhaodai congshu* and *Tanji congshu* used the format of the *jing* 經 (classic) and *pu* 譜 (register), both long-standing genres for scholarly investigation, but they wittily parodied them to delve into mundane objects in a casual and playful manner. Chosŏn writers imitated such registers on various kinds of snakes ("Shepu" 蛇譜), pigeons ("Gejing" 鴿經), and bamboo ("Zhupu" 竹譜) in Zhang Chao's compilations and created similar works, such as Yu Tŭk-kong's *Palhapgyŏng* 鵓鴿經 (Classic of Domestic Pigeons), Yi Sŏ-gu's 李書九 (1754–1825) *Nok aengmugyŏng* 綠鸚鵡經

(Classic of Green Parrots, 1771), Yi Ok's 李鈺 (1760–1815) *Yŏn'gyŏng* 煙經 (Classic of Tobacco, 1810), Kim Ryŏ's 金鑢 (1766–1812) *Uhae iŏ po* 牛海異漁譜 (Register of Unusual Fish in Uhae [Chinhae]), and Sim Yun-ji's 沈允之 (fl. 1748) *Ch'omok hwahwe po* 草木花卉譜 (Register of Trees, Grasses, and Flowers).[70] These creations of Chosŏn writers, though started with playful curiosity, leaned toward compiling new knowledge about ordinary things that were not traditionally deemed worthy of scholarly investigation. The proliferation of such writings became part of a newly emerging interest in accumulating knowledge in the name of "Broad Learning" (*pakhak* 博學), which extended the bounds of knowledge beyond the Confucian classics and antiquity to encompass contemporary topics and practical matters.[71]

The emergence of interest in compiling practical knowledge also extended to include knowledge of Korea, spurring scholars to investigate localities and identities.[72] *Tongyŏn po* 東硯譜 (Register of Eastern [Korean] Inkstones) followed the format of the registers of Chinese inkstones included in *Tanji congshu*, such as *Mantang mopin* 漫堂墨品 (The Classification of Ink by Mantang [Song Luo]) and *Yanlin* 硯林 (A Forest of Inkstones), but it aimed to produce a Korean counterpart. In a similar fashion, Yu Huai's record of courtesans in Nanjing, "Banqiao zaji," was followed by a record of courtesans in Pyŏngyang, a city known for its flamboyant courtesan culture in the Chosŏn dynasty. Korean writers' shift in focus to their own culture further resulted in the systematic assembly and organization of knowledge of the Korean peninsula. Following the format of Zhang Chao's compilations, for example, Pak Chi-wŏn launched a huge compilation of information on Korea around 1784. His *Samhan ch'ongsŏ* 三韓叢書 (Collectanea of Three Korean Kingdoms) sought to bring together the scattered records about Korea that were found in Chinese books. In collecting materials for his compilation, Pak Chi-wŏn not only read a wide range of imported Chinese books,[73] but also collaborated with members of his coterie who

70. Kim Yŏng-jin, "Chosŏn hugi sirhakp'a," 956.

71. Ibid., 957–58.

72. Kang Myŏng-gwan, *Chŏson sidae munhak yesul*, 271–72.

73. See Pak Chong-ch'ae, *Yŏkchu Kwajŏngnok*, 135–36, for an incomplete list of Chinese books that Pak Chi-wŏn referenced.

were familiar with imported Chinese books, including those who had been to Beijing as envoys.[74] Although the compilation remained incomplete, its claim for the need to accumulate knowledge about the indigenous culture would not have been motivated without the flow of large numbers of books imported from another culture.

In short, the reverberations from reading Zhang Chao's compilations were varied, ranging from experiments with new literary styles to the perusal of information about ordinary things and to the systematic organization of knowledge about the Korean Peninsula. The outcome reveals that, although the imported book itself remained a stable and immutable entity, the readings of Chosŏn readers were far from being dictated by the original context and made up but one phase of a larger field of textual interaction in which each reading and interpretation asserted discursive and social significance according to the Chosŏn intellectuals' needs at the time, particularly the growing interest in broadening the boundaries of scholarly knowledge. The elite's attempt to redefine what was deemed scholarly pursuit was increasingly at odds with King Chŏngjo's need to reaffirm moral and aesthetic principles that were derived from a strictly defined state orthodoxy—which led him to set off the extensive literary inquisition campaign beginning in 1792.

Censoring *Tanji congshu* as Evidential Research

The vigorous circulation of imported Chinese books among Chosŏn literati and the newly emerging literary and intellectual trends caught the attention of King Chŏngjo. He himself kept up with intellectual and cultural trends of the Qing by reading imported Chinese books, and he frequently asked envoys to look for books for his personal pleasure. He even asked the tribute missions to find a copy of the *Siku quanshu* as soon as he heard the news of its compilation.[75] At the same

74. The friends who helped Pak Chi-wŏn compile his work included literati such as Yi Tŏng-mu, Pak Che-ga, Yu Tŭk-kong, and Yi Sŏ-gu, who had visited Beijing as envoys and who were avid readers of the imported Chinese books. See ibid., 963.

75. Since only seven manuscript copies of *Siku quanshu* were produced, the envoys instead brought back another imperial compilation, *Gujin tushu jicheng* 古今圖書集成. Chŏngjo 1/2/24, in *Chŏngjo sillok*, in *Chosŏn wangjo sillok*.

time, however, he was aware of the growing popularity of reading Chinese books among Chosŏn literati and voiced concern about the reading boom: "When I see the books recently purchased in Beijing, there isn't a single book about practical matters like ritual, music, the art of war, law, finance, grain, weaponry, and so on. They are only vulgar, eccentric, trivial, and ludicrous, which only gratifies the momentary pleasure of reading!"[76]

Although King Chŏngjo had been uneasy about the literati's fascination with books imported from Qing, the literary inquisition itself was triggered by an event related to the spread of Catholicism in his kingdom. In 1785, the Ministry of Punishment (*Ch'ujo* 秋曹) discovered a group of elites discussing Catholic dogma and performing a Catholic service. Chŏngjo was appalled to hear of this, but since the elites involved were from the political sect known as the Southerners (*Namin* 南人), whom he depended on as his political allies, he played down the significance of the incident. He considered the attraction to Catholicism to be due to the introduction of the new books from Qing China, however, and issued orders prohibiting the importation of Chinese books in 1786 and 1787. Four years later, in 1791, a group of Catholics who spoke of the veneration of ancestors as idolatry burned their ancestral tablets. This act was considered one of the worst forms of treason, challenging as it did the fundamental Confucian rituals and social order based on ancestor worship. The furor that resulted led to the execution of two Catholics and the punishment of everyone associated with them.

As alarming as Chŏngjo found Catholicism to be, however, he regarded it as a mere symptom. For him, the root of the problem was to be found in the unorthodox ideas that were infiltrating Chosŏn from Qing China through books, and he identified these heterodox ideas not merely in Catholicism but also in fiction and literary collections of the late Ming and early Qing periods. He therefore asserted that "if you want to ban Western learning [Catholicism], then you must first go after storytellers' miscellanies [fiction] and ban them; if

76. "近看燕中新購之書, 如禮樂兵刑錢穀甲兵等, 有實用者, 一不概見, 只以鄙俚不經冗瑣可笑之事, 苟求一時之悅眼。" Chŏngjo, "Iltŭngnok" 日得錄, in *Hongjae chŏnsŏ*, reprint of Changsŏgak's manuscript, 162.22.

you want to ban storytellers' miscellanies, then you must first go after late Ming and early Qing literary collections and ban them."[77] How were these seemingly disparate entities—Catholicism, works of fiction, and late Ming and early Qing literary collections—connected? Why did King Chŏngjo identify late Ming and early Qing literary collections as the origin of "heterodox ideas"?

In fact, one does not know which late Ming and early Qing literary collections Chŏngjo was specifically targeting, as various, often contradictory literary and philosophical works of the late Ming and early Qing were being read by Chosŏn intellectuals at the time.[78] Ambiguous as it may sound, Chŏngjo identified the problem with the seventeenth-century literary collections in question as their writing style (*munch'e* 文體). Referring to this style as "casual short prose" (*sop'um*), Chŏngjo defined it as "eccentric," "superficial," and "uncouth," in that it was concerned only with discussing small and trivial matters far from the moral principles of the Confucian classics and sages:

> Recent scholars have gradually degenerated and their writing styles become more vulgar every day. Even when I take a look at their official documents, I find that they are written in the style of fictional accounts and casual short prose (*p'aegwan sop'um*). The literati all imitate and use the Confucian classics and their commentaries, but [merely] savoring the taste [of the classics] is of no use. [Their writings are] superficial and

---

77. "欲禁西洋之學, 先從稗官雜記, 禁之; 欲禁稗官雜記, 先從明末清初文集禁之。" Chŏngjo 15/10/24, in *Chŏngjo sillok*, in *Chosŏn wangjo sillok*.

78. The gap between the production of Chinese books and their reading by Chosŏn readers caused by the time lag of book importation enabled Chosŏn readers to encounter diachronic Chinese literary and intellectual development synchronically. Eighteenth-century Chosŏn readers were thus introduced to both seventeenth- and eighteenth-century Chinese books simultaneously, which presented apparently opposing literary and intellectual positions that had evolved gradually in the Chinese context. For example, they read the works of the Archaist school writers who imitated old models—specifically advocating the emulation of poetic models of the past—side by side with works of the Gong'an school (Gong'an pai 公安派) and the Jingling school (Jingling pai 竟陵派), which had emerged from strong opposition to the Archaist school. In addition, the Chosŏn intellectuals read the books of late Ming *Yangming xue* 陽明學 together with early Qing evidential research (*kaozheng xue* 考證學) that reacted against the metaphysical emphasis on the human mind in *Yangming xue*.

uncouth, lacking the literary style of the ancients; [they are also] sorrowful and frivolous, and do not have the voice proper to times of prosperity. This is not a trivial concern in terms of the ways of our age.

近來士趨漸下, 文風日卑。 雖以功令文字觀之, 稗官小品之體, 人皆做用經傳, 菽粟之味, 便歸弁髦。浮淺奇刻, 全無古人之體; 噍殺輕薄, 不似治世之聲, 有關世道, 實非細憂。[79]

At first, it may seem as if the so-called casual short prose is nothing but a writing style. However, talented youth with shallow knowledge tend to dislike the familiar and prefer the new. They competitively imitate [this casual short prose], unaware of being indulged in it as if obscene sounds and perverted countenance delude men's minds. The harm [casual short prose does] extends to criticize the sages, oppose the classics, despise order, and mislead meanings. Furthermore, one branch of casual short prose is the evidential research of names and things. This is a short step to heterodox scholarship [Western learning]. Thus I say that if we are to get rid of such heterodox scholarship, we must first rid [our kingdom] of this casual short prose.

所謂小品, 初不過文墨筆硯間事。年少識淺薄有才藝者, 厭常喜新, 爭相摸倣, 駸駸然如淫聲邪色之蠱人心術, 其弊至於非聖反經蔑倫悖義而後已。況小品一種, 則名物考證之學, 一轉而入於邪學。予故曰: 欲祛邪學, 宜先祛小品。[80]

According to Chŏngjo, the problem with writing style, or *munch'e*, was not merely an issue of the casual short prose style (*sop'um*) as opposed to the ancient-prose style (*komun*). Rather, it became an ideological position toward the classics—that is, for or against the Neo-Confucian orthodoxy that the state had legitimized. For instance, Chŏngjo argued that, in contrast to ancient prose, which was devoted to the explication of the meanings of the Confucian classics and the manifestation of moral principles, casual short prose tended to delve into mundane, trivial, or extraordinary subjects, and imbued them with excessive emotion and literary embellishment. As a consequence, the concerns of casual short prose were likely to stray from the orthodox understanding of the classics and to induce people to become attracted to

79. Chŏngjo 16/10/19, in *Chŏngjo sillok*, in *Chosŏn wangjo sillok*.
80. Chŏngjo, "Iltŭngnok," in *Kugyŏk Hongjae chŏnsŏ*, 16:76.

"heterodox scholarship," that is, Catholicism. In addition, casual short prose served as a pretext for writers who lacked skill in working within the model of classical prose to fill their works with encyclopedic and historical investigations of "errors in geography, names, and genealogy in the works of the ancients."[81] In effect, he asserted that, if the literati indulged themselves in reading texts such as late Ming and early Qing literary collections, they would stray from the sanctioned Neo-Confucian approach, thereby posing a threat to the ideological foundation of his regime.

In this narrowly redefined orthodoxy, anything different from Neo-Confucianism was labeled an "aberrant form of literature," a catchall that included not only Catholicism but the newly emerged branches of Confucianism in late Ming and early Qing, such as the Yangming school (*Yangming xue* 陽明學) and evidential scholarship (*kaozheng xue* 考證學).[82] In fact, whereas the Chosŏn literati generally railed against the Yangming school, the works of early evidential scholars were widely read before the literary inquisition, and scholars did not perceive these works to be in serious opposition to the Neo-Confucian orthodoxy. Chŏngjo himself initially praised the scholarship of early Qing evidential scholars such as Gu Yanwu 顧炎武 (1613–82) and Mao Qiling 毛奇齡 (1623–1713) for its extensive and thorough use of textual evidence in historical investigation.[83] But when the Chŏngjo's literary inquisition labeled any approach to the Confucian classics other than Neo-Confucianism as "derailment of orthodox scholarship," this heralded his rejection of evidential scholarship.

Although the literary collections of the late Ming and early Qing periods were criticized as a category at large, King Chŏngjo singled out Zhang Chao's *Tanji congshu* as a typical example of evidential scholarship.[84] As noted at the beginning of this chapter, Chŏngjo himself had earlier been drawn to *Tanji congshu*'s broad inclusion of topics and eager to import it from Qing China. During his literary inquisition, however,

81. Ibid., 16:58.
82. Chŏngjo 11/11/8, in *Sŭngjŏngwŏn ilgi*.
83. An Se-hyŏn, "Munch'e panchŏng," 146–47.
84. Chŏngjo, "Ch'aengmun," in *Hongjae chŏnsŏ*, reprint of Changsŏgak's manuscript, 50.46b–47a.

he censured not only *Tanji congshu* but also a number of works by members of Zhang Chao's coterie from which his compilations excerpted, such as Niu Xiu's *Gusheng* and Zhou Lianggong's *Yinshuwu shuying*, insisting that their selections were too loose and cursory.[85] This remark was in the same vein as the high official and scholar Sŏ Hyŏng-su's 徐瀅修 (1749–1824) criticism of *Tanji congshu* and *Zhaodai congshu*. Sŏ commented that the inferiority of such compilations as *Tanji congshu* and *Zhaodai congshu* derived from their inclusion of works pertinent to trivial (*yŏngnyŏng swaeswae* 零零瑣瑣) and superfluous (*puch'we hyŏnu* 付贅懸疣) matters.[86] In other words, King Chŏngjo held *Tanji congshu* up as an example of the extent to which evidential research had fallen into meaningless erudition by focusing on superfluous knowledge.

Whether *Tanji congshu* can be categorized as a book of evidential research is, however, a matter of contention. Not only did Zhang Chao and his coterie reveal no particular intellectual orientation in compiling the book, but the eighteenth-century Qing compilers of *Siku quanshu* also commented that the frivolity of the pieces selected for *Tanji congshu* disqualified it as evidential research. In addition to disparaging playful and light perusal as superficiality,[87] they denigrated the selected scholarly treatises, stating that they did not evince the careful discernment characteristic of the rigorous standard of evidential research. For example, the compilers of the *Siku quanshu* reprimanded the early Qing classicist Yan Ruoqu's 閻若璩 (1638–1704) "Mengzi kao"

85. Ibid.
86. Sŏ Hyŏng-su, "Tap Sŏng Misŏ Taejung" 答成秘書大中, in *Myŏnggo chŏnjip*, *juan* 5, 261.
87. Rejecting any justification for the playful nature of *xiaopin*, the comments on *Tanji congshu* by the compilers of *Siku quanshu* focused on the frivolity of the pieces selected. The commentators picked out two examples, "Daishi" 黛史 (A History of Women's Cosmetics) and "Xiaoxing pu" 小星譜 (A Manual on How to Treat Concubines), and criticized them as too demeaning for works of the literati. In addition, they also cited the example of "Yuanyang die" 鴛鴦牒 (Certificate of Couples), an imaginary match-making between historical celebrities and emperors and empresses, and condemned its immoral, ludicrous treatment of historically respected figures and royalty. Their scorn even led them to cry out: "This piece should be burned; how could paper be soiled by such writing!" 其書可燒, 奈何以穢簡牘也! Yong Long et al., *Siku quanshu zongmu*, 1:1140.

孟子考 (Investigation of the Chronology of Mencius) because it used evidence from miscellaneous works in contrast to previous sages who had relied on the classics alone.[88] Their strict rule for proper use of evidence is also clear in their reading of Wu Shouyi's 吳守一 "Chunqiu rishi zhiyi" 春秋日食質疑 (Query on Solar Eclipses in the *Spring and Autumn Annals*) in *Zhaodai congshu*, in which they found a number of errors. Addressing and correcting each error scrupulously, the compilers stated: "Although this book calculates the date one thousand years after the fact, it ought to seek to have the fewest errors. [But this book] does not show enough meticulousness."[89]

Thus, though both the Qing compilers of *Siku quanshu* and King Chŏngjo were critical toward *Tanji congshu*, their positions were completely opposite: the compilers considered *Tanji congshu* as failing to meet the standards of evidential research, whereas the king perceived it as a typical example of evidential research. Despite different understandings of *Tanji congshu* derived from their differences in focus—the lack of methodological rigor for the Qing compilers versus the inappropriate boundaries of research for Chŏngjo—the radically different perception of evidential research itself reveals how much its definition was overshadowed by the political agenda that each monarch emphasized. In contrast to Qing censorship, which attempted to establish official sanction for evidential research against Song learning,[90] Chŏngjo's seemingly parochial definition of "evidential scholarship" was driven by his ideological need to resist expanding the boundaries of knowledge beyond those of the Neo-Confucian model that undergirded his regime.

The emphasis of Chŏngjo's literary inquisition was not primarily on suppressing the unorthodox ideas conveyed by the imported Chinese books, however. Previously, the typical pattern of censorship involved implementing a strict ban on the books in question and punishing the relevant parties. For example, Chŏngjo's father, King Yŏngjo 英祖

---

88. Ibid., 1:534. The censors also criticized Yan Ruoqu's other work "Mao Zhu shishuo" 毛朱詩說, selected in *ZDCS*, on the grounds that it contains "a number of arguments out of context without evidence" 多懸揣臆斷之詞. Ibid., 1:146.

89. "生數千載之後, 必欲求歲差於秒忽之間, 亦未見其悉得." Ibid., 1:262.

90. Guy, *Emperor's Four Treasuries*, 38–66, 121–56.

(r. 1724–1776), discovered passages that denigrated the genealogy of the founder of the Chosŏn dynasty in a book imported from China, *Mingji jilüe* 明紀輯略 (Abbreviation of Ming Annals), in 1771. The harsh censorship was not limited to destruction of the book itself but extended to the execution and demotion to the status of slaves of all individuals who imported, owned, or sold the book. In contrast, Chŏngjo was little concerned with eradicating the problematic books. Although he issued two orders prohibiting the importation of Chinese books, in 1791 and again 1794, he acknowledged that removing copies from the possession of individuals would merely cause commotion to no avail.[91] He did not find the complete banning of Chinese books possible or likely to be effective in correcting the problem he identified, because the problem did not lie in certain ideas and books but in the active venues of circulation among the elite literati through which they shared books, ideas, and knowledge that were increasingly uncontrollable by the state.

Instead of thorough suppression of the problematic Chinese books, therefore, King Chŏngjo's literary inquisition was a public performance that was meant to serve as a warning, mainly targeting the elites and attempting to confine their reading and writing to the redrawn boundary of state-sanctioned orthodoxy. In 1792 he singled out the works of two scholars, Nam Kong-ch'ŏl 南公轍 (1760–1840) and Yi Ok (1760–1813), criticizing a memorial of Nam's and an examination paper of Yi's for including phrases and expressions that were often used in late Ming and early Qing literary collections. He ordered the high official Nam Kong-ch'ŏl to make a confession and prohibited the national academy student Yi Ok from applying for the civil service examinations. Several renowned writers and officials of the time, including Yi Sang-hwang, Kim Cho-sun, Sim Sang-kyu 沈象奎 (1766–1838), and Yi Tŏng-mu, were subsequently apprehended on charges of writing "aberrant forms of literature" and ordered to write confessions. These confessions were publicized in the court gazettes (*chopo* 朝報) as examples of how their corrupt literary style could be rectified.[92] Beginning in 1792, King Chŏngjo also publicly disseminated the officially

---

91. Chŏngjo 19/7/25, in *Chŏngjo sillok*, in *Chosŏn wangjo sillok*.

92. Chŏngjo 16/10/24, Chŏngjo 16/11/3, Chŏngjo 16/11/8, in ibid. For the details of each individual case, see Pak Kyun-sŏp, "Munch'e panch'ŏng tokpŏp."

sanctioned writing style by publishing collections of works of royal scholars trained at Kyujanggak (*ch'ogye munsin* 抄啓文臣), the Royal Library.[93] Compared to the draconian punishments in previous censorship campaigns, these efforts of Chŏngjo in rectifying the writings of the literati were relatively mild: the literati targeted by his literary inquisition were not punished but required to submit a confession, and most of them later resumed their official positions.[94] Since his literary inquisition was aimed not at certain particular targets but at discouraging the private venues of communication among the literati community at large, its focus lay on reinstating the old model of state-dominated communication by singling out some leading writers and punishing them as an example.

Epilogue: The Unabated Elite Channel of Communication

Zhang Chao's imprints figured not only at the beginning but also at the end of King Chŏngjo's literary inquisition. In 1793, during the literary inquisition, King Chŏngjo pointed to Pak Chi-wŏn's work as the main example of a degenerated literary style. Pak Chi-wŏn was one of the most popular and influential writers in the eighteenth century, and his record of traveling to Beijing as a member of a tribute mission, titled *Yŏrha ilgi* 熱河日記 (The Diary of Travel to Jehol), exerted a deep influence on the literati community in various ways. Keenly aware of this book's popularity, King Chŏngjo asked the high official Nam Kong-ch'ŏl, whom he had earlier reproached for writing in a style influenced by imported Chinese books, to ask Pak Chi-wŏn to submit a confession in a "pure and proper style" (*sunjŏng chi mun* 純正之文).[95]

The rectification of writing by Chŏngjo was prescribed, but it was not implemented as intended because the literati received and interpreted his order based on their private networks of communication.

---

93. Chŏng Ok-cha, "Chŏngjo ŭi ch'ogye munsin kyoyuk."

94. Nam Kong-ch'ŏl, Yi Sang-hwang, and Sim Sang-kyu all became prime minster later in their careers.

95. Pak Chi-wŏn, "Wŏnsŏ pu" 原書附, in *Kugyŏk Yŏnam chip*, 1:135–37.

Nam Kong-ch'ŏl himself attempted to give Pak Chi-wŏn some leeway when it came to King Chŏngjo's order by adding his own opinions about the king's instruction. At the end of the letter in which he conveys Chŏngjo's order, he sympathizes with Pak Chi-wŏn and advises him to take some time in writing his confession: "The order is bitter and difficult [to follow]. It would be good to submit one or two volumes of writing to criticize the literature of Ming and Qing. Or a couple of or three or four volumes of records of landscapes in Yŏngnam province [where Pak Chi-wŏn was living at that time] in the pure and proper manner would be good."[96] By creating works that were in keeping with Chŏngjo's criticism of late Ming and early Qing literary styles or landscape writings that were supposedly apolitical, Nam Kong-ch'ŏl implied that Pak Chi-wŏn could avoid the king's furor and immediate official censure.

Pak Chi-wŏn's response did not conform completely to Chŏngjo's instructions. Although his reply to the king shows his intention to subject himself to the royal order in a most polite and respectful manner,[97] it appears that Pak Chi-wŏn did not submit his writings immediately,[98] because in 1797, when he finally met King Chŏngjo in person to accept appointment as a county magistrate in Ch'ungch'ŏng province 忠清道, Chŏngjo asked him whether or not he had changed his writing style. At the time, Chŏngjo was concerned with recording the itinerary of a certain Yi Pang-ik 李邦翼, a commoner who had drifted from the Korean island of Cheju to Qing China, and he asked Pak Chi-wŏn to reorganize it using a "proper" writing style.

In "Sŏ Yi Pang-ik sa" 書李邦翼事 (Record of the Shipwreck of Yi Pang-ik), written in response to the order of the king,[99] Pak Chi-wŏn used a structure of double account: each part of Yi Pang-ik's oral testi-

96. "命題苦不易。以排斥明清學, 作一二卷文字, 上送為好耶。不然則南中山水記一二卷, 或三四卷, 醇正著出好耶。" Ibid., 1:47.

97. Pak Chi-wŏn, "Tap Nam Chikgak Kong-ch'ŏl sŏ" 答南直閣公撤書, in *Kugyŏk Yŏnam chip*, 1:132–35.

98. Pak Chong-ch'ae, *Yŏkchu Kwajŏngnok*, 135–36. Apparently, this was not an option for literati who had a lower social status than Pak Chi-wŏn. For example, Yi Tŏng-mu's son Yi Kwang-kyu 李光葵 (b. 1795) recorded that the death of his father, the renowned writer of the status of illegitimate sons (*sŏŏl* 庶孽), was caused by anxiety over Chŏngjo's order to submit a confession in 1792. See his "Sŏngo pukŭn yusa" 先考府君遺事, in *Kugyŏk Ch'ŏngjanggwan chŏnsŏ*, 4:236–37.

99. Pak Chi-wŏn, "Sŏ Yi Pang-ik sa," in *Kugyŏk Yŏnam chip*, 2:117–42.

mony was followed by his comment beginning with "nota bene" (*ansŏl* 按說), in which Pak Chi-wŏn presented his verification of the information contained in the testimony. His thorough investigation of the information in the oral testimony, which included a detailed examination of Qing cities, buildings, and geography, was all supported by textual evidence, which reveals the wide knowledge of Qing China that Pak Chi-wŏn must have acquired from reading a number of imported Chinese books.[100] In fact, when Pak Chi-wŏn was ordered to complete this text, he sent several letters to members of his coterie, including Pak Che-ga and Yu Tŭk-kong, asking them to search the Chinese books in their possession not only for historical evidence but also for models of the writing style he sought. He specifically asked their opinion, noting in the letter that "the writing style ought to be like 'Xu Xiake zhuan' 徐霞客傳 [in *Yu Chu xinzhi*] and 'Feng Changbai shan ji' 封長白山記 [in *Zhaodai congshu*], and I wonder what you think."[101]

It is hard to ascertain whether King Chŏngjo was satisfied with Pak Chi-wŏn's work because he died in 1800, most likely before receiving it. But this episode reveals that the intention of the literary inquisition was not fully realized, for Pak Chi-wŏn not only made use of the common writing style of evidential research in verifying information, which King Chŏngjo detested during his literary inquisition, but also consulted a number of Chinese books that the literary inquisition had problematized, including books of Zhang Chao such as *Yu Chu xinzhi* and *Zhaodai congshu*. In spite of Chŏngjo's campaign, therefore, Pak Chi-wŏn's letters demonstrate that the circulation of imported Chinese books was far from dying out and that they were still easily accessible via his elite network—the private circuit of transmission over which King Chŏngjo had attempted to regain control in his literary inquisition by reasserting that the essential function of writing was only to serve the orthodoxy of the state.

---

100. Kim Mun-sik, "Sŏ Yi Pang-ik sa," 214–18.

101. "文體似當如霞客傳、長白山記，未知如何。" Chŏng Min and Pak Ch'ŏl-sang, "Yonam sŏnsaeng sŏgan ch'ŏp," 381. See also Pak Chi-wŏn's letters to his coterie in *Koch'ujang chagŭn tanji rŭl ponaeni*, 79, 82. Since both "Xu Xiake zhuan" and "Feng Changbai shan ji" were travel records, Pak Chi-wŏn must have thought that they would be the proper works for his "Sŏ Yi Pang-ik sa," a testimony of the travel from Qing to Chosŏn, to be modeled on.

CONCLUSION

Publishing and the Making of Textual Authority

A pressing concern for scholars of Chinese print culture is that the generally understood universal effects of print be reassessed in the specific Chinese context. By shifting the view of the popularity of print from an involuntary outcome of technological ascendancy to the deliberate choice of appropriation, this book has given due weight to the role of writers as active agents in shaping the significance of print. It has examined the ways in which the literati's appropriation of the increasingly dominant material presence and growing social force of print reshaped their textual production and circulation in the seventeenth century and also followed that appropriation's ramifications into the eighteenth century. The investigation of writers' publishing practices has underscored the contingent nature of print's effects, shedding light on the inextricable enmeshment of print with the traditional medium of the manuscript, with peer patronage, and with the socially embedded gift economy that had been sustained by the cohesive literati community. In other words, seventeenth-century writers' appropriation of the print medium reveals their concerted efforts to seek the prestige attached to the exclusive and privileged manuscript culture of elite coteries in combination with the contemporary publicity, market value, and widespread cultural influence provided by print in the rapidly expanding book market.

In a sense, the publishing practice of Zhang Chao and Wang Zhuo resembles modern academic publishing. They relied on the deep-seated belief that a writer's standing was determined by the recognition that resulted from vetting by his peers. At the outset, therefore, the publishing practice of Zhang Chao and Wang Zhuo was geared toward attaining recognition for their texts from their peer community because they construed peer recognition to be more important than popularity with anonymous readers in the commercial book market. Wang Zhuo once commented on the centrality of peer evaluation to establish the reputation of a book:

> The publisher clearly knows the lack of ability of the writer but puts on false embellishments to invite profit and seek fame. He thinks that he can publish it, but learned men already scorn this practice. If more and more people come to scorn the practice, such books will not be able to circulate in present times. How could one thus expect them to be transmitted forever?
>
> 明知其人之不能, 必多方假飾, 為邀利弋名之計。彼方自以為得而識者早已鄙之, 鄙之者衆, 其書終不克行于當時。安望其千古哉?[1]

In order to gain the endorsement of "learned men" who deemed a book worthy of being printed and widely disseminated, Zhang Chao and Wang Zhuo relied heavily on the long-standing convention of the manuscript culture that garnered peer patronage: Zhang Chao tightly controlled the production and circulation of his printed text within selective literati circles, and Wang Zhuo not only foregrounded peer endorsement in the form of paratextual materials external to the text but also embedded such endorsement as an inlay in the narrative structure. Rather than using the indiscriminate power of print to create an egalitarian community, the power that is so celebrated by the modern discourse of the printing revolution, Zhang Chao and Wang Zhuo instead employed print as a medium of distinction, competitively distinguishing themselves and their close coterie from other literati groups as well as from readers at large served by the commercial book market.

At the same time, however, the publishing practice of Zhang Chao and Wang Zhuo also demonstrates that contemporary publicity, wide dissemination, and high market value became important because

---

1. Wang Zhuo, "Yu Wu Meiji" 與吳枚吉, in *Chidu oucun* 2.9b, in *Xiaju tang ji*, reprinted in *Qingdai shiwen ji huibian*, 144:188.

they could and did supplement the increasingly weakening authority of peer patronage in establishing textual authority. The diversification and stratification of the literati community by the social, economic, and political transformation of late imperial China unsettled the cohesion of literati groups and challenged the consensus notion of literary worth, which was supposed to yield immortality in the due course of time. Unlike earlier writers, therefore, seventeenth-century writers increasingly felt that a work's merit could not bring them the recognition that they deserved, whereas publishing could.[2] Without the contemporary recognition that print could deliver, that is, their works would not even have the opportunity to be properly evaluated. Jiang Zhilan, a seventeenth-century writer and medical practitioner from Huizhou, therefore, refused to wait for his work to be recognized after his death. Instead he sought recognition while he was alive, declaring: "I do not want to hide [my works] silently away on a famous mountain; I desire to pass them on to someone [who will publish them]!"[3] This sentiment contrasts starkly with that expressed in the Grand Historian Sima Qian's 司馬遷 (ca. 145–86 BCE) most often-quoted phrase, "hiding away books on a famous mountain," until their worth would be eventually recognized.[4] The optimistic belief in the seamless conjunction between merit and recognition expressed in Sima Qian's dictum was not convincing to seventeenth-century writers, who had become skeptical about merit as ensuring recognition in the absence of publishing.

2. For example, the Hangzhou writer Chai Shitang remarked, "If there is indeed no one who recognizes the worth [of the work], the work will not be transmitted despite its beauty; if the book is not commended [in print], it will not be celebrated despite its excellence" 誠以人無賞識, 雖美勿傳; 書之表章, 有佳不顯也. *CDYS* 15.15b.

3. "故不欲默默藏之名山, 欲傳之其人耳。" *CDYS* 10.32a.

4. "藏之名山。" Sima Qian, *Shiji*, 10:3320. With this famous phrase, writers often comforted themselves that their work would be acknowledged, provided it deserved recognition. For example, one of the most controversial thinkers and popular writers of the sixteenth century, Li Zhi, alluded to this phrase as the reason for naming his book *Cangshu* 藏書 (A Book to Keep Hidden), thereby ensuring that his work would eventually receive the proper reception: "So I intended to hide it. I meant for it to be hidden in a mountain to await someone of a later generation, a Ziyun 子雲 [who recognizes its value] to come" 故欲藏之, 言當藏於山中以待後世子雲也. Li Zhi, "Zixu," in *Fenshu Xu Fenshu*, 1. Handler-Spitz's translation in Handler-Spitz, Lee, and Saussy, *Book to Burn*, 4.

The production and circulation of *Tanji congshu* and *Zhaodai congshu* by Zhang Chao and Wang Zhuo illustrate the cooptation of the contested relationship between merit and recognition by the expanding presence of the book market: Zhang Chao and Wang Zhuo believed that, as long as they produced a high-quality text vetted by peer recognition, it would garner fame, broad market appeal, and commercial success. Although their involvement with the commercial book market was premised on the notion that high market value was a by-product of peer acknowledgment, a belief in the reverse causality also emerged at the same time—that is, books with a high market value came to be deemed highly valued books. For example, Jiang Zhilan contended that commercial success was clear evidence of the merit of a book. In defense of his open pursuit of money in the commercial market, he remarked:

> In the past, people said that fine writing makes a clanking sound [like that of a metal musical instrument] when it is cast to the ground. I would say that if the clanking sound just indicates the fine quality of the work, the writing is not particularly worthwhile; but, if the clanking sound indicates real gold, then the writing is indeed worthwhile. Alas, when will our writing be "golden writing" in the sense of real gold!
> 昔人謂文章擲地, 當作金聲。蘭謂: 若作金聲玉振之金字, 殊不足貴; 惟作金銀之金, 方可貴耳。嗟乎! 吾儕筆墨, 何日可作金銀之金也! [5]

Jiang Zhilan here takes a well-known phrase from *Shishuo xinyu*, "making a clanking sound when it is cast to the ground" (*zhidi jinsheng* 擲地金聲)—which originally praised well-rhymed poetry that sounded almost like music—but, playing on the homonyms of the character *jin* 金—signifying both a "metal" musical instrument and "gold" in monetary currency—he makes the point that a fine work is expected to earn commercial success. In this way, Jiang Zhilan justifies his involvement in the commercial book market based on the idea that a work's literary worth is demonstrated by how well it sells. The commercial value of the book thus emerged as an

5. *CDYS* 8.29b.

alternative to the doubtful efficacy of coterie patronage in establishing textual value.

The intricate interplay between peer patronage and market value in shaping textual authority in the seventeenth century was at odds with the eighteenth-century state's attempt to reinstate its authority in determining textual value. Although the censorship campaigns of the Qianlong emperor and King Chŏngjo were engineered by different political agendas, both attempted to reaffirm imperial power as the only legitimate grantor of textual authority—not the literati community, the commercial book market, or a combination of the two. The eighteenth-century censorship campaigns thus exemplified the increasing tension and competition among the literati community, the commercial book market, and political authority in determining what made a piece of writing deserving of publication. The publishing practices of writers and their reverberations clearly reveal the ways in which the impact of print manifested in far-reaching contests over the relationship among reputation, commercial success, and imperial endorsement in shaping textual authority in the rapidly changing social, economic, and political conditions of late imperial China.

APPENDIX

Bibliographical Notes on Extant Editions of Zhang Chao

The editions recorded in this appendix are original editions of Zhang Chao or reprints of original editions, printed mostly from the Kangxi (1662–1722) to Qianlong (1736–95) periods, that I personally examined. I use traditional Chinese bibliographical terms to describe the physical characteristics of the editions. For example, I keep the original Chinese term *juan* 卷, a standard bibliometric unit in traditional China, which designates either a fascicle in the physical volume (*ce* 冊) or a chapter as a content division (*zhang* 章 or *hui* 回), and so can range in length from a just a handful to hundreds of pages.[1]

Zhang Chao published more than forty titles,[2] but, since most of them have disappeared over time, the extant titles number only nineteen. Besides his own writings and anthologies that collect his contemporaries' works, Zhang Chao also printed the works of his late father and collections by friends. The following bibliographical notes on the nineteen extant titles are accordingly divided into two categories: extant writings by Zhang Chao and anthologies he collected and published (fourteen in total, some in several editions); and other writers'

---

1. For a detailed explanation of traditional Chinese bibliographical terms and their English translations, see Edgren, *Chinese Rare Books*, 15; and Chia, *Printing for Profit*, 43.

2. Zhang Yi's postface, in Zhang Chao, *Yu Chu xinzhi*, 1760 reprint edition in the National Taiwan University Library.

works published by Zhang Chao (two works by his father plus three other collections, for a total of five).[3]

Extant Writings by Zhang Chao and Anthologies He Collected and Published

1. *JIULÜ* 酒律 AND *XIAJIU WU* 下酒物 (1677)

Jiulü and *Xiajiu wu* are a joint publication of some of Zhang Chao's early writings. They belong to the genre of drinking games and word-play that the literati of the time played at their gatherings and drinking parties. *Jiulü* was later reprinted in the first collection of *Tanji congshu*. The date of *Jiulü* is not known, but it must be one of Zhang Chao's early imprints, since his preface is dated 1677.[4] According to the cover page of the copy in the National Library of China, this work was initially designed to be a joint publication of *Xiajiu wu*, *Jiulü*, and *Tangshi jiudi* 唐詩酒底, but there is no extant joint publication of all three. Only joint publications of *Jiulü* and *Xiajiu wu*, and also of *Jiulü* and *Tangshi jiudi* (see no. 2), survive.

Jiulü, one *juan*; *Xiajiu wu*, two *juan*. Seven lines, sixteen characters; white fore edge (*baikou* 白口); single borderline (*danbian* 單邊); 13.9 × 10.6 cm. Prefaces by Gu Cai 顧彩 and an unidentified man; a short preface (*xiaoyin* 小引) by Zuixiang zhuren 醉鄉主人 (i.e., Zhang Chao) dated 1677; and the table of contents are attached. *Xiajiu wu* is signed "The gentleman in retirement Zhang Shanlai edited" (*Xinzhai jushi Zhang Shanlai ji* 心齋居士張山來輯), and *Jiulü* is signed "Master of Intoxication, [illegible character] Shuiyue from Qinghe collated" (*Zuixiang zhuren Qinghe [illegible character] Shuiyue ding* 醉鄉主人清

---

3. A considerable number of Zhang Chao's works, particularly his poems, appeared in the anthologies that his contemporaries compiled. For a list of collections that selected Zhang Chao's poems, see Liu Hewen, "Zhang Chao zhushu zongkao."

4. *Jiulü* might not have been printed in 1677, but it must have been printed by 1682 at the latest because its preface is included in *Xinzhai liaofu ji*, published in 1682.

河□水月定). Available in the National Library of China and the Harvard-Yenching Library.[5]

2. *JIULÜ* 酒律 AND *TANGSHI JIUDI* 唐詩酒底

Jiulü and *Tangshi jiudi* are a joint publication of Zhang Chao's drinking games. Since *Jiulü* is also in the joint collection of *Jiulü* and *Xiajiu wu* (see no. 1), it is not certain whether it was originally conceived as part of the joint collection or as a separate work that later became part of a joint collection along with either *Xiajiu wu* or *Tangshi jiudi*.

Tangshi jiudi is a collection of verses of Tang poetry that are classified into groups, such as "beauty," "spring," "lantern," "fallen flowers," "the Vega festival," "apricot tree," "wind," "the setting sun," and "oriole." It is also a kind of drinking game, and the last page records the rules of the game. Unfortunately, there is no record or preface indicating the date the work was printed.

Jiulü, one *juan*; *Tangshi jiudi*, two *juan*. Seven lines, sixteen characters; white fore edge; single borderline; "Xinzhai" 心齋 below the center-fold (*banxin* 版心); 13.9 × 10.6 cm. The first four pages are missing. *Tangshi jiudi* is signed "The gentleman in retirement Zhang Shanlai edited" (*Xinzhai jushi Zhang Shanlai ji* 心齋居士張山來輯), and a preface by an unidentified man is attached. Available in the Shanghai Library.

3. *XINZHAI LIAOFU JI* 心齋聊復集 (1682)

Xinzhai liaofu ji is a collection of Zhang Chao's early writings, including a variety of genres such as rhapsody, preface, biography, critical essay, letter, manifesto, memorial, postscript, explanation, record, debate, account of origins (*yuanqi* 緣起), eulogy, funeral oration, and epitaph.[6] Although the preface by Wu Qi 吳綺 is dated 1682, it is not certain whether it was first printed in 1682 because it contains not only

5. The Harvard-Yenching Library copy is the same as the one in the National Library of China except that it does not have the preface by the unidentified man and the last page of *Xiajiu wu*.

6. *CDOC* 3.19b.

memorials written in 1683 and 1684,[7] but also a eulogy for the Kangxi emperor's southern tour that began in 1689.[8] It is difficult to determine the exact date of publication, but I surmise two possibilities: (1) given that the two extant copies show a difference in the number of comments attached, it was first printed in 1682 and then reprinted later with additional writings; or (2) although the book was completed and the preface was received in 1682, it was eventually printed sometime after 1689, that is, when all the writings and comments were gathered. Deng Changfeng supposes that it was printed around 1684, but he does not provide any evidence to support the argument.[9]

One *juan*, four volumes (*ce* 冊). Eight lines, eighteen characters; white fore edge; single borderline; single fishtail (*yuwei* 魚尾); "Yiqing-tang" 詒清堂 below the centerfold; 18.1 × 13.2 cm. The preface by Wu Qi dated 1682 and the table of contents are attached. The book title on the cover page is different from edition to edition.[10] Available in the Beijing Normal University Library, the Fudan University Library, and the Naikaku Bunko 內閣文庫 in Japan. The Fudan University Library copy is reprinted in *Siku jinhuishu congkan bubian* 四庫禁燬書叢刊補編, vol. 85, and *Qingdai shiwen ji huibian* 清代詩文集彙編, vol. 177.

7. *Xinzhai liaofu ji* 53a, 57a, 62a, 71a, 73a. Beijing Normal University Library edition.

8. See "Nanxun song" 南巡頌, in *Xinzhai liaofu ji* 115a–117a. Beijing Normal University Library edition.

9. Deng Changfeng, "*Yu Chu xinzhi* de banke yu Zhang Chao de shengping," in *Ming Qing xiqujia kaolüe xubian*, 169.

10. The Fudan University Library copy has a cover page that says "Zhang Shanlai from Huizhou wrote" 新安張山來著, "*Xinzhai liaofu ji*" 心齋聊復集, "the second collection of the poetry collection will follow" (*erji shiji sichu* 二集詩集嗣出), and "retention of the blocks of Yiqing tang" (*Yiqing tang cangban* 詒清堂藏板). In contrast, the Princeton University Library Hishi Collection copy, which is a photo-reprint copy of the Naikaku Bunko edition, has a cover page titled "*Xinzhai liaofu ji, First Collection*" (*Xinzhai liaofu ji chuji* 心齋聊復集初集). When I visited Naikaku Bunko in June 2009, the edition there did not have a cover page. My guess is that the edition in the Naikaku Bunko originally did have a cover page but that the recent binding may have inadvertently omitted the cover page (and the preface by Wu Qi). Because the Hishi Collection in the Princeton University Library was made in the late 1960s or early 1970s, it apparently preserves the original condition of the book including the pages that the current Naikaku Bunko copy does not contain.

4. *XINZHAI ZAZU* 心齋雜俎 (KANGXI REIGN)

Xinzhai zazu is a collection of Zhang Chao's twenty miscellaneous writings. Among them, "Shu bencao" 書本草, "Pingua" 貧卦, "Huaniao chunqiu" 花鳥春秋, "Bu huadi shiyi" 補花底拾遺, "Wanyue yue" 玩月約, and "Yinzhong baxian ling" 飲中八仙令 are also included in the extra collection of *Tanji congshu* (see no. 7). The exact date of *Xinzhai zazu* cannot be determined, but it appears to be one of the early imprints of Zhang Chao because it is often mentioned with other early imprints, such as *Xinzhai liaofu ji* and *Xiajiu wu*, in the letters of Zhang Chao's friends.[11] Considering the avoidance of taboo characters (*bihui* 避諱), the extant copies seem to have been printed in the Kangxi reign.

Two *juan*. Eight lines, eighteen characters; white fore edge; single borderline; single fishtail; "Yiqing tang" below the centerfold; 18.4 × 13.3 cm. Prefaces by Wu Sugong 吳肅公, Min Yiwei 閔奕位, Yin Shu 殷曙, and Zhang Zong 張熜; and the table of contents are attached at the front of the first *juan*. Available in the National Library of China, the Beijing University Library, and the Shanghai Library.[12]

5. *YU CHU XINZHI* 虞初新志 (1684–1704)

Yu Chu xinzhi is a collection of classical short tales. The original edition published by Zhang Chao himself does not survive; only reprint editions are extant. It is difficult to track down the genealogies of the extant editions because the censorship campaign during the Qianlong reign expurgated the editions; as a result, the included works vary depending on the edition.[13] The extant reprint editions of *Yu Chu xinzhi* are generally divided into three groups.[14]

11. See, for example, *CDYS* 10.32a.
12. The order of the prefaces is different in different copies. The National Library of China copy has an impaired postscript written in cursive style at the end, whereas the Shanghai Library copy does not have Zhang Zong's preface.
13. See chapter 4 for a detailed explanation of the censorship of *Yu Chu xinzhi*.
14. I find Kim Yŏng-jin's detailed bibliographical study of the reprint editions that are available in Korean and Taiwan universities by far the most useful research for the textual history of *Yu Chu xinzhi*. See Kim Yŏng-jin, "*U Ch'o sinji*," 203–32.

5.1a. Reprint edition by Zhang Yi 張繹 in 1760

Twenty *juan*. Nine lines, twenty characters; white fore edge; single fishtail; "Yiqing tang" below the centerfold; 11 × 8.2 cm. Preface by Zhang Chao dated 1683; the table of contents, indicating the source of each work; and the postscript by Zhang Yi, Zhang Chao's grand-nephew, are attached. This edition is titled *Yu Chu xinzhi*, and phrases such as "reprint in sleeve edition" (*chongkan xiuzhen* 重刊袖珍), "sold by Guhuan lou in Dingjia Bay in Yangzhou" (*Yangzhou Dingjia wan Guhuan lou fadui* 揚州丁家灣古歡樓發兌), and "pirates must be prosecuted even if from 1,000 *li* away" (*fanke qianli bijiu* 翻刻千里必究) are written on the lower left side, whereas the phrase "retention of the blocks of Yiqing tang" (*Yiqing tang cangban* 詒清堂藏板) appears on the right side. Available in the National Library of China, the Taiwan University Library, and the University of Tokyo Library.[15]

5.1b. Reprint of the edition by Zhang Yi of 1760, after the censorship in 1769

All the physical characteristics of this edition are the same as of the original 1760 edition, but this edition reveals traces of the censorship by the Qianlong emperor: (1) in the table of contents, the titles of Qian Qianyi's 錢謙益 two works "Xu Xiake zhuan" 徐霞客傳 and "Shu Zheng Yangtian shi" 書鄭仰田事 are blacked out; (2) although the text of "Xu Xiake zhuan" has been removed from the actual volume, depending on the edition, the text of "Shu Zheng Yangtian shi" is either omitted from or kept in the volume;[16] and (3) with the removal of "Xu Xiake zhuan," the second text in the volume, "Da tiechui zhuan" 大鐵椎傳 is now first, and its centerfold is carved with the characters "from [pages] 1 to 6" 一至六. It seems that, since "Xu Xiake zhuan" originally ranged from pages 1 to 5 in the edition, when it was removed, the later printing therefore added "from 1 to" 一至 right

15. The University of Tokyo Library copy has no warning of prosecution of an illegal reprint.
16. The National Library of China edition omits "Shu Zheng Yangtian shi" in the actual volume, whereas the Ewha Womans University Library edition retains it.

before the original character for "page 6" 六 on the first page of "Da tiechui zhuan."[17] Available in the National Library of China and the Ewha Womans University Library in Korea.[18]

5.2. Luo Shunzhang's 羅舜章 reprint edition after the censorship of 1769

Twenty *juan*. Nine lines, twenty characters; white fore edge; single fishtail; 10.2 × 8.4 cm. The preface by Zhang Chao dated 1683 and the table of contents, indicating the source of each work, are attached. The postscript by Zhang Yi is not included. This edition was collated and reprinted by Luo Shunzhang from Huizhou (*Xin'an Luo Xingtang Shunzhangshi jiao* 新安羅興堂舜章氏校).[19] The cover page is titled *Yu Chu xinzhi* and includes phrases such as "reprint in sleeve edition" (*chongkan xiuzhen* 重刊袖珍) and "retention of the blocks of Yiqing tang" (*Yiqing tang cangban* 詒清堂藏板). This edition is very similar to the 1760 edition in 5.1, but it is not a direct reprint (*fuke* 覆刻) of that edition because some of the titles in the 5.1 edition have been carved incorrectly. For example, "Qi nüzi zhuan" 奇女子傳 in the 5.1 edition was mistakenly carved as "Qi dazi zhuan" 奇大子傳 in the 5.2 edition, "Wang Cuiqiao zhuan" 王翠翹傳 was carved as "San Cuiqiao zhuan" 三翠翹傳, and "Jixian ji" 乩仙記 was carved as "Luanxian ji" 乱仙記. In addition, the removed works of Qian Qianyi, namely, "Xu Xiake zhuan" and "Shu Zheng Yangtian shi," and also Xu Fang's 徐芳 "Liu furen xiaozhuan" 柳夫人小傳 have been replaced by "Jiang Zhenyi xiansheng zhuan" 姜貞毅先生傳, "Sun Wenzheng Huang Shizhai liang yishi" 孫文正黃石齋兩逸事, and "Gusheng zhuan" 賈生傳, respectively. Finally, the last work in the volume, "Banqiao zaji" 板橋雜記, has been removed. Available in the National Library of China and the Korea University Library.

17. See chapter 4 for the details of the censorship of *Yu Chu xinzhi*.

18. Whereas there is no cover page for the National Library of China copy, the Ewha Womans University Library copy contains a torn cover page.

19. Luo Shunzhang also collated Zhang Chao's *Xi'nang cunjin*. See extant text no. 11.

5.3a. Qianlong reprint edition

Twenty *juan*. Nine lines, twenty characters; white fore edge; single fishtail; 18.6 × 13.4 cm. The preface of Zhang Chao dated 1683; "Editorial Principles"; the table of contents (the source of each work is not recorded); and the postscript by Zhang Chao dated 1700 are attached at the end. There is a cover page titled *Yu Chu xinzhi*. Available in the National Library of China, the Qinghua University Library, the Shanghai Library, the Naikaku Bunko, and the University of Chicago Library.[20] In particular, both the Naikaku Bunko copy and the National Library of China copy have a red stamp saying: "Special Announcement: according to the catalog of banned books, the blocks of three writings of Qian Qianyi were extracted and sent to the Book Service of Zhejiang Province and were destroyed."[21] This edition is reprinted in *Siku jinhuishu congkan* 四庫禁燬書叢刊, *zibu* vol. 38.[22]

5.3b. Qianlong reprint edition

All the physical characteristics of this edition are the same as of the 5.3a edition except that there is no cover page, no red stamp of censorship, and no "Yiqing tang" in the centerfold. The last work, "Banqiao zaji," is also not included; instead there is the indication "end of twenty *juan*" 卷二十大終 after the work of Wang Jia 汪价 (*juan* 19). Available in the National Library of China, Beijing University Library, and Institute for Advanced Studies on Asia (Tōyō Bunka Kenkyūjo) at the University of Tokyo. This edition is reprinted in *Xuxiu Siku quanshu* 續修四庫全書, vol. 1783.[23]

20. Some of the National Library of China editions do not have Zhang Chao's postscript.

21. "謹遵飭禁書目, 將錢謙益文三篇抽板, 送浙江書局銷毀訖特白。"

22. *Siku jinhuishu congkan* claims that it has reprinted the original 1700 edition of *Yu Chu xinzhi*, but in fact it comprises Qianlong reprints.

23. Despite *Xuxiu Siku quanshu*'s indication that it is a reprint of the 1700 edition, it in fact comprises Qianlong reprints.

6. *SHIHUAN* 詩幻 (1686)

Shihuan is a collection of Zhang Chao's 185 poems. The collected poems are not of the ordinary kind, but ones similar to wordplay, that is, a way of showing off one's skill and dexterity in creating poetry. The first *juan* contains poems that are supposed to fit given rules, such as including all the characters in the sexagenarian cycle, the dozen animals, the numbers, the names of local counties, mountains, ancient peoples, famous beauties, medicines, flowers, birds, books, tunes of popular songs, dramas, or rhyming the character of the antonym. The second *juan* has poems composed by selecting verses from famous works, such as *Wenxuan* 文選, *Xixiang ji* 西廂記, and *Caotang shiyu* 草堂詩餘.

Two *juan*. Eight lines, eighteen characters; white fore edge; single borderline; single fishtail; 17.6 × 13.2 cm. Prefaces by Gu Cai 顧彩 dated 1685 and by Wang Zheng 王正 dated 1686 are attached. The only extant copy is available in the Qinghua University Library.[24]

7. *TANJI CONGSHU* 檀几叢書 (1695–97)

Tanji congshu is a compilation of 157 miscellaneous writings by contemporaries of Zhang Chao. It includes a variety of genres of short prose pieces, as Wang Zhuo boasts in the "Editorial Principles":

> In ancient times, there was an efficacious sandalwood desk made of seven valuables. On the table were characters, which would appear at one's will. This book is replete with all kinds of writings, such as Confucian classics, commentaries to the classics, histories, philosophy, literature, rites and etiquette, family codes of conduct, and bits and pieces about local products. Those who want to look through these writings will find them as soon as they flip the pages. This collectanea is thus named after that sandalwood desk.[25]

24. *Zhang Shanlai shiji* 張山來詩集 in the National Central Library of Taiwan contains poems with titles similar to the ones in *Shihuan*. It is a collection of Zhang Chao's 194 poems, selected as the last *juan* in Ge Lun's 葛崙 (n.d.) *Ganyun shuwu xinbian* 干筠書屋新編 (eight *juan*).

25. Wang Zhuo, "Editorial Principles," in the first collection of *TJCS*, 4.

古有七寶靈檀几，几上有文字，隨意所及，文字輒現。今書中為經、為
傳、為史、為子集、為禮節大端、為家門訓戒、為土物瑣屑，種種畢具。有
意披覽，展卷即得，名曰檀几。

Although *Tanji congshu* was a product of Wang Zhuo and Zhang
Chao's collaborative effort, many scholars suppose that this book was
printed in Xiaju tang, Wang Zhuo's studio in Hangzhou, because
"Xiaju tang" is recorded on its centerfold. But, according to the circumstances recorded in the letters of *Chidu yousheng* and *Chidu
oucun* (see no. 12), it is certain that Zhang Chao took charge of printing the whole collection in Yangzhou.[26] The compilation had three
installments—the first collection (*yiji* 一集), printed in 1695; the second collection (*erji* 二集), printed in 1697; and the extra collection (*yuji*
餘集), also printed in 1697. It was not distributed as a complete three-
collection set, as we see today, but instead distributed separately in
sequential order.[27] The extant editions are, therefore, of three kinds:
three-collection editions, two-collection editions, and single-collection
editions.

7.1. Three-collection edition

In the three-collection edition, the first and second collections are fifty
juan each, and the extra collection is two *juan* (*shangxia* 上下). Nine
lines, twenty characters; white fore edge; single borderline; "Xiaju
tang" below the centerfold only in the first collection; 17.9 × 13.5 cm.
White or yellow cover page titled *Tanji congshu*. Prefaces by Wu Sugong,

---

26. Wang Zhuo, preface in the second collection of *TJCS*, 203; Zhang Chao, preface in the first collection of *ZDCS*, 2; and Wu Sugong, preface in the first collection
of *TJCS*, 2.

27. Based on the cover page of the Library of Congress copy, it is evident that the
first collection, the second collection, and the supplementary collection were distributed separately. The cover page of the first collection is partially torn, but we can
clearly see the advertisement for the upcoming second collection: "the second collection will follow" 二集嗣出 (see Fig. 3.1). In addition, the cover page of the second
collection also advertised the forthcoming publication of the extra collection: "extra
collection will follow" 餘集嗣出.

Wang Zhuo, and Zhang Chao dated 1695, "Editorial Principles" by Wang Zhuo, and the table of contents are attached in the first volume of the first collection; prefaces by Wang Zhuo and Zhang Chao, "Editorial Principles" by both Wang Zhuo and Zhang Chao dated 1697, and the table of contents are attached in the first volume of the second collection; and prefaces by Wang Zhuo and Zhang Chao, and the table of contents are attached in the first volume of the extra collection. The order and the location of prefaces show minor differences among editions. Available in the National Library of China, the Beijing University Library, the Shanghai Library, the Princeton University Library, the Harvard-Yenching Library, the Cornell University Library, the University of Hong Kong Library, the Naikaku Bunko, the Tokyo University Institute for Advanced Studies on Asia, the National Diet Library of Japan, the Ewha Womans University Library, and the Kyujanggak Library of Korea.[28]

7.2. Two-collection edition

The two-collection edition comprises the first and second collections of *Tanji congshu* without the extra collection. All the physical characteristics are the same as of the 7.1 edition. Available in the Shanghai Library, the Zhejiang Library, and the Library of Congress.[29]

7.3. Single-collection edition

The single-collection edition consists of the first collection of *Tanji congshu* only. All the physical characteristics are the same as of the 7.1 edition. Available in the National Library of China, the Beijing University Library, and the Shanghai Library.[30]

---

28. The Kyujanggak Library copy has only two volumes: the second collection from *juan* 21 to 27, and the *xiajuan* of the extra collection.
29. The Zhejiang Library copy does not have a cover page.
30. The Beijing University Library copy does not have Zhang Chao's preface.

8. *ZHAODAI CONGSHU* 昭代叢書 (1697–1703)

Zhaodai congshu is a collection of casual short prose pieces by contemporaries of Zhang Chao. It consists of three collections (*jia yi bing* 甲乙丙) of a total of 150 *juan*—each collection having fifty *juan*—printed in 1697, 1700, and 1703, respectively. The extant copies are divided into two editions: one is a two-collection edition that contains only the first two collections; the other is a three-collection edition. Many library catalogs regard the two-collection edition as an impaired version, but, as in the example of *Tanji congshu*, it is possible that *Zhaodai congshu* was not initially made into a three-collection set but circulated separately in two installments.

8.1. Three-collection edition

Three collections in 150 *juan*. Nine lines, twenty characters; white fore edge; single borderline; "retention of the blocks of Yiqing tang" below the centerfold only in the first collection; 18 × 13.6 cm. There is no cover page. Prefaces by You Tong 尤侗 dated 1697 and by Zhang Chao, "Selection Principles" (*Xuanli* 選例), and table of contents are attached to the first collection; preface by Zhang Chao, "Editorial Principles," and table of contents are attached at the front of the second collection; and prefaces by Zhang Chao dated 1703 and by Zhang Jian 張漸 dated 1703, "Editorial Principles," and table of contents are attached at the front of the third collection. Available in the Shanghai Library and the Korea University Library.[31]

8.2a. Two-collection edition (Kangxi reign)

This two-collection edition consists of the first collection (fifty *juan*) and the second collection (fifty *juan*). Other physical characteristics are the same as of the 8.1 edition. The preface by Zhang Chao, "Editorial Principles," and table of contents are attached in the first collection;

---

31. In the Korea University Library copy of *ZDCS, juan* 26 to 31 are missing in the first collection, and *juan* 42 to 50 are omitted in the second collection. In addition, there is no third collection.

the preface by Zhang Chao, "Editorial Principles," and table of contents are also attached in the second collection. Available in the Kyujanggak Library.

8.2b. Two-collection edition (Kangxi reign)

This two-collection edition consists of the first collection (fifty *juan*) and the second collection (forty *juan*). Compared to the 8.2a edition, the last ten *juan* in the second collection are not included, but it is not certain whether this is an impaired edition. It is possible that this edition was an earlier edition than the 8.2a edition, the last ten *juan* of which were attached later. Other physical characteristics are the same as of the 8.2a edition. It has a yellow cover page titled *Zhaodai congshu*. The second collection has the preface by Zhang Chao and "Editorial Principles" but is without the table of contents. Available in the Princeton University Library, the Harvard-Yenching Library, and the Beijing University Library.[32]

8.2c. Reprint (chongke 重刻) of two-collection edition (Qianlong reign)

This reprint consists of the first collection (fifty *juan*) and the second collection (either forty or fifty *juan*, as explained below). It follows the same physical characteristics as the 8.2b edition, but it is a reprint edition of the Qianlong period because it avoids the characters that were taboo under the Qianlong reign. For example, the character *li* 曆 has been changed into the character *li* 歷 throughout "Xueli shuo" 學曆說 in the first collection because the character 曆 had to be avoided in the Qianlong period. In addition, some of the works are rearranged in the reprint. Works such as "Changchunyuan yushi gongji" 暢春苑御試恭紀 and "Shengyun congshuo" 聲韻叢說, originally included in the second collection in the 8.2b edition, have been moved into the first collection,

32. In the Beijing University Library copy, the table of contents lists forty *juan*, but in fact this copy includes all of the original fifty *juan* because the numbering of *juan* 30 to 40 is duplicated on what are actually *juan* 41 to 50.

from which the works "Guaiyu" 怪語 and "Banqiao zaji" have been removed; and "Beiyue hengshan lisi shangquyang kao" 北嶽恆山歷祀上曲陽考, "Sannian fuzhi kao" 三年服制考, "Geyan jinlu" 格言僅錄, and "Shenyi" 身易, which were originally in the third collection, have been moved into the second collection, from which the works "Di shiyi duan jin" 第十一段錦 and "Guangsi dianyi" 廣祀典議 have been removed.

There are two types of this reprint edition. First, there are the editions in which the table of contents of the second collection lists only forty *juan* even though the volume in fact includes all fifty *juan* in the text proper. They are available in the Beijing University Library, the University of Hong Kong Library, the Columbia University Library, the University of Tokyo Library, the National Diet Library of Japan, the National Library of Korea, and the Korea University Library.[33] Second, there are editions in which the table of contents of the second collection lists forty *juan* and the actual content also contains forty *juan*. Available in the National Library of China, Naikaku Bunko, the Institute for Advanced Studies on Asia at the University of Tokyo, and the Kyujanggak Library.[34]

8.2d. Reprint (fanke 翻刻) of two-collection edition from Wumen 吳門 Saoye shanfang 埽葉山房 (Qianlong reign)

The physical characteristics and the table of contents of this reprint of the two-collection edition are exactly the same as of the 8.2c edition. Only the typeface is different. Available in the Beijing University Library and the Columbia University Library.[35]

33. Part of the University of Hong Kong Library copy is supplemented by handwritten transcription, such as *juan* 2 and parts of *juan* 24 and *juan* 35 in the first collection, and parts of *juan* 26, *juan* 30, and *juan* 40 in the second collection. The copies in the National Library of Korea and the University of Tokyo Library only have the second collection, and the Korea University Library copy omits *juan* 7 to 18, 25 to 30, and 35 to 37.

34. The Kyujanggak Library copy leaves out *juan* 1 to 15.

35. The Columbia University Library copy does not have the preface by You Tong.

9. *SISHU ZUNZHU HUIYI JIE* 四書尊注會意解 (1697)

Sishu zunzhu huiyi jie is a collection of commentaries to the Four Books (*Sishu* 四書). It was written by Zhang Jiuda 張九達, complemented and collated by his son Zhang Yongde, and printed by Zhang Chao. It was so popular that it was later reprinted many times by commercial publishers in Fujian and Jiangxi provinces while Zhang Chao was still alive.[36] In addition, it was exported to Japan in 1709. *Hakusai shomoku* 舶載書目, a seventeenth-century catalog listing Chinese books exported to Japan, has a record of this book saying that it was six *juan* in sixteen volumes and published by Daisong lou 岱宋樓.[37]

Thirty-six *juan*. Prefaces by Zhang Chao dated 1697 and by Zhang Yongde dated 1697, and "Editorial Principles" are attached. It is signed "supplemented by Zhang Yongde from Guangling [Yangzhou]" (*Guangling Zhang Yongde Zichang bu* 廣陵張庸德紫裳補) and "consulted by Zhang Chao from Huizhou" (*Xin'an Zhang Chao Shanlai can* 新安張潮山來參). The disciples and family members of Zhang Yongde and Zhang Chao also participated in making the book as collators and proofreaders. The Chinese Academy of Social Sciences Library copy is reprinted in *Siku jinhuishu congkan bubian*, vol. 2.

10. *BIGE* 筆歌 (1698)

Bige is a collection of Zhang Chao's northern plays (*zaju* 雜劇) and popular songs. In the middle of the text are attached comments by several of Zhang Chao's friends, such as Wu Qi, Gu Cai, Xu Song 徐崧, Zheng Xudan 鄭旭旦, Kong Shangren, and Cui Daiqi 崔岱齊. According to Deng Changfeng, it was completed before 1684, but the printing was done around 1698.[38]

---

36. *CDOC* 11.12b; Zhang Chao, "Editorial Principles," in the third collection of *ZDCS*, 343–44.

37. Ōba, *Hakusai shomoku*, 1:13–14. It is possible that Daisong lou 岱宋樓 is a typo for Daibao lou 貸寶樓, the bookshop to which Zhang Chao entrusted the woodblocks of the book. *CDOC* 11.10a–13a. However, the number of *juan* is different from the number in the extant edition.

38. Deng Changfeng, *Ming Qing xiqujia kaolüe xubian*, 164.

Two *juan*, two volumes. The first *juan* contains "Kaige" 凱歌 (one
zhe) and four northern plays, "Mutianzi jueyu kuaiaoyou" 穆天子絕
域快遨遊, "Wan Sizong qiongtu shangtongku" 阮嗣宗窮途傷痛哭,
"Liu Zihou qiqiao huanguanshang" 柳子厚乞巧換冠裳, and "Mi Yuan-
zhang baishi jupaohu" 米元章拜石具袍笏, and the second *juan* contains
thirteen popular songs (*siqu* 詞曲). Preface by Wu Qi 吳綺 is attached.
There is one extant copy in Tianyi ge 天一閣 in Ningbo[39] and a transcribed copy that was made in the early twentieth century in the Zhejiang Library.

11. *XI'NANG CUNJIN* 奚囊寸錦 (1707)

Xi'nang cunjin is a collection of Zhang Chao's riddles, consisting of one
hundred riddles and answers. The first *juan* comprises a riddle illustrated on the left side and a clue to solve the riddle on the right side;
the second *juan* contains the answers to the riddles in order. It seems
to have been published when Zhang Chao was alive,[40] but only the
later reprint editions are extant.

11.1. *1764 reprint from Qingyuan ge* 清遠閣 *edition*

This 1764 reprint consists of three *juan* (*shangzhongxia* 上中下). The
first *juan* and the second *juan* are in nine lines, twenty-one characters;
double borderline; "the possession of [woodblocks by] Qingyuan ge"
(*Qingyuan ge cang* 清遠閣藏) below the centerfold. The third *juan* is in
eight lines, eighteen characters; double borderline; "the possession of
[woodblocks by] Qingyuan ge" below the centerfold. The first *juan*
contains seventy riddles and the clues for them. The second *juan* has

39. See Zhou Miaozhong, *Qingdai xiqu shi*, 170. I have not seen this copy, but all
the characteristics that Zhou Miaozhong describes are the same as those of the transcribed copy in the Zhejiang Library that I examined.
40. Zhang Chao mentioned that he circulated *Xi'nang cunjin* in manuscript first
since he lacked the financial wherewithal to print it. But he eventually printed it, as
he states in the "Editorial Principles." The book must have been completed before
1707, considering that An Duansu's preface is dated 1707, but it is not certain
whether this indicates the completion of the manuscript copy or of the printed
book.

one hundred answers and the remaining thirty riddles and clues. The cover page is titled *Xi'nang cunjin*, with such phrases as "the original copy of Mr. Zhang Shanlai" (*Zhang Shanlai xiansheng yuanben* 張山來先生原本), "Luo Shunzhang 羅舜章 from Congchuan 潀川 collated," and "Qingyuan ge 清遠閣 edition." Warning phrases in red ink "retention of the blocks" (*benya cangban* 本衙藏版) and "pirates must be prosecuted" (*fanke bijiu* 翻刻必究) are also inserted. Prefaces by Luo Shunzhang dated 1764, An Duansu 庵端肅 dated 1707, and Gu Cai; "Editorial Principles"; and table of contents are attached. The preface by Zhang Chao is attached to the front of the first and second *juan*. Available in the Naikaku Bunko. Both the Harvard-Yenching Library and the Princeton University Library (Hishi Collection) have a photo-reprint copy of the Naikaku Bunko's copy.[41]

11.2. 1820 reprint of Qingyuan ge edition

This 1820 reprint (*chongkan* 重刊) of the Qingyuan ge edition is collated by Li Wenshou 李文綬, Yin Biao 殷杓, Mei Zhiyuan 梅植元 (b. 1794) of Yangzhou, Wang Sengbao 王僧保, and Wu Lianyang 吳連颺 of Yizheng 儀徵. Two *juan*. The cover page is titled *Xi'nang cunjin*, with the phrase "[Wang] Yingxiang (style name Guling) wrote in the seventh month in the autumn of Gengchen year of the Jiaqing reign (1820)" (*Jiaqing gengchen qiu qiyue Guling Yingxiang ti* 嘉慶庚辰秋七月古靈應祥題). Prefaces by Luo Shunzhang dated 1764, Gu Cai, and An Duansu dated 1707; table of contents; "Editorial Principles"; prefatory remarks 題詞 (*tici*) of Tuipu 退圃 and Mei Zhiyuan; list of collators; and postscript by Zhang Chao are attached to the front of the first *juan*. The other characteristics of format are the same as of the 1764 edition (the 11.1 edition), except that there is no signature of Qingyuan ge in the centerfold. Available in the National Library of China, the Beijing University Library, the Zhejiang Library, and the

---

41. In the copies in the Princeton University Library and the Harvard-Yenching Library, the first *juan* only contains seventy riddles and the accompanying seventy hints. The second *juan* has the seventy answers, then suddenly, after ten missing pages, the riddles and accompanying clues from 71 to 100 continue with no answers.

University of Hong Kong Library.[42] It is reprinted in *Siku jinhuishu congkan, zibu* vol. 1.

12. *CHIDU YOUSHENG* 尺牘友聲
AND *CHIDU OUCUN* 尺牘偶存

Chidu yousheng and *Chidu oucun* are collections of correspondence between Zhang Chao and his coterie over the course of twenty-six years, from 1677 to 1703. *Chidu yousheng* is a collection of letters sent to Zhang Chao, and *Chidu oucun* is the collection of Zhang's letters in reply. *Chidu yousheng* contains about 1,000 letters of Zhang Chao's friends, whereas *Chidu oucun* records about 450 replies. The renowned bibliographer Sun Dianqi 孫殿起 (1894–1958) recorded that there was a 1684 edition of *Chidu oucun*,[43] but no Kangxi edition survives. Only the 1780 reprint edition is available.

Chidu yousheng consists of three collections, each of which has five *juan*. Eight lines, twenty characters; white fore edge; single borderline; no fishtail; "Xinzhai" 心齋 below the centerfold; 18.3 × 11.5 cm. The yellow cover page is titled *Chidu yousheng, First Collection* (*Chidu yousheng chuji* 尺牘友聲初集) and includes phrases such as "definitive edition of Xinzhai" (*Xinzhai dingben* 心齋定本), "retention of the blocks" (*benya cangban* 本衙藏版), and "engraved in the autumn of Gengzi year of the Qianlong reign (1780)" (*Qianlong Gengzi qiu juan* 乾隆庚子秋鐫). Preface by Cai Fangbing 蔡方柄 dated 1684 and the list of letter writers are attached to the first *juan* of the first collection.

Chidu oucun is in eleven *juan*. All the physical characteristics are the same as those of *Chidu yousheng* except that the size of the blocks is smaller, 18 × 11.5 cm. The prefaces by Chen Di 陳軝 and Cong □ (illegible character) are attached to the front of the first *juan*. The cover page is titled *Chidu yousheng oucun* and includes phrases such as "retention of the blocks" and "engraved in the autumn of Gengzi year of the Qianlong reign (1780)."

---

42. The cover page and the first two pages in the second volume are missing in the University of Hong Kong Library copy. The Zhejiang Library copy only has sixty riddles.

43. Sun Dianqi, *Qingdai jinshu zhijian lu*, 12.

Both are available in the Beijing University Library, the National Library of China, the Zhejiang Library, the Qinghua University Library, the Library of Congress, and Columbia University Library. Depending on the editions, however, the number of prefaces is different.[44]

13. *JI LI TAIBO SHI* 集李太白詩

Ji Li Taibo shi is a joint publication of *Ji Li Taibo shi*, one *juan* (fifty poems); *Ji Du* 集杜, two *juan*;[45] and *Ji Du Yanzi shi* 集杜雁字詩, one *juan*. Since the poems in the collection belong to *Jizi shi* 集字詩, assorted poetry that selects each line from different existing poems and makes them into a whole new poem, this book is a collection of Zhang Chao's new poems using lines taken from poems by the two most famous poets of the Tang dynasty, Li Bai 李白 (701–62) and Du Fu 杜甫 (712–70). Zhang Chao identifies the original source next to each poem.

Four *juan*. Eight lines, twenty characters; white fore edge; single borderline; "Yiqing tang" below the centerfold; 18.5 × 13.3 cm. Preface by Wu Sugong and postscript by Fang Qijin 方淇蓋 are attached to *Ji Li Taibo shi*; the author Zhang Chao's own preface and short prefaces by Hong Jiazhi 洪嘉植 and Yu Lanshuo 余蘭碩 are attached to *Ji Du*; and a preface by Zhu Shen 朱慎 is attached to *Ji Du Yanzi shi*. Available in the National Library of China.

14. *YOUMENGYING* 幽夢影

Youmengying is a collection of aphorisms and maxims written by Zhang Chao with attached comments by his friends and family members. Its original title was *Xiangmengying* 香梦影 (Fragrant Dream Shadows), but, following the advice of his friends, Zhang Chao changed

---

44. For example, the preface by Cong □ (illegible character) and the last three *juan* are missing in the National Library of China copy. The Zhejiang Library copy and the Qinghua University Library copy lack the third collection of *Chidu yousheng* and the preface by Cong □. The Columbia University Library copy and the Library of Congress copy also lack the preface by Cong □.

45. The first *juan* comprises five-syllable poems, and the second *juan* is titled *Meihua shi* 梅花詩 (Poems of Apricot Blossom).

its title to *Youmengying*.[46] There is only one extant early Qing edition, of which the exact date of print is not known, although it is surmised that it was printed before the Qianlong reign, considering the observance of taboo characters (*bihui*).

Two *juan*. Eight lines, eighteen characters; attached comments are carved in smaller characters in two lines in a column and in the upper side of the margin (*shumei* 書眉 or *tiantou* 天頭); white fore edge; double borderline; single fishtail; 18.2 × 13.4 cm. Prefaces by Yu Huai, Shi Pang 石龐, Sun Zhimi 孫致彌, and Wang Zhuo are attached to the front of the first *juan*; postscripts by Jiang Zhilan and Zhang Zong are attached to the end of the second *juan*. Available in the National Library of China, the Beijing University Library, and the Shanghai Library.[47]

There are also two reprint editions. The first one is the Daoguang 道光 (1820–50) edition. One *juan*. Nine lines, twenty characters; attached comments are small characters in two lines in a column; white fore edge; double borderline; single fishtail; "Shikai tang" 石楷堂 below the centerfold; 17.8 × 12.3 cm. Prefaces by Yu Huai, Sun Zhimi, and Shi Pang, and postscripts by Zhang Zong, Jiang Zhilan, and Yang Fuji dated 1775 are attached. It is included in the separate collection (*bieji* 別集) of the Daoguang reprint of *Zhaodai congshu*; the first collection of *Chenfengge congshu* 晨風閣叢書; and the first collection of *Guoxue zhenben wenku* 國學珍本文庫.

The second reprint is the Guangxu 光緒 (1875–1908) edition. Two *juan*. Nine lines, twenty characters; attached comments are small characters in two lines in a column; black fore edge; double borderline; single fishtail; 12.7 × 9.2 cm. Prefaces by Shi Pang and Sun Zhimi, and postscripts by Jiang Zhilan and Ge Yuanxu 葛元煦 dated 1879 are attached. It is included in the second box of *Xiaoyuan congshu* 嘯園叢書, the first collection of *Cuilanggan guan congshu* 翠琅玕舘叢書, the sixth collection of *Gujin shuobu congshu* 古今說部叢書, the section of miscellaneous works (*zapin* 雜品) of *Yishu congshu* 藝術叢書, and the philosophy part (*zibu* 子部) of *Yuyuan congshu* 芋園叢書.

46. *CDYS* 5.8a.

47. One of the two Shanghai Library editions does not have prefaces by Yu Huai and Shi Pang and the postscript by Zhang Zong.

Other Literati Writers' Works Published by Zhang Chao

1. ZHANG XIKONG 張習孔, *YIQING TANG JI* 詒清堂集

Twelve *juan*, supplements (*buyi* 補遺) four *juan*. Eight lines, nineteen characters; white fore edge; single borderline; single fishtail; 19 × 13 cm. Prefaces by Wu Weiye 吳偉業 dated 1669, Zhou Lianggong 周亮工 dated 1667, Mr. Huang 黃氏, Lei Yilong 雷一龍, and Shi Runzhang 施閏章 dated 1660; and the table of contents are attached. The cover page is titled *Yiqing tang ji*, with phrases such as "written by Master Huangyue [Zhang Xikong]" (*Huang Yuegong xiansheng zhu* 黃岳公先生著) and "retention of the blocks" (*benya cangban* 本衙藏版). According to Wu Weiye's preface, Zhang Chao printed this book after his father's— Xikong's—death. Available in the National Library of China. Reprinted in *Siku quanshu cunmu congshu bubian* 四庫全書存目叢書補編, vol. 1.

2. ZHANG XIKONG, *DAYI BIANZHI* 大易辨志 (OR *ZHOUYI BIANZHI* 周易辨志) (1690)

Twenty-four *juan*. Nine lines, twenty-five characters; white fore edge; single borderline; single fishtail; 21 × 12 cm. Prefaces by Cao Zhenji 曹貞吉, Jiang Chao 蔣超, and Zhang Xikong are attached. Available in the Harvard-Yenching Library.

3. DENG HANYI 鄧漢儀, THE THIRD COLLECTION OF *SHIGUAN* 詩觀 (1690)

Shiguan has three collections: the first collection has twelve *juan*; the second collection has fourteen *juan* with a collection of women's writing in one *juan*; and the third collection has thirteen *juan* with a collection of women's writing in one *juan*. The original compiler and publisher, Deng Hanyi, died before all three collections were completed. Zhang Chao was then asked by Deng Hanyi's son to complete the unfinished third collection.[48] Kangxi Shenmo tang 慎墨堂 edition.

---

48. Zhang Chao's preface, in the third collection of *Shiguan*, in *Siku jinhuishu congkan*, *jibu* 2:512.

Available in the Chinese Academy of Social Sciences Library and the Nanjing Library. Reprinted in *Siku quanshu cunmu congshu bubian*, vols. 39–40; *Siku jinhuishu congkan, jibu* vols. 1–3; and *Siku quanshu cunmu congshu, jibu* vol. 273.

4. WU SUGONG 吳肅公, *DUSHU LUNSHI* 讀書論世 (1698)

Sixteen *juan,* four volumes. Nine lines, twenty characters; commentary carved in small characters in double columns; double borderline; white fore edge; single fishtail; "possession of blocks of Yiqing tang" in the centerfold; 19 × 13.8 cm. The prefaces by Wu Sugong and Zhang Chao dated 1698 are attached. It is signed "written by Wu Sugong (style name Qingyan) from Xuancheng" (*Xuancheng Wu Sugong Qingyan zhu* 宣城吳肅公晴巖著) and "consulted by Zhang Chao of Tiandu [Huizhou]" (*Tiandu Zhang Chao Shanlai can* 天都張潮山來參). Available in the People's University Library and the Beijing University Library.

5. ZHUO ERKAN 卓爾堪, *HEKE CAO TAO XIE SANJIA SHI* 合刻曹陶謝三家詩 (1706)

Eight *juan.* Eleven lines, twenty-one characters; white fore edge; double borderline; single fishtail; 19 × 14.6 cm. The prefaces by Zhang Chao, Zhang Shikong 張師孔, and Zhuo Erkan are attached at the front of the first *juan.* The book was originally edited and collated by Zhuo Erkan, but, since he lacked the financial capacity to print it, Zhang Chao and Zhang Shikong took it over.[49] It is thus indicated on the book that it was the collaboration of these three. Available in the Beijing University Library and the National Central Library of Taiwan as a transcribed copy.[50]

49. *CDOC* 11.3a.
50. The National Central Library copy does not have the preface by Zhang Shikong.

Bibliography

An Se-hyŏn 안세현. "Munch'e panchŏng ŭl tullŏssan kŭlssŭgi wa munch'e non-jaeng" 문체반정을 둘러싼 글쓰기와 문체 논쟁. *Ŏmun nonjip* 어문논집 54 (2006): 137–72.

An Tae-hoe 안대회. "18–19 segi ŭi chugŏ munhwa wa sangsang ŭi chŏngwŏn" 18–19 세기 주거문화와 상상의 정원. *Chindan hakpo* 진단학보 97 (2004.6): 111–38.

An Tae-hoe 안대회, Yi Ch'ŏr-hŭi 이철희, Yi Hyŏn-il 이현일 et al., eds. *Chosŏn hugi Myŏng-Ch'ŏng munhak kwallyŏn charyojip* 조선후기 명청문학 관련자료집. Seoul: Sŏnggyun'gwan taehakkyo ch'ulp'anbu, 2012.

Barr, Allan H. "Novelty, Character, and Community in Zhang Chao's *Yu Chu xinzhi*." In *Trauma and Transcendence in Early Qing Literature*, ed. Wilt L. Idema, Wai-yee Li, and Ellen Widmer, 282–309. Cambridge, MA: Harvard University Asia Center, 2006.

Blair, Ann. *Too Much to Know: Managing Scholarly Information before the Modern Age*. New Haven: Yale University Press, 2010.

Brokaw, Cynthia J. *Commerce in Culture: The Sibao Book Trade in the Qing and Republic Periods*. Cambridge, MA: Harvard University Asia Center, 2007.

———. "On the History of the Book in China." In *Printing and Book Culture in Late Imperial China*, ed. Cynthia Brokaw and Kai-wing Chow, 3–54. Berkeley and Los Angeles: University of California Press, 2005.

Brook, Timothy. "Censorship in Eighteenth-Century China: A View from the Book Trade." *Canadian Journal of History* 23.2 (1998): 177–96.

———. *The Chinese State in Ming Society*. London and New York: RoutledgeCurzon, 2005.

———. "Communications and Commerce." In *The Cambridge History of China*, vol. 8, ed. Frederic W. Mote and Denis Twitchett, 579–707. Cambridge, UK: Cambridge University Press, 1998.

———. *The Confusions of Pleasure: Commerce and Culture in Ming China*. Berkeley and Los Angeles: University of California Press, 1999.

———. *Praying for Power: Buddhism and the Formation of Gentry Society in Late Ming China*. Cambridge, MA: Harvard University Asia Center, 1993.

Bussotti, Michela. *Gravures de Hui: Étude du livre illustré chinois*. Paris: École française d'Extrême-Orient, 2001.

Bussotti, Michela, and Jean-Pierre Drège, eds. *Imprimer sans profit? Le livre non commercial dans la Chine impériale*. Genève: Librairie Droz, 2015.

Cai Yi 蔡毅, ed. *Zhongguo gudian xiqu xuba huibian* 中國古典戲曲序跋彙編. 4 vols. Ji'nan: Qilu shushe, 1989.

Cao Chen 曹臣 (b. 1583). *Shehua lu* 舌華錄. Annotated by Yu Yueheng 喻岳衡. Changsha: Yuelu shushe, 1985.

Carlitz, Katherine. "Printing as Performance: Literati Playwright-Publishers of the Late Ming." In *Printing and Book Culture in Late Imperial China*, ed. Cynthia J. Brokaw and Kai-wing Chow, 267–303. Berkeley and Los Angeles: University of California Press, 2005.

Chan Hok-lam. *Control of Publishing in China, Past and Present*. Canberra: Australian National University, 1983.

Chang, Kang-i Sun. *The Late Ming Poet Chen Tsu-lung: Crisis of Love and Loyalism*. New Haven: Yale University Press, 1991.

Chartier, Roger. *The Order of Books*. Stanford: Stanford University Press, 1992.

Chen Dakang 陳大康. "Wang Zhuo he tade *Jin Shishuo*" 王晫和他的今世說. *Ming Qing xiaoshuo yanjiu* 明清小說研究 (1994.1): 121–28.

Chen Ding 陳鼎 (b. 1650). *Liuxi waizhuan* 留溪外傳. In *Congshu jicheng xubian* 叢書集成續編, vol. 30. Shanghai: Shanghai shudian, 1994.

Chen, Jack. "Knowing Men and Being Known: Gossip and Social Networks in the *Shishuo Xinyu*." In *Idle Talk: Gossip and Anecdote in Traditional China*, ed. Jack Chen and David Schaberg, 55–70. Berkeley and Los Angeles: University of California Press, 2014.

Chen Jiru 陳繼儒 (1558–1639). *Taiping qinghua* 太平清話. In *Shuoku* 說庫, ed. Wang Wenru 王文濡. Reprint of 1915 edition. 2 vols. Taipei: Xinxin shuju, 1963.

Chen Shi 陳軾 (fl. 1640). *Daoshan tang houji* 道山堂後集. Reprinted in *Qingdai shiwenji huibian* 清代詩文集彙編, vol. 62. Shanghai: Guji chubanshe, 2010.

Chen Wanyi 陳萬益. *Wan Ming xiaopin yu Mingji wenren shenghuo* 晚明小品與明季文人生活. Taipei: Daan chubanshe, 1988.

Chen Wenxin 陳文新. "*Jin Shishuo* yu Wang Zhuo xintai" 今世說與王晫心態. *Ming Qing xiaoshuo yanjiu* 明清小說研究 (1990.1): 168–78.

Chen Yuji 陳玉璂 (fl. 1667). *Xuewen tang wenji* 學文堂文集. Reprinted in *Congshu jicheng xubian* 叢書集成續編, vol. 126. Shanghai: Shanghai shudian, 1994.

Chen Zilong 陳子龍 (1608–47). *Huang Ming jingshi wenbian* 皇明經世文編. 1639 edition reprinted in *Xuxiu Siku quanshu* 續修四庫全書, vol. 1655. Shanghai: Guji chubanshe, 1995.

Cherniack, Susan. "Book Culture and Textual Transmission in Sung China." *Harvard Journal of Asiatic Studies* 54 (1994): 5–125.

Chia, Lucille. "Of Three Mountains Street: The Commercial Publishers of Ming Nanjing." In *Printing and Book Culture in Late Imperial China*, ed. Cynthia J. Brokaw and Kai-wing Chow, 107–83. Berkeley and Los Angeles: University of California Press, 2005.

———. *Printing for Profit: The Commercial Publishers of Jianyang, Fujian (11th–17th Centuries)*. Cambridge, MA: Harvard University Asia Center, 2003.

Chia, Lucille, and Hilde de Weerdt, eds. *Knowledge and Text Production in an Age of Print: China, Tenth–Fourteenth Centuries*. Leiden: Brill, 2011.

Cho Hŭi-ryong 趙熙龍 (1789–1866). *Hosan oegi* 壺山外記. Reprinted in *Yŏhang munhak ch'ongsŏ* 여항문학총서. Seoul: Yŏgang, 1991.

Cho Su-sam 趙秀三 (1762–1849). *Ch'ujae chip* 秋齋集. Reprinted in *Yŏhang munhak ch'ongsŏ* 여항문학총서. Seoul: Yŏgang, 1991.

Ch'ŏn Hye-bong 천혜봉. *Han'guk sŏjihak* 韓國書誌學. Seoul: Minŭmsa, 1991.

———. *Ko inswae* 古印刷. Seoul: Taewŏnsa, 1989.

Chŏng Ch'ang-gwŏn 정창권. *Hollo pyŏsŭl hamyŏ kŭdae rŭl saenggak hanora* 홀로 벼슬하며 그 대를 생각하노라. Seoul: Sagyejŏl, 2003.

Chŏng Min 정민. *18 segi hanchung chisigin ŭi munye konghwaguk* 18세기 한중지식인의 문예공화국. Seoul: Munhak tongne, 2014.

———, ed. *Pukkyŏng Yurich'ang: 18, 19 segi Tong Asia ŭi munhwa kŏjŏm* 북경 유리창: 18–19세기 동아시아의 문화거점. Seoul: Minsogwŏn, 2013.

Chŏng Min 정민 and Pak Ch'ŏl-sang 박철상, trans. "Yonam sŏnsaeng sŏgan ch'ŏp" 연암 선생 서간첩. *Taedong hanmunhak* 대동한문학 22 (2005): 311–93.

Chŏng Ok-cha 정옥자. "Chŏngjo ŭi ch'ugye munsin kyoyuk kwa munch'e chŏngch'aek" 정조의 추계문신교육과 문체정책. *Kyujanggak* 6 (1982): 116–39.

———. *Chŏngjo ŭi munye sasang kwa kyujanggak* 정조의 문예사상과 규장각. Seoul: Hyohyŏng ch'ulp'an, 2001.

———. *Chosŏn hugi munhwa undong sa* 조선후기문화운동사. Seoul: Iljogak, 1993.

Chŏng Sang-gi 鄭尙驥 (1678–1752). *Nongp'o mundap* 農圃問答. Trans. Yi U-Sŏng. Seoul: Han'gilsa, 1992.

Chŏng Yag-yong 丁若鏞 (1762–1836). *Kugyŏk Tasan simunjip* 국역다산시문집. Seoul: Minjok munhwa ch'ujinhoe, 1985.

———. *Tasan simunjip* 茶山詩文集. http://db.itkc.or.kr.

———. *Yŏyudang chŏnsŏ* 與猶堂全書. http://db.itkc.or.kr.

Chŏngjo 正祖 (1752–1800). *Kugyŏk Hongjae chŏnsŏ* 國譯弘齋全書. 18 vols. Seoul: Minjok munhwa ch'ujinhoe, 1997.

———. *Hongjae chŏnsŏ* 弘齋全書. Reprint of Changsŏgak's manuscript. 5 vols. Seoul: Munhwajae kwalliguk changsŏgak samuso, 1978.

Chosŏn wangjo sillok 朝鮮王朝實錄. Ed. Kuksa p'yŏnch'an wiwŏnhoe 國史編纂委員會. http://sillok.history.go.kr.

Chow, Kai-wing. *Publishing, Culture, and Power in Early Modern China*. Stanford: Stanford University Press, 2003.

Chu Renhuo 褚人獲 (b. 1635). *Jianhu ji* 堅瓠集. 4 vols. Shanghai: Guji chubanshe, 2012.

Clunas, Craig. *Elegant Debts: The Social Art of Wen Zhengming, 1470–1559*. London: Reaktion Books, 2004.

———. *Superfluous Things: Material Culture and Social Status in Early Modern China*. Honolulu: University of Hawai'i Press, 1991.

Connery, Christopher Leigh. *The Empire of the Text: Writing and Authority in Early Imperial China*. Lanham: Rowman and Littlefield, 1998.

Crossley, Pamela Kyle. *A Translucent Mirror: History and Identity in Qing Imperial Ideology*. Berkeley and Los Angeles: University of California Press, 1999.

Dai Mingshi 戴名世 (1653–1713). *Nanshan ji ouchao* 南山集偶抄. Reprinted in *Xuxiu Siku quanshu* 續修四庫全書, vol. 1418. Shanghai: Guji chubanshe, 1995.

Dai Tingjie 戴廷杰 (Pierre-Henri Durand). *Dai Mingshi nianpu* 戴名世年譜. Beijing: Zhonghua shuju, 2004.

———. "Yasu gongrong, xiayu hujian: Kangxi nianjian Huizhou shangji Yangzhou wenshi he xuanjia Zhang Chao qiren qishi" 雅俗共融，瑕瑜互見：康熙年間徽州商籍揚州文士和选家張潮其人其事. Trans. Xu Minglong 許明龍, *Faguo hanxue* 法國漢學 13 (2010): 544–658.

———. "*Youmengying* banke kaolun" 幽夢影版刻考論. *Wenxian jikan* 文獻季刊 4 (2011): 38–50.

Deng Changfeng 鄧長風. *Ming Qing xiqujia kaolüe xubian* 明清戲曲家考略續编. Shanghai: Guji chubanshe, 1997.

Deng Hanyi 鄧漢儀 (1617–89). *Shiguan* 詩觀. Reprinted in *Siku jinhuishu congkan* 四庫禁燬書叢刊, *jibu* vol. 512. Beijing: Beijing chubanshe, 1997–99.

Deng Zhicheng 鄧之誠. *Qingshi jishi chubian* 清詩紀事初編. 2 vols. Beijing: Zhonghua shuju, 1965.

Dennis, Joseph R. *Writing, Publishing, and Reading Local Gazetteers in Imperial China, 1100–1700*. Cambridge, MA: Harvard University Asia Center, 2015.

Ding Naifei. *Obscene Things: The Sexual Politics in Jin Ping Mei*. Durham: Duke University Press, 2002.

Du Guiping 杜桂萍. *Qingchu zaju yanjiu* 清初雜劇研究. Beijing: Renmin wenxue chubanshe, 2005.

Edgren, Sören. "The *Fengmianye* (Cover Page) as a Source for Chinese Publishing History." In *Higashi Ajia shuppan bunka kenkyū, Niwatazumi* 東アジア出版文化研究：にわたずみ, ed. Isobe Akira 磯部彰, 261–67. Tokyo: Chisen shokan, 2004.

Edgren, Sören et al., eds. *Chinese Rare Books in American Collections*. New York: China House Gallery, China Institute of America, 1985.

Eisenstein, Elizabeth. *The Printing Revolution in Early Modern Europe*. Cambridge, UK: Cambridge University Press, 1983.

Elman, Benjamin. "Collecting and Classifying: Ming Dynasty Compendia and Encyclopedia (*Leishu*)." *Extrême-Orient, Extrême-Occident* (2007):131–57.

Evon, Gregory. "Tobacco, God, and Books: The Perils of Barbarism in Eighteenth-Century Korea." *Journal of Asian Studies* 73.2 (2014): 641–59.

Feng, Linda Rui. *City of Marvel and Transformation: Chang'an and Narratives of Experience in Tang Dynasty China*. Honolulu: University of Hawai'i Press, 2016.

Finnane, Antonia. *Speaking of Yangzhou: A Chinese City, 1550–1850*. Cambridge, MA: Harvard University Asia Center, 2004.

Genette, Gérard. *Paratexts: Thresholds of Interpretation*. Cambridge, UK: Cambridge University Press, 1997.

Goodrich, Luther C. *The Literary Inquisition of Ch'ien-lung*. New York: Paragon Book Reprint Corp, 1966.

Gōyama Kiwamu 合山究. *Yūmuei* 幽夢影. Tokyo: Meitoku shuppansha, 1977.

Grafton, Anthony, Elizabeth Eisenstein, and Adrian Johns. "AHR Forum: How Revolutionary Was the Print Revolution?" *American Historical Review* 107.1 (Feb. 2002): 84–128.

Greenbaum, Jamie. *Chen Jiru (1558–1639): The Background to, Development and Subsequent Uses of Literary Personae*. Leiden: Brill, 2007.

Gu Guorui 顧國瑞 and Liu Hui 劉輝. "'Chidu oucun,' 'Yousheng' ji qizhong de xiqu shiliao" 尺牘偶存、友聲及其中的戲曲史料. *Wenshi* 文史 15 (1982): 263–74.

Guo Chengkang 郭成康 and Lin Tiejun 林鉄鈞. *Qingchao wenziyu* 清朝文字獄. Beijing: Junzhong chubanshe, 1990.

Guy, R. Kent. *The Emperor's Four Treasuries: Scholars and the State in the Late Ch'ienlung Era*. Cambridge, MA: Harvard University Press, 1987.

Han Chae-rak 韓在洛 (1775–ca. 1833). *Nokp'a chapki* 綠波雜記. Trans. Yi Ka-wŏn and Hŏ Kyŏng-jin. Seoul: Kimyŏng sa, 2007.

Hanan, Patrick. "The Text of the *Chin P'ing Mei*." *Asia Major* 9.1 (1962): 1–57.

Handler-Spitz, Rivi, Pauline C. Lee, and Haun Saussy, eds. and trans. *A Book to Burn and a Book to Keep Hidden: Selected Writings of Li Zhi*. New York: Columbia University Press, 2016.

Hangzhou fuzhi 杭州府志. Taipei: Chengwen chubanshe, 1974.

He, Yuming. *Home and the World: Editing the "Glorious Ming" in Woodblock-Printed Books of the Sixteenth and Seventeenth Centuries*. Cambridge, MA: Harvard University Asia Center, 2013.

Hegel, Robert E. *Reading Illustrated Fiction in Late Imperial China*. Stanford: Stanford University Press, 1998.

Heijdra, Martin. "Technology, Culture and Economics: Movable Type versus Woodblock Printing in East Asia." In *Higashi Ajia shuppan bunka kenkyū, Niwatazumi* 東アジア出版文化研究: にわたずみ, ed. Isobe Akira 磯部彰, 223–40. Tokyo: Chisen shokan, 2004.

Henry, Eric. "The Motif of Recognition in Early China." *Harvard Journal of Asiatic Studies* 47.1 (1987): 5–30.

Ho, Wai-Kam. "Late Ming Literati: Their Social and Cultural Ambience." In *The Chinese Scholar's Studio*, ed. Chu-Tsing Li and James Watt, 23–36. New York: Asia Society Galleries, 1987.

Hong Kil-ju 洪吉周 (1786–1841). *Hanghae pyŏngham* 沆瀣丙函. 2 vols. P'aju: T'aehak sa, 2006.

Hong Sŏn-p'yo 홍선표 et al., comps. *17–18 segi Chosŏn ŭi oeguk sŏjŏk suyong kwa toksŏ munhwa: mongnok kwa haeje* 17–18 세기 조선의 외국서적 수용과 독서문화: 목록과 해제. Seoul: Hyean, 2006.

Hong Tae-yong 洪大容 (1731–83). "Yŏn'gi" 燕記. In *Tamhŏnsŏ* 湛軒書, vol. 4. Seoul: Minjok munhwa ch'ujinhoe, 1986.

Hou Zhongyi 侯忠義 and Wang Rumei 王汝梅, eds. *Jin Ping Mei ziliao huibian* 金瓶梅資料彙編. Beijing: Beijing daxue chubanshe, 1985.

Hsiao, Li-Ling. *The Eternal Present of the Past: Illustration, Theater, and Reading in the Wanli Period, 1573–1619*. Leiden: Brill, 2007.

Hsieh, Daniel. *Love and Women in Early Chinese Fiction*. Hong Kong: Chinese University Press, 2008.

Hu Yinglin 胡應麟 (1551–1602). *Shaoshi shanfang bicong* 少室山房筆叢. Shanghai: Shanghai shudian chubanshe, 2009.

Huang Aiping 黃愛平. *Siku quanshu zuanxiu yanjiu* 四庫全書纂修研究. Beijing: Renmin daxue chubanshe, 1989.

Huang Lie 黃烈, comp. *Jiangsu caiji yishu mulu* 江蘇采集遺書目錄. Reprint of the manuscript. 4 vols. Shanghai: Shanghai hezhong tushuguan, 1943.

Huang, Martin. *Literati and Self-Re/Presentation: Autobiographical Sensibility in the Eighteenth-Century Chinese Novel.* Stanford: Stanford University Press, 1995.

Huang Tingjian 黃廷鑑 (1762–1841). *Di liu xianxi wenchao* 第六絃溪文抄. Reprinted in *Congshu jicheng chubian* 叢書集成初編, vol. 2462. Shanghai: Shangwuyin shuguan, 1935–40.

Huang Zhouxing 黃周星 (1611–80). *Chongding Tang shikuai* 重訂唐詩快. Shudai caotang 書帶草堂 edition. National Library of China.

———. *Xiawei tang bieji* 夏為堂別集. Reprinted in *Qingdai shiwen ji huibian* 清代詩文集彙編, vol. 37. Shanghai: Guji chubanshe, 2010.

———. *Xiawei tang bieji ciyu* 夏為堂別集詞餘. National Library of China.

Hummel, Arthur. "Ts'ung Shu." *Journal of the American Oriental Society* 51.1 (1931): 40–46.

Idema, Wilt L., trans. *Personal Salvation and Filial Piety: Two Precious Scroll Narratives of Guanyin and Her Acolytes.* Honolulu: University of Hawai'i Press, 2008.

———. "Zang Maoxun as a Publisher." In *Higashi Ajia shuppan bunka kenkyū, Niwatazumi* 東アジア出版文化研究: にわたずみ, ed. Isobe Akira 磯部彰, 19–30. Tokyo: Chisen shokan, 2004.

Idema, Wilt L., Wai-yee Li, and Ellen Widmer, eds. *Trauma and Transcendence in Early Qing Literature.* Cambridge, MA: Harvard University Asia Center, 2006.

Inglis, Alister D. "A Textual History of Hong Mai's *Yijian zhi.*" *T'oung Pao* 93.4/5 (2007): 283–368.

Inoue Susumu 井上進. *Chūgoku shuppan bunkashi: shomotsu sekai to chi no fūkei* 中国出版文化史: 書物世界と知の風景. Nagoya: Nagoya daigaku shuppankai, 2002.

Jackson, Leon. *The Business of Letters: Authorial Economies in Antebellum America.* Stanford: Stanford University Press, 2008.

Jardine, Lisa. *Worldly Goods: A New History of the Renaissance.* New York: W. W. Norton and Company, 1996.

Ji Tongcheng Fang Dai liangjia shu'an 記桐城方戴兩家書案. Reprinted in *Congshu jicheng xubian* 叢書集成續編, vol. 25. Taipei: Xinwenfeng chuban gongsi, 1991.

Johns, Adrian. *The Nature of the Book: Print and Knowledge in the Making.* Chicago: University of Chicago Press, 1998.

Johnson, David, Andrew Nathan, and Evelyn Rawski, eds. *Popular Culture in Late Imperial China.* Berkeley and Los Angeles: University of California Press, 1985.

Kafalas, Philip A. *In Limpid Dream: Nostalgia and Zhang Dai's Reminiscences of the Ming.* Norwalk: Eastbridge, 2007.

Kang Myŏng-gwan 강명관. *Ch'aek pŏlledŭl Chosŏn ŭl mandŭlda* 책벌레들 조선을 만들다. Seoul: P'urŭn yŏksa, 2007.

———. *Chosŏn sidae ch'aek kwa chisik ŭi yŏksa: Chosŏn ŭi ch'aek kwa chisik ŭn Chosŏn sahoe wa ŏttŏk'e mannago heŏjyŏssŭlkka?* 조선시대 책과 지식의 역사: 조선의

책과 지식은 조선 사회와 어떻게 만나고 헤어졌을까? Seoul: Ch'ŏnnyŏn ŭi sangsang, 2014.

———. *Chosŏn sidae munhak yesul ŭi saengsŏng konggan* 조선시대 문학 예술의 생성 공간. Seoul: Somyŏng ch'ulp'an, 1999.

———. "Munch'e wa kukka changch'i" 문체와 국가장치. *Munhak kwa kyŏnggye* 문학 과 경계 2 (2001): 120–42.

Kasai Naomi 笠井直美. "Gogun hōkanrō shomoku" 吳郡寶翰樓書目. *Tōkyō daigaku tōyō bunka kenkyūsho kiyō* 東京大学東洋文化研究所紀要 164 (2013.12): 53–113.

Katsuyama Minoru. "Mindai ni okeru bōkaku bon no shuppan jōkyō nitsuite: Mindai zenpan no shuppanshū kara miru kenyō bōkaku bon nitsuite" 明代における坊刻 本の出版狀況について: 明代全般の出版數から見る建陽坊刻本について. In *Higashi Ajia shuppan bunka kenkyū, Niwatazumi* 東アジア出版文化研究: に わたずみ, ed. Isobe Akira 磯部彰, 83–100. Tokyo: Chisen shokan, 2004.

Kim Kwan-ung 김관웅 et al. "Hojŏ ŭi chŏng: Hwang Pi-yŏl kwa Pak Che-ga, Yu Tŭk-kong saiŭi kyoyu e taehan kojŭng" 호저의 정: 황비열과 박제가, 유득공 사이의 교유에 대한 고증. *Kyujanggak* 규장각 38 (2011): 153–76.

Kim Mun-sik 김문식. "Sŏ Yi Pang-ik sa e nat'ananŭn Pak Chi-wŏn ŭi chiri kojŭng" 서이방익사에 나타나는 박지원의 지리 고증. *Han'guk sirhak yŏn'gu* 한국실학연구 15 (2008): 193–225.

Kim Sŏng-jin 김성진. "Yŏng-Chŏng yŏn'gan ŭi sidaesang kwa sop'umch'e sanmun ŭi taedu" 영정 연간의 시대상과 소품체 산문의 대두. *Han'guk munhak nonch'ong* 한국문학논총 12 (Nov. 1991): 93–114.

Kim Yŏng-jin 김영진. "Chosŏn hugi chungguk sahaeng kwa sŏch'aek munhwa" 조선 후기 중국 사행과 서책 문화. In *19 segi Chosŏn chisigin ŭi munhwa chihyŏngdo* 19 세기 조선 지식인의 문화 지형도, ed. Hanyang taehakkyo Han'gukhak yŏn'guso, 591–648. Seoul: Hanyang taehakkyo ch'ulp'anpu, 2006.

———. "Chosŏn hugi sirhakp'a ŭi ch'ongsŏ p'yŏnch'an kwa kŭ ŭimi" 조선 후기 실학 파의 총서 편찬과 그 의미. In *Han'guk hanmunhak yŏn'gu ŭi sae chip'yŏng* 한국 한문학 연구의 새 지평, ed. Yi Hye-sun, 949–83. Seoul: Somyŏng ch'ulp'an, 2005.

———. "*U Ch'o sinji* ŭi p'anbon kwa Chosŏn hugi munindŭl ŭi Myŏng-Ch'ŏng sop'um yŏldok" 우초신지의 판본과 조선 후기 문인들의 명청 소품 열독. In *Chosŏn hugi sop'ummun ŭi silch'e* 조선 후기 소품문의 실체, ed. An Tae-hoe, 203–32. Seoul: T'aehak sa, 2003.

Kim Yŏng-min 김영민. "Chosŏn chunghwa chuŭi ŭi chaegŏmt'o" 조선중화주의의 재검토. *Han'guk sa yŏn'gu* 한국사 연구 162 (2013): 211–52.

Kong Shangren 孔尚任 (1648–1718). *Kong Shangren quanji* 孔尚任全集. Ed. Xu Zhen-gui 徐振貴. 4 vols. Ji'nan: Qilu shushe, 2004.

Kornicki, Peter. *The Book in Japan: A Cultural History from the Beginnings to the Nine-teenth Century*. Honolulu: University of Hawai'i Press, 2001.

Knight, Jeffrey Todd. *Bound to Read: Compilations, Collections, and the Making of Re-naissance Literature*. Philadelphia: University of Pennsylvania Press, 2013.

Kye Sŭng-bŏm 계승범. "Chosŏn ŭi 18 segi wa t'al chunghwa munje" 조선의 18세기와 탈중화문제. *Yŏksa hakpo* 역사학보 213 (2012): 71–96.

Lang Ying 郎瑛 (1487–ca. 1566). *Qixiu leigao* 七修類稿. 2 vols. Beijing: Zhonghua shuju, 1961.

Ledyard, Gari. "Korean Travelers in China over Four Hundred Years, 1488–1887." *Occasional Papers on Korea* 2 (March 1974): 1–42.

Legge, James. *The Four Books: Confucian Analects, The Great Learning, The Doctrine of the Mean, and the Works of Mencius.* Shanghai: The Chinese Book, 1930.

Lei Mengchen 雷夢辰. *Qingdai gesheng jinshu huikao* 清代各省禁書彙考. Beijing: Beijing tushuguan chubanshe, 1989.

Lerer, Seth. "Medieval English Literature and the Idea of the Anthology." *PMLA* 118.5 (2003): 1251–60.

Li Dou 李斗 (1749–1817). *Yangzhou huafang lu* 揚州畫舫錄. Beijing: Zhonghua shuju, 2004.

Li Fang 李昉 (925–96) et al., comps. *Taiping guangji* 太平廣記. Beijing: Renmin wenxue chubanshe, 1959.

Li Huan 李桓 (1827–91), comp. *Guochao shixian leizheng* 國朝耆獻類徵. Guangxu edition. Cornell University Library.

Li Mengsheng 李夢生. *Zhongguo jinhui xiaoshuo baihua* 中國禁毀小説百話. Shanghai: Shanghai shudian, 2006.

Li, Wai-yee. "The Collector, the Connoisseur, and Late-Ming Sensibility." *T'oung Pao* 81 (1995): 269–302.

———. "The Late-Ming Courtesan: Invention of a Cultural Ideal." In *Writing Women in Late Imperial China*, ed. Ellen Widmer and Kang-i Sun Chang, 46–73. Stanford: Stanford University Press, 1997.

———. "The Rhetoric of Spontaneity in Late-Ming Literature." *Ming Studies* 35 (August 1995): 32–52.

———. "Shibian yu wanwu" 世變與玩物. *Zhongguo wenzhe yanjiu jikan* 中國文哲研究集刊 33 (2008.9): 35–76.

———. "Shishuo xinyu and the Emergence of Chinese Aesthetic Consciousness in the Six Dynasties." In *Chinese Aesthetics: The Ordering of Literature, the Arts, and the Universe in the Six Dynasties*, ed. Zong-qi Cai, 237–76. Honolulu: University of Hawai'i Press, 2004.

———. *Women and National Trauma in Late Imperial Chinese Literature.* Cambridge, MA: Harvard University Asia Center, 2014.

Li Wenzao 李文藻 (1730–78). "Liuli chang shusi ji" 琉璃廠書肆記. In *Liuli chang xiaozhi* 琉璃廠小志, ed. Sun Dianqi 孫殿起. Beijing: Beijing guji chubanshe, 1982.

Li Xiaorong. "Gender and Textual Politics during the Qing Dynasty: The Case of the Zhengshi Ji." *Harvard Journal of Asiatic Studies* 69.1 (2009): 75–107.

Li Yanshi 李延昰 (1628–97). *Nanwu jiuhua lu* 南吳舊話錄. Reprinted in Shanghai, n.d. Cornell University Library.

Li Yu 李漁 (1610–80). *Chidu chuzheng* 尺牘初徵. Reprint of 1660 edition in *Siku jinhuishu congkan* 四庫禁燬書叢刊, vol. 153. Beijing: Beijing chubanshe, 1997.

———. *Liweng yijiayan chuji* 笠翁一家言初集. Reprinted in *Siku jinhuishu congkan bubian* 四庫禁燬書叢刊補編, vol. 85. Beijing: Beijing chubanshe, 2005.

Li Zhi 李贄 (1527–1602). *Fenshu Xu Fenshu* 焚書續焚書. Beijing: Zhonghua shuju, 1975.

Lin Yutang. *The Importance of Living.* New York: John Day Company, 1940.

Liu Dakui 劉大魁 (1697–1779). *Shexian zhi* 歙縣志. Collated by Zhang Peifang 張佩芳. Reprint of 1771 edition. 5 vols. Taipei: Chengwen chubanshe, 1975.

Liu Hewen 劉和文. *Zhang Chao yanjiu* 張潮研究. Hefei: Anhui daxue chubanshe, 2011.

———. "Zhang Chao zhushu zongkao" 張潮著述綜考. *Hefei xueyuan xuebao* 合肥學院學報 21.3 (Aug. 2004): 27–30.

Liu Shangheng 劉尚恒. *Guji congshu gaishuo* 古籍叢書概說. Shanghai: Guji chubanshe, 1989.

———. *Huizhou keshu yu cangshu* 徽州刻書與藏書. Yangzhou: Guangling shushe, 2003.

Liu Yiqing 劉義慶 (403–44). *Shishuo xinyu* 世說新語. Beijing: Huaxia chubanshe, 2000.

Liu Zongyuan 柳宗元 (773–819). *Liu Zongyuan ji* 柳宗元集. 4 vols. Beijing: Zhonghua shuju, 1979.

Lo, Andrew. "Amusement Literature in Some Early Ch'ing Collectanea." In *The Power of Culture: Studies in Chinese Cultural History*, ed. Willard J. Peterson, Andrew Plaks, and Ying-shih Yü, 275–303. Hong Kong: Chinese University Press, 1994.

Love, Harold. *The Culture and Commerce of Texts: Scribal Publication in Seventeenth-Century England*. Amherst and Boston: University of Massachusetts Press, 1993.

Lowry, Kathryn A. *The Tapestry of Popular Songs in Sixteenth- and Seventeenth-Century China: Reading, Imitation, and Desire*. Leiden: Brill, 2005.

Lu Lin 陸林. "Qingchu zongji *Shiguan* suoshou Huizhou shijia sanlun" 清初總集詩觀所收徽州詩家散論. *Huixue* 徽學 2 (2002): 289–306.

———. "Sheren Zhang Chao yu *Yu Chu xinzhi*" 歙人張潮與虞初新志. *Gudian wenxue zhishi* 古典文學知識 5 (2001): 97–103.

Ma Chung-rak 마중락. "Chŏngjo cho komun puhŭng undong ŭi sasang kwa paegyŏng" 정조조 고문 부흥 운동의 사상과 배경. *Han'guksaron* 한국사론 14 (1986): 51–103.

McDermott, Joseph P. "The Ascendance of the Imprint in China." In *Printing and Book Culture in Late Imperial China*, ed. Cynthia J. Brokaw and Kai-wing Chow, 55–104. Berkeley and Los Angeles: University of California Press, 2005.

———. "The Making of a Chinese Mountain, Huangshan: Politics and Wealth in Chinese Art." *Asian Cultural Studies* 17 (1989): 145–77.

———. *A Social History of the Chinese Book: Books and Literati Culture in Late Imperial China*. Hong Kong: Hong Kong University Press, 2006.

McKenzie, D. F. *Making Meaning: "Printers of the Mind" and Other Essays*. Ed. Peter D. McDonald and Michael F. Suarez, S.J. Amherst and Boston: University of Massachusetts Press, 2002.

McKitterick, David. *Print, Manuscript and the Search for Order, 1450–1830*. Cambridge, UK: Cambridge University Press, 2003.

Meyer-Fong, Tobie. *Building Culture in Early Qing Yangzhou*. Stanford: Stanford University Press, 2003.

———. "Packaging the Men of Our Times: Literary Anthologies, Friendship Networks, and Political Accommodation in the Early Qing." *Harvard Journal of Asiatic Studies* 64.1 (2004): 5–56.

Miu Yonghe 繆咏禾. "Mao Jin Jigu ge de chuban shiye" 毛晉汲古閣的出版事業. In *Zhongguo chuban shiliao* 中國出版史料, ed. Song Yuanfang 宋原放 et al., 1:592–615. Wuhan: Hubei jiaoyu chubanshe, 2004.

Naegak pangsŏrok 內閣訪書錄. Reprinted in *Kyujanggak* 13 (1990): 61–207.

Needham, Joseph. *Science and Civilization in China*, vol. 5.1. Cambridge, UK: Cambridge University Press, 1985.

Nie Xian 聶先 (fl. 1679). *Baiming jia cichao* 百名家詞鈔. Kangxi Jinchang 金閶 Lüyin tang 綠蔭堂. National Library of China.

Nugent, Christopher M. B. *Manifest in Words, Written on Paper: Producing and Circulating Poetry in Tang Dynasty China*. Cambridge, MA: Harvard University Asia Center, 2010.

Ōba Osamu 大庭脩, ed. *Hakusai shomoku* 舶載書目. 2 vols. Fukita: Kansai daigaku tōzai gakujutsu kenkyūjo, 1972.

Okamoto Sae 岡本さえ. *Shindai kinsho no kenkyū* 清代禁書の研究. Tokyo: Tōkyō daigaku shuppankai, 1996.

Ōki Yasushi 大木康. "Chugoku: Minmatsu no shuppan jijou" 中國：明末の出版事情. *Edo bungaku* 江戶文學 18 (1997): 160–65.

———. *Chūgoku Minmatsu no media kakumei: shomin ga hon o yomu* 中国明末のメディア革命：庶民が本を読む. Tokyo: Tōsui shobō, 2009.

———. *Chūgoku yūri kūkan: Min Shin Shinwai gijo no sekai* 中国遊里空間：明清秦淮妓女の世界. Tokyo: Seidosha, 2002.

———. *Minmatsu kōnan no shuppan bunka* 明末江南の出版文化. Tokyo: Kenbun shuppan, 2004.

———. "Minshin ryōdai ni okeru shōhon" 明清兩代における鈔本. In *Mindaishi kenkyūkai sōritsu sanjūgo-nen kinen ronshū* 明代史研究會創立三十五年紀念論集. Tokyo: Kyūko shoin, 2003.

Orgel, Stephen. *Spectacular Performances: Essays on Theatre, Imagery, Books, and Selves in Early Modern England*. Manchester and New York: Manchester University Press, 2011.

Pak Chi-wŏn 朴趾源 (1737–1805). *Koch'ujang chagŭn tanji rŭl ponaeni: Yŏnam Pak Chi-wŏn i kajok kwa pŏt ege ponaen p'yŏnji* 고추장 작은 단지를 보내니: 연암 박지원이 가족과 벗에게 보내온 편지. Trans. Pak Hŭi-byŏng. P'aju: Tol pegae, 2005.

———. *Kugyŏk Yŏnam chip* 國譯燕巖集. Trans. Sin Ho-yŏl and Kim Myŏng-ho. Seoul: Minjok munhwa ch'ujinhoe, 2004.

———. *Yŏrha ilgi* 熱河日記. Trans. Ri Sang-ho. 2 vols. Seoul: Pori, 2004.

Pak Chong-ch'ae 朴宗采 (1780–1835). *Yŏkchu Kwajŏngnok* 譯注過庭錄. Ed. and trans. Kim Yun-ju. Seoul: T'aehaksa, 1997.

Pak Hyŏn-gyu 박현규. "Chosŏn Pak Che-ga Yu Tŭk-kong kwa Ch'ŏng hwaga Na Ping ŭi hwayŏn" 조선 박제가 유득공과 청 화가 나빙의 화연. *Han'gukhak nonjip* 한국학논집 50 (2013): 69–96.

———. "Chosŏn sasintŭl i kyŏnmunhan pukkyŏng yurich'ang" 조선 사신들이 견문한 북경 유리창. In *Yŏnhaengnok yŏn'gu ch'ongsŏ* 연행록 연구총서, vol. 10, 233–63. Seoul: Hakkobang, 2006.

Pak Kyun-sŏp 박균섭. "Munch'e panch'ŏng tokpŏp" 문체반정 독법. *Kukhak yŏn'gu* 국학연구 16 (2010): 609–45.

Pak Sa-ho 朴思浩 (b. 1784). *Simjŏn ko* 心田稿. In *Kugyŏk Yŏnhaengnok sŏnjip* 국역 연행록 선집. Seoul: Minjok munhwa ch'ujinhoe, 1976.

Pan Shuguang 潘樹廣. "Ming yimin Huang Zhouxing ji qi yiqu" 明遺民黃周星及其
逸曲. *Wenxue yichan* 文學遺產 2 (2001): 134–37.

Park, J. P. *Art by the Book: Printing Manuals and the Leisure Life in Late Ming China.*
Seattle: University of Washington Press, 2012.

Pattinson, David. "The Market for Letter Collections in Seventeenth-Century China."
Chinese Literature: Essays, Articles, Reviews 28 (2006): 125–57.

Poovey, Mary. *Genres of the Credit Economy: Mediating Value in Eighteenth- and
Nineteenth-Century Britain.* Chicago: University of Chicago Press, 2008.

Qian Daxin 錢大昕 (1728–1804). *Shijia zhai yangxin lu* 十駕齋養新錄. In *Sibu beiyao*
四部備要, case 206. Shanghai: Zhonghua shuju, 1936.

Qian Hang 錢杭 and Cheng Zai 承載. *Shiqi shiji Jiangnan shehui shenghuo* 十七世紀
江南社會生活. Hangzhou: Zhejiang renmin chubanshe, 1996.

Qian Nanxiu. *Spirit and Self in Medieval China: The "Shih-shuo hsin-yü" and Its Legacy.*
Honolulu: University of Hawai'i Press, 2001.

Qingdai shiwen ji huibian bianzuan weiyuanhui 清代詩文集彙編編纂委員會. *Qingdai shiwen ji huibian* 清代詩文集彙編. Shanghai: Guji chubanshe, 2009–10.

Qingshi liezhuan 清史列傳. 20 vols. Beijing: Zhonghua shuju, 1987.

Ren Songru 任松如. *Siku quanshu dawen* 四庫全書答問. Chengdu: Bashu shushe, 1988.

Rowe, William T. "Political, Social and Economic Factors Affecting the Transmission
of Technical Knowledge in Early Modern China." In *Cultures of Knowledge: Technology in Chinese History*, ed. Dagmar Schäfer, 25–44. Leiden: Brill, 2012.

Roy, David T. "The Case for T'ang Hsien-tsu's Authorship of the *Jin Ping Mei*." *Chinese
Literature: Essays, Articles, Reviews* 8.1–2 (1986): 31–62.

St. Clair, William. *The Reading Nation in the Romantic Period.* Cambridge, UK: Cambridge University Press, 2004.

Shang Wei. "*Jin Ping Mei* and Late Ming Print Culture." In *Writing and Materiality in
China*, ed. Judith T. Zeitlin and Lydia H. Liu, 187–238. Cambridge, MA: Harvard
Universtiy Asia Center, 2003.

Shen Chu 沈初 et al., eds. *Zhejiang caiji yishu zonglu* 浙江採集遺書總錄. Yonsei University Library, Seoul.

———. *Zhejiang caiji yishu zonglu* 浙江採集遺書總錄. Shanghai: Guji chubanshe, 2011.

Shen Defu 沈德符 (1578–1642). *Wanli yehuo bian* 萬曆野獲編. Reprint of 1959 edition.
Taipei: Xinxing shuju, 1976.

Shields, Anna M. *One Who Knows Me: Friendship and Literary Culture in Mid-Tang
China.* Cambridge, MA: Harvard University Asia Center, 2015.

Sima Chaojun 司馬朝軍. *Siku quanshu zongmu bianzuan kao* 四庫全書總目編纂考.
Wuchang: Wuhan daxue chubanshe, 2005.

———. *Siku quanshu zongmu yanjiu* 四庫全書總目研究. Beijing: Shehui kexue wenxian chubanshe, 2004.

Sima Qian 司馬遷 (ca. 145–86 BCE). *Shiji* 史記. 10 vols. Beijing: Zhonghua shuju, 1982.

Sin Sang-mok 신상목, Chang Chae-sŏk 장재석, and Cho Ch'ŏl-lae 조철래, trans.
Kanyŏksi ilgi 刊役時日記. Andong: Han'guk kukhak chinhŭngwŏn, 2015.

Sŏ Hyŏng-su 徐瀅修 (1749–1824). *Myŏnggo chŏnjip* 明皐全集. In *Han'guk munjip
ch'onggan* 한국문집총간. Seoul: Minjok ch'ujin wiwŏnhoe, 2001.

Son, Suyoung. "Between Writing and Publishing Letters: Publishing a Letter about Book Proprietorship." In *A History of Chinese Letters and Epistolary Culture*, ed. Antje Richter, 878–99. Leiden: Brill, 2015.

———. "Reading an Authorless Text: The Reception of *Jin Ping Mei* in Manuscript and Print." *Chungguk ŏmunhak nonjip* 중국어문학논집 81 (2013.8): 439–55.

Song Chae-yong 송재용. *Chosŏn sidae sŏnbi iyagi: Miam ilgi rŭl t'onghae kwagŏ wa hyŏnjae rŭl poda* 조선시대 선비이야기: 미암일기를 통해 과거와 현재를 보다. Seoul: Chei aen ssi, 2008.

Song Lihua 宋莉華. *Ming Qing shiqi de xiaoshuo chuanbo* 明清時期的小說傳播. Beijing: Zhongguo shehui kexue chubanshe, 2004.

Su Shi 蘇軾 (1036–1101). *Su Shi quanji* 蘇軾全集. 3 vols. Shanghai: Guji chubanshe, 2000.

Sun Congtian 孫從添 (1692–1767). "Cangshu jiyao" 藏書紀要. Trans. Achilles Fang, "Bookman's Manual." *Harvard Journal of Asiatic Studies* 14.1/2 (June 1951): 215–60.

Sun Dianqi 孫殿起, ed. *Liuli chang xiaozhi* 琉璃廠小志. Beijing: Beijing guji chubanshe, 1982.

———. *Qingdai jinshu zhijian lu waibian* 清代禁書知見錄外編. In *Qingdai jinshu zhijian lu* 清代禁書知見錄. Shanghai: Shangwuyin shuguan, 1957.

Sŭngjŏngwŏn ilgi 承政院日記. http://sjw.history.go.kr/main/main.jsp.

Tang Shunzhi 唐順之 (1507–60). *Tang Jingchuan wenji* 唐荊川文集. 12 vols. Reprint of Shanghai Hanfen lou 涵芬樓 edition. Shanghai: Shangwuyin shuguan, 1922.

Tsien, Tsuen-hsuin. "Technical Aspects of Chinese Printing." In *Chinese Rare Books in American Collections*, ed. Sören Edgren et al., 16–25. New York: China House Gallery, China Institute of America, 1985.

Wakeman, Frederic, Jr. "Romantics, Stoics, and Martyrs in Seventeenth-Century China." *Journal of Asian Studies* 43.4 (Aug. 1984): 631–65.

Wang Ayling 王璦玲. "Ming Qing shuhuai xiefen zaju zhi yishu tezhi yu chengfen" 明清抒懷寫憤雜劇之藝術特質與成分. *Ming Qing wenzhe yanjiu jikan* 明清文哲研究集刊 13 (1998): 37–120.

Wang Bin 王彬. *Jinshu wenziyu* 禁書文字獄. Beijing: Zhongguo gongren chubanshe, 1992.

———. *Qingdai jinshu zongshu* 清代禁書總述. Beijing: Zhongguo shudian, 1999.

Wang Guiping 王桂平. *Qingdai Jiangnan cangshujia keshu yanjiu* 清代江南藏書家刻書研究. Nanjing: Fenghuang chubanshe, 2008.

Wang Guoyuan 汪國垣, annot. *Tangren xiaoshuo* 唐人小說. Taipei: Yuandong tushu gongsi, 1956.

Wang Nengxian 王能憲. *Shishuo xinyu yanjiu* 世說新語研究. Nanjing: Jiangsu guji chubanshe, 2000.

Wang Qi 汪淇 (fl. 1600–68) and Xu Shijun 徐士俊 (1602–81), eds. *Fenlei chidu xinyu* 分類尺牘新語. Shanghai: Guangyi shuju, 1917.

Wang, Yugen. *Ten Thousand Scrolls: Reading and Writing in the Poetics of Huang Tingjian and the Late Northern Song*. Cambridge, MA: Harvard University Asia Center, 2011.

Wang Zhongmin 王重民, comp. *Bianli Siku quanshu dang'an* 辨理四庫全書檔案. 2 vols. Beijing: Beiping tushuguan, 1934.

Wang Zhuo 王晫 (b. 1636), comp. *Jin Shishuo* 今世説. In *Aoya tang congshu* 奧雅堂 叢書. Reprint of 1853 edition. Taipei: Hualian chubanshe, 1965.

———, comp. *Jin Shishuo* 今世説. Reprinted in *Xixiu Siku quanshu* 續修四庫全書, *zibu* 子部 vol. 1175. Shanghai: Guji chubanshe, 1985.

———, comp. *Lanyan ji* 蘭言集. 24 *juan*. National Library of China.

———. *Qiangdong zachao* 墻東雜鈔. 4 *juan*. National Library of China and Beijing University Library.

———, comp. *Qianqiu yadiao* 千秋雅調. National Library of China.

———, comp. *Wenjin* 文津. National Library of China.

———. *Xiaju tang ji* 霞舉堂集. 35 *juan*. Beijing University Library. Reprinted in *Qing-dai shiwen ji huibian* 清代詩文集彙編, vol. 144. Shanghai: Guji chubanshe, 2009.

———. *Xiaju tang ji* 霞舉堂集. 7 *juan*. National Library of China.

———. *Xiaju tang quanji dingben* 霞舉堂全集定本. 19 *juan*. Reprint of Shulin 書林 Zhenxiu tang 振秀堂 edition in Naikaku Bunko. Photo-reprint copy in the Hishi Collection in the Princeton University Library.

———. *Xialiu ci* 峽流詞. 3 *juan*. National Library of China.

———. *Zazhu shizhong* 雜著十種. 10 *juan*. National Library of China. Reprinted in *Siku quanshu cunmu congshu* 四庫全書存目叢書, vol. 165. Ji'nan: Qilu shushe, 1995–97.

———. *Zhuye ting zaji; Jin Shishuo* 竹葉亭雜記 今世說. Shanghai: Guji chubanshe, 2012.

Wang Zhuo and Zhang Chao, eds. *Tanji congshu* 檀几叢書. Facsimile reprint of 1695 edition in Shanghai Library. Shanghai: Guji chubanshe, 1991.

West, Stephen. "Text and Ideology: Ming Editors and Northern Drama." In *Ming Qing xiqu guoji yantao hui lunwen ji* 明清戲曲國際研討會論文集, ed. Hua Wei 華瑋 and Wang Ayling 王瓊玲, 1:237–83. Taipei: Zhongyang yanjiuyuan zhongguo wen-zhesuo yanjiusuo, 1998.

Widmer, Ellen. "Between Worlds: Huang Zhouxing's Imaginary Garden." In *Trauma and Transcendence in Early Qing Literature*, ed. Wilt L. Idema, Wai-yee Li, and Ellen Widmer, 249–81. Cambridge, MA: Harvard University Asia Center, 2006.

———. "The Huanduzhai of Hangzhou and Suzhou: A Study in Seventeenth-Century Publishing." *Harvard Journal of Asiatic Studies* 56.1 (1996): 77–122.

Wu Cheng 吳澄 (1249–1331). *Wu Wenzheng ji* 吳文正集. Reprinted in *Siku quanshu zhenben erji* 四庫全書珍本二集, vol. 322. Taipei: Taiwan shangwuyin shuguan, 1971.

Wu Chengxue 吳承學. *Wan Ming xiaopin yanjiu* 晚明小品研究. Nanjing: Jiangsu guji chubanshe, 1998.

Wu Gan 吳敢. *Jin Ping Mei pingdianjia Zhang Zhupo nianpu* 金瓶梅評點家張竹坡 年譜. Shenyang: Liaoning renmin chubanshe, 1987.

Wu Jingzi 吳敬梓 (1701–54). *The Scholars*. Trans. Yang Hsien-yi and Gladys Yang. Peking: Foreign Language Press, 1957.

Wu Shuyin 吳書蔭. "Dui 'Ming yimin Huang Zhouxing ji qi yiqu' de buzheng" 對'明 遺民黃周星及其逸曲'的補正. *Wenxue yichan* 文學遺產 5 (2003): 128–30.

Wu Weizu 吳慰祖, collated. *Siku caijin shumu* 四庫採進書目. Beijing: Shangwuyin shuguan, 1930.

Wu Zhefu 吳哲夫. *Qingdai jinhui shumu yanjiu* 清代禁燬書目研究. Taipei: Jiaxin shuinigongsi wenhua jijinhui, 1969.

Wu Zhenfang 吳震方 (fl. 1679), comp. *Shuoling* 說鈴. Reprinted in *Congshu jicheng xubian* 叢書集成續編, vol. 96. Shanghai: Shanghai shudian, 1994.

Xie Guozhen 謝國楨. *Ming Qing biji tancong* 明清筆記談叢. Shanghai: Guji chubanshe, 1981.

———. *Ming Qing zhi ji dangshe yundong kao* 明清之際黨社運動考. Taipei: Taiwan Shangwuyin shuguan, 1967.

Xie Zhaozhe 謝肇淛 (1567–1624). *Wu zazu* 五雜俎. Shenyang: Liaoning jiaoyu chubanshe, 2001.

Xie Zhengguang 謝正光. "Tanlun Qingchu shiwen dui Qian Muzhai pingjia zhi zhuanbian" 探論清初詩文對錢牧齋評價之轉變. In *Qingchu shiwen yu shiren jiaoyou kao* 清初詩文與士人交遊考, 61–108. Nanjing: Nanjing daxue chubanshe, 2001.

Xie Zhengguang and She Rufeng 佘汝豐, eds. *Qingchu ren xuan Qingchu shi huikao* 清初人選清初詩彙考. Nanjing: Nanjing daxue chubanshe, 1998.

Xu Qiu 徐釚 (1636–1708), ed. *Ciyuan congtan jiaojian* 詞苑叢談校箋. Annot. Wang Baili 王百里. Beijing: Renmin wenxue chubanshe, 1988.

Xu Wei 徐渭 (1521–93). *Xu Wei ji* 徐渭集. 4 vols. Beijing: Zhonghua shuju, 1983.

Xu Xuelin 徐學林. *Huizhou keshu* 徽州刻書. Hefei: Anhui renmin chubanshe, 2005.

Yao Jinyuan 姚覲元 (fl. 1843) and Sun Dianqi 孫殿起 (1894–1958), eds. *Qingdai jinshu zhijian lu; Qingdai jinhui shumu buyi er* 清代禁書知見錄 清代禁燬書目補遺二. Shanghai: Shangwuyin shuguan, 1957.

Ye Dehui 葉德輝 (1864–1927). *Shulin qinghua; Shulin yuhua* 書林清話 書林餘話. Changsha: Yuelu shushe, 1999.

Ye Mengzhu 葉夢珠 (b. 1624). *Yueshi bian* 閱世編. Shanghai: Guji chubanshe, 1981.

Yi Chae-jŏng 이재정. *Chosŏn ch'ulp'an chusik hoesa* 조선출판주식회사. Seoul: Antiquus, 2008.

Yi Chon-hŭi 이존희. "Chosŏn chŏn'gi ŭi taemyŏng sŏch'aek muyŏk" 조선 전기의 대명 서책 무역. *Chindan hakpo* 진단학보 44 (1977): 53–78.

Yi Hak-kyu 李學逵 (1770–1835). *Nakhasaeng chip* 洛下生集. http://db.itkc.or.kr.

Yi Ik 李瀷 (1681–1763). *Sŏngho sasŏl* 星湖僿說. http://db.itkc.or.kr.

Yi Kyu-gyŏng 李圭景 (1788–1856). *Oju yŏnmun changjŏn san'go* 五洲衍文長箋散稿. Seoul: Tong'guk munhwasa, 1958.

———. *Oju yŏnmun changjŏn san'go* 五洲衍文長箋散稿. http://db.itkc.or.kr.

Yi Min-hŭi 이민희. *16–19 segi sŏjŏk chunggaesang kwa sosŏl sŏjŏk yut'ong kwan'gye yŏn'gu* 16–19 세기 서적 중개상과 소설 서적 유통 관계 연구. Seoul: Yŏknak, 2007.

Yi Ok 李鈺 (1760–1815). *Yŏkchu Yi Ok chŏnjip* 역주 이옥 전집. Seoul: Somyŏng ch'ulp'an, 2001.

Yi Tŏng-mu 李德懋 (1741–93). *Ch'ŏngjanggwan chŏnsŏ* 青莊館全書. http://db.itkc .or.kr.

———. *Kugyŏk Ch'ŏngjanggwan chŏnsŏ* 國譯青莊館全書. Trans. Minjok ch'ujin wiwŏnhoe. 13 vols. Seoul: Sol, 1981.

Yi Ŭi-hyŏn 李宜顯 (1669–1745). "Kyŏngja yŏnhaeng chapchi" 庚子燕行雜識. In *Kugyŏk yŏnhaengnok sŏnjip* 國譯燕行錄選集. Seoul: Minjok munhwa ch'ujinhoe, 1976.

Yŏksa hakhoe 역사학회, ed. *Chŏngjo wa 18 segi: Yŏksa rosŏ 18 segi, Sŏgu wa Tong Asia ŭi pigyosajŏk sŏngch'al* 정조와 18세기: 역사로서 18세기, 서구와 동아시아의 비교사적 성찰. Seoul: P'urŭn yŏksa, 2013.

Yong Long 永瑢 (1744–90) et al., eds. *Siku quanshu zongmu* 四庫全書總目. 2 vols. Beijing: Zhonghua shuju, 1965.

Yu Chae-yŏp 유재엽. "Chosŏn chunggi ŭi tosŏ ch'ulp'an e kwanhan ilgoch'al" 조선 중기의 도서 출판에 관한 일고찰. *Ch'ulp'an chapchi yŏn'gu* 출판잡지연구 11.1 (2003): 88–96.

Yu Man-ju 俞晩柱 (1755–88). *Hŭmyŏng* 欽英. Reprint. 6 vols. Seoul: Sŏul taehakkyo kyujanggak, 1997.

———. *Ilgi rŭl ssŭda: Hŭmyŏng sŏnjip* 일기를 쓰다: 흠영 선집. Ed. and trans. Kim Ha-ra. P'aju: Tol pegae, 2015.

Yu Pong-hak 유봉학. *Chosŏn hugi hakkye wa chisigin* 조선 후기 학계와 지식인. Seoul: Singu munhwasa, 1998.

Yu Tŭk-kong 柳得恭 (1748–1807). *Yŏngjae chip* 泠齋集. http://db.itkc.or.kr.

Yuan Hongdao 袁宏道 (1568–1610). *Yuan Zhonglang quanji* 袁中郎全集. Taipei: Wenxing shudian, 1965.

Yuan Yi 袁逸. "Mingdai shuji jiage kao" 明代書籍價格考. In *Zhongguo chuban shiliao* 中國出版史料, ed. Song Yuanfang 宋原放 et al., 2:518–30. Wuhan: Hubei jiaoyu chubanshe, 2004.

Yun Chae-min 윤재민. "Munch'e panchŏng ŭi chaehaesŏk" 문체반정의 재해석. *Kochŏn munhak yŏn'gu* 고전문학연구 21 (2002): 69–94.

Zeitlin, Judith T. "Shared Dreams: The Story of the Three Wives' Commentary on *The Peony Pavilion.*" *Harvard Journal of Asiatic Studies* 54.1 (1994): 127–79.

Zhang Chao 張潮 (1650–ca. 1707), ed. *Chidu oucun* 尺牘偶存. 1780 reprint edition in the Beijing University Library.

———, ed. *Chidu yousheng* 尺牘友聲. 1780 reprint edition in the Beijing University Library.

———. *Xi'nang cunjin* 奚囊寸錦. Photo-reprint copy in the Hishi Collection in the Princeton University Library.

———. *Xinzhai liaofu ji* 心齋聊復集. 4 vols. Reprinted in *Siku jinhuishu congkan bubian* 四庫禁燬書叢刊補編, vol. 85. Beijing: Beijing chubanshe, 2005.

———. *Xinzhai liaofu ji* 心齋聊復集. 4 vols. 1682 edition. Beijing Normal University Library.

———. *Xinzhai zazu* 心齋雜俎. Beijing University Library.

———. *Youmengying* 幽夢影. Beijing University Library.

———. *Youmengying* 幽夢影. Annot. Wang Feng 王峰. Beijing: Zhonghua shuju, 2010.

———. *Yu Chu xinzhi* 虞初新志. Reprinted in *Siku jinhuishu congkan* 四庫禁燬書叢刊, vol. 38. Beijing: Beijing chubanshe, 1997–99.

———. *Yu Chu xinzhi* 虞初新志. 1760 reprint by Zhang Yi 張譯. Taiwan University Library.

———. *Yu Chu xinzhi* 虞初新志. Shanghai: Guji chubanshe, 2012.

Zhang Chao, ed. *Zhaodai congshu* 昭代叢書. Reprint of Daoguang 道光 Shikai tang 石楷堂 edition. Shanghai: Guju chubanshe, 1990.

Zhang Chao and Zhang Yongde 張庸德, eds. *Sishu zunzhu huiyi jie* 四書尊注會意解. 1697 edition in *Siku jinhuishu congkan* 四庫禁燬書叢刊, vol. 2. Beijing: Beijing chubanshe, 2005.

Zhang Dai 張岱 (1597–1684). *Taoan mengyi* 陶庵夢憶. Annot. Yu Xuezhou 于學周 and Tian Gang 田剛. Qingdao: Qingdao chubanshe, 2005.

Zhang Shenyu 張慎玉 and Zhao Yi 趙益. "Zhang Chao *Youmengying* zhi chengshu ji qi tongfeng xiaopin congshu lüelun" 張潮幽夢影之成書及其同朋小品叢書略論. *Anhui wenxian yanjiu jikan* 安徽文献研究集刊 1 (2004): 143–58.

Zhang Xikong 張習孔 (b. 1606). *Yiqing tang ji* 詒清堂集. 1669 Yiqing tang 詒清堂 edition. National Library of China.

———. *Xin'an Zhangshi xuxiu zongpu* 新安張氏續修宗譜. 1659 edition. National Library of China.

Zhang Xiumin 張秀民. *Zhongguo yinshua shi* 中國印刷史. Collated by Han Qi 韓琦. 2 vols. Hangzhou: Zhejiang guji chubanshe, 2006.

Zhang Ying. *Confucian Image Politics: Masculine Morality in Seventeenth-Century China*. Seattle: University of Washington Press, 2017.

Zheng Shuruo 鄭澍若 (fl. 1802). *Yu Chu xuzhi* 虞初續志. Beijing: Xinhua shudian, 1986.

Zheng Weizhang 鄭偉章. *Wenxian jia tongkao* 文獻家通考. 3 vols. Beijing: Zhonghua shuju, 1999.

Zhou Miaozhong 周妙中. *Qingdai xiqu shi* 清代戲曲史. Zhengzhou: Zhongzhou guji, 1987.

Zhou Qingyuan 周清源, ed. *Xihu erji* 西湖二集. 2 vols. Hangzhou: Zhejiang renmin chubanshe, 1981.

Zhu Fuwei 朱富烓. *Yangzhou shishu* 揚州史述. Suzhou: Suzhou daxue chubanshe, 2001.

Zhu Yixuan 朱一玄 and Liu Yuchen 劉毓忱, eds. *Rulin waishi ziliao huibian* 儒林外史資料彙編. Tianjin: Nankai daxue chubanshe, 2003.

Index

Harvard-Yenching Institute Monograph Series

(titles now in print)